ATE DUE

ANTECEDENTS OF REVOLUTION:
ALEXANDER I AND THE POLISH KINGDOM, 1815-1825

FRANK W. THACKERAY

EAST EUROPEAN MONOGRAPHS, BOULDER
DISTRIBUTED BY COLUMBIA UNIVERSITY PRESS
NEW YORK

1980

EAST EUROPEAN MONOGRAPHS, NO. LXVII

Frank W. Thackeray is Assistant Professor of History
at Indiana University Southeast

Copyright © 1980 by Frank W. Thackeray
Library of Congress Card Catalog Number 80-66053
ISBN 0-914710-61-3

Printed in the United States of America

FOR KATHY

FOR KATHY

TABLE OF CONTENTS

	LIST OF ABBREVIATIONS	viii
	INTRODUCTION	1
1.	THE ANTECEDENTS: POLAND REBORN, 1812-1815	6
2.	THE CONSTITUTIONAL MONARCHY: TSAR ALEXANDER'S "LIBERAL" EXPERIMENT, 1815	16
3.	AN AUSPICIOUS BEGINNING: THE POLISH CONGRESS KINGDOM, 1815-1818	36
4.	STRAINED RELATIONS: THE AUTOCRACTIC EMPIRE AND THE CONSTITUTIONAL MONARCHY	54
5.	THE SUCCESSION CRISIS: GRAND DUKE CONSTANTINE, RUSSIA, AND POLAND, 1819-1823	79
6.	A NEW DEPARTURE: NOVOSIL'TSOV'S RISE TO POWER, 1820-1825	93
7.	REACTION TRIUMPHANT: THE FINAL PHASE OF TSAR ALEXANDER'S POLISH POLICY, 1820-1825	113
	EPILOGUE	132
	CONCLUSION	145
	NOTES	149
	BIBLIOGRAPHY	182
	INDEX	193

ACKNOWLEDGMENTS

The preparation and publication of this book owes much to the generous financial support extended to me by several institutions. A Fulbright Doctoral Dissertation Research Grant to Poland enabled me to conduct archival research during 1972-1973. A summer faculty fellowship from Indiana University Southeast allowed me to devote the summer of 1978 to the manuscript. A grant from Indiana University's President's Council on the Social Sciences speeded publication.

I am deeply indebted to the archivists of the Central Archive of Old Records in Warsaw and the Polish Library in Paris for their invaluable help and inexhaustible patience. For similar reasons I wish to acknowledge the staffs of the University of Warsaw library, the National Library in Warsaw, the Warsaw Public Library, the Library of Congress, the New York Public Library, the Indiana University library, and the Indiana University Southeast library.

During my stay in Poland, several Polish scholars freely contributed their time and expertise. While I can never adequately repay ltem, I want to take this opportunity to thank Professors Stefan Kieniewicz, Jerzy Skowronek, and Hanna Dylagowa. The manuscript benefited greatly from Professor R.E. McGrew's careful reading and the perceptive suggestions which he offered. Naturally, I alone am responsible for the opinions expressed in this study and for any of its shortcomings.

Finally, I wish to extend my heartfelt thanks to those without whose aid this project would never have been completed: Jola Polanowska, Hanna and Irena Drzewiecka, Gisela Hill, the late Roland Cannan, A. Eaton-Irving, and W.R. Miller.

LIST OF ABBREVIATIONS

A.G.A.D.	Archiwum Główne Akt Dawnych w Warszawie (The Central Archive of Old Records in Warsaw)
K.N.	Kanceleria Nowosilcowa (Novosil'tsov's Chancellery)
K.T.K.	Kanceleria Tajna Wielkiego Księcia Konstantina (Grand Duke Constantine's Secret Chancellery)
P.R.A.	Protokoły Rady Administracyjnej Królestwa Polskiego (Minutes of the Polish Kingdom's Administrative Council)
R.S.	Rada Stanu Królestwa Polskiego (State Council of the Kingdom of Poland)
K.R.S.W.i.P.	Komisja Rządowa Spraw Wewnętrznych i Policji (The Interior Ministry)
B.P.P.	Biblioteka Polska w Paryżu (The Polish Library in Paris)
A.W.K.K.	Archiwum Wielkiego Księcia Konstantego (Grand Duke Constantine's Archive) folio no. 340.
R.P.A.C.	Różne Pisma Adama Czartoryskiego (Various Letters of Adam Czartoryski) folio no. 54

INTRODUCTION

The vexatious question of Poland's position among European states and even its fundamental right to exist as a political entity has confounded and exasperated European statesmen for more than two centuries. However, in terms of Russo-Polish relations the problem has persisted for almost a millennium. Although Poles and Russians are contiguous people sharing common Slavic origins, over the centuries their institutions, behavioral patterns, and frames of cultural reference have assumed radically different forms. The Poles looked westward for their inspiration and their models. They embraced Latin Christianity and prided themselves on membership in the European community of nations. Consequently, Poland developed the religious, cultural, social and political configurations peculiar to western Europe. The Russians, on the other hand, turned to Byzantium for their Christianity and accepted Byzantine influences and traditions. With the Mongol invasion, the Russians found themselves not only cut-off from their previously slender contacts with Europe, but isolated as well from the Byzantine matrix.

In addition to nourishing uniquely Russian institutions and attitudes which diverged greatly from those then sprouting in the West, the Mongol conquest also destroyed the weakened remnant of Kiev Rus'. When the Mongol wave receded, two states based on antagonistic religious, cultural, social and political traditions emerged to engage in a protracted struggle to control the land which formerly comprised the western half of Kiev Rus'. One power consisted of the Europeanized Poles jointed to the temporarily mighty and abnormally extended Lithuanian principality. The respective dynasties merged in 1386 to produce a loose union of Poland and Lithuania which the 1569 Lublin Union solidified. Practically, however, the Poles dominated from the outset. They spread Roman Catholicism as well as Polish customs, language and opinions over the Lithuanian lands. The second power was Muscovite Russia, the strongest political and military force to emerge from appanage Russia. Orthodox in religion and autocratic in government, Muscovy, with its unique social and cultural forms, stood far removed from the European norm and presented a sharp contrast to its Polish-Lithuanian rival.

Both states entertained expansionist ambitions, and both evinced a real determination to rule the one-time Kievan lands. Stretching to encompass not only these territories but also former Kievan lands lying far to the east, Poland-Lithuania enjoyed great initial success. In the early seventeenth century, the western warriors occupied Moscow and seized the Muscovite throne. But this was a transitory victory. The balance of forces shifted as the Polish-Lithuanian Commonwealth entered a period of prolonged decline while the Muscovite principality revitalized itself. By the opening of the eighteenth century, an ascendant Muscovite Russia had appropriated the Kievan territories and was moving beyond them into the Polish-Lithuanian heartland.

The new balance was a consequence of Poland's exhaustion from almost continual warfare, but it owed as well to Poland's political system. The *Liberum Veto* and an elective kingship contributed to anarchy, acute regionalism, and the failure to enact vital social and economic reforms. What was worse, Poland showed the weakness in an advanced way at the very time Russia was undergoing growth and consolidation. Indeed, Russia faced an unexpected yet pleasant problem: how to deal with her fallen adversary. Confronted with the choice of indirect domination over Poland-Lithuania, or piecemeal annexation of the Commonwealth's easternmost possessions, Peter the Great decided upon the former course.

This decision shaped Russo-Polish relations throughout most of the eighteenth century. Successive Russian rulers supported weak and pliant candidates for the Polish throne and cultivated Polish aristocractic circles distinguished by their pro-Russian orientation. Catherine the Great deviated from this course when she joined the Germanic powers in partitioning Poland in 1772. The shock of the first partition stimulated spirited Polish efforts at reform. When these efforts culminated in a new constitution (1791), Catherine, heeding the call of a Polish *fronde*, not only destroyed the charter but also once again partitioned the country with Prussia's help. This action provoked Kościuszko's revolt which, in turn, brought on the third and final partition.

Although Poland disappeared from the European map, the Poles retained and nurtured the memory of the community and the geopolitical borders which existed prior to 1772. Re-establishment of the Polish state on its old geographical if not political base became an obsession with the Poles and acted as a major determinant in their subsequent history. Moreover, eighteenth century events, particularly the partitions, inaugurated a new era in Russo-Polish relations characterized by three fresh considerations which fundamentally shaped the Polish question well into the twentieth century.

First, the lengthy Russo-Polish struggle ceased to be a purely private conflict between the two largest Slavic powers. It now assumed a decidedly European character by virtue of Austrian and Prussian involvement as well as Russian expansion into the continent's heartland.

Second, the problem no longer remained a matter of relatively pure and simple territorial adjustments on Europe's easternmost borderlands. The question now became the complicated and confused issue of restoring a long-standing European state.

Lastly, all those who proposed to deal with the situation soon discovered that the parameters prescribed by eighteenth century events strictly limited their field of activity. Force of arms decided the matter then, and as history shows, force of arms was to continue to play the decisive role in the Polish question.

Cognizant of the Polish question's importance for Russia as well as Europe, Tsar Alexander I attempted to preserve and strengthen Russian hegemony over Polish-Lithuanian lands without alarming the European powers. Moreover, believing that Polish acquiescence was essential for his policy's success, he searched for a formula which would at least mollify the Poles if not satisfy them entirely. Only after Napoleon's defeat, however, could Alexander turn his full attention to Poland. At the Congress of Vienna he forced the creation of the Polish Congress Kingdom and claimed its crown. The tsar regarded the new Polish state as a fitting vehicle with which to achieve his Polish goals. One major aim of this monograph will be to explore the formation, evolution and execution of Alexander's Polish policy as it appeared in the Congress Kingdom. This approach will also furnish the opportunity to examine and define Alexander's views on constitutionalism and liberalism as well as provide insight into the tsar's character and personality.

During and after the Congress of Vienna, Alexander's Polish policy provoked decided reaction among educated and politicized Russians. Although frequently overlooked, these responses played an important role in the formulation and development of nineteenth century Russian nationalist and conservative thought. A second theme will be to identify and inspect these Russian reactions to Alexander's Polish policy.

A third major topic will be Congress Poland's administrative structure and its supervision of daily events. Under the direction of Grand Duke Constantine Pavlovich and the Imperial Commissioner, N.N. Novosil'tsov, Poland's administrative system developed distinct attitudes which shaped its decision-making procedures as well as the methods employed to implement those decisions.

Finally, this monograph will consider indigenous Polish opposition to both the form and substance of Alexander's policy. Specifically, this study will investigate student secret societies as well as parliamentary opposition in terms of their political and intellectual foundations, their principal objectives and their achievements. Perforce, this includes a discussion of reaction or overreaction by the tsar and the Kingdom's administrators to what they viewed as a serious but unwarranted threat to their authority.

This study relies greatly on primary sources (government documents, official reports and personal letters) housed at Archiwum Głowne Akt Dawnych w Warszawie (The Central Archive of Old Records in Warsaw), Biblioteka Polska w Paryżu (The Polish Library in Paris), and Biblioteka Czartoryskich w Krakowie (The Library of the Czartoryskis in Cracow). Among the most valuable collections are Novosil'tsov's Chancellery (Kancelaria Nowosilcowa) which contains much of the Imperial Commissioner's official correspondence with both St. Petersburg and the Congress Kingdom's administrators, the Minutes of the Polish Kingdom's Administrative Council (Protokoły Rady Administracyjnej Królestwa Polskiego), and Grand Duke Constantine's Secret Chancellery (Kanceleria Tajna Wielkiego Księcia Konstantina) which contains the records of Constantine's secret police. These collections are housed at Archiwum Głowne Akt Dawnych. In Paris, Archiwum Wielkiego Księcia Konstantego (Grand Duke Constantine's Archive) contains a useful potpourri including a series of Novosil'tsov's reports to Alexander.

The Library of Congress transliteration system for the Russian language has been adopted but with minor modifications such as the use of "ov" for "ev" in familiar names (for example, Novosil'tsov for Novosil'tsev), the dropping of the hard sign (*tverdyi znak*) and the elimination of the soft sign (*miagkii znak*) when it falls at the end of a word or name. All dates are New Style (Gregorian calendar) unless specifically noted. During

Introduction

the nineteenth century the Julian calendar, or Old Style (O.S.), was twelve days behind the Gregorian calendar. Geographical names present a difficult problem. Shifting borders as well as ethnic sensitivities defy an easy or logical solution. However, since this study will principally focus on Polish events, the author has decided to use Polish place names for the most part. The only exceptions to this rule will be those instances where the Poles, during 1815-1830, found themselves in the distinct minority (e.g., Breslau instead of Wrocław), and where the English reader's sensibilities demand an Anglicized form (e.g., Warsaw instead of Warszawa; Cracow instead of Krakow).

CHAPTER 1

The Antecedents: Poland Reborn, 1812-1815

The nineteenth century witnessed several attempts to revive Poland and to restore her to the ranks of the European states. Napoleon was the first to try a Polish restoration, but his efforts were neither sincere nor successful. The Duchy of Warsaw (1807-1815), little more than a thinly disguised French satellite, served to stimulate Napoleon's ambitions.[1] It also gave him a strategic position on Russia's borders. Many Poles, however, looked on the Duchy of Warsaw as the initial step toward their country's rebirth, though some understood that Bonaparte did not favor their ambition to create a strong state occupying prepartition borders. Still, many supported Napoleon to the bitter end because he "was the only ruler who acted vigorously on behalf of the resuscitation of Poland... his acts on her behalf far exceeded those of any other sovereign."[2]

Nevertheless, even with Napoleon at the height of his popularity in Poland, the Russian tsar, Alexander I, tried to win over the Polish landlords. Well before Napoleon's invasion of Russia, Alexander had indicated to several prominent Poles that he was committed to the regeneration of the Polish state. Certainly the major reason for Alexander's sympathetic attitude toward the Poles was his hope of detaching them from Napoleon. However, his friendly overtures reveal something else. Within these preliminary proposals one can distinguish two long-standing Russian objectives: control—either direct or indirect—over the Poles, and expansion westward. These discussions also indicated that the emperor, pressing to achieve his goals, proposed to captivate the Poles with mild and conciliatory treatment, while smothering European objections in a blanket of high-minded phrases.

Not unexpectedly, the tsar encountered widespread opposition to his Polish plans, especially after Polish troops played a prominent role in Napoleon's invasion of Russia. Internationally, Alexander's allies were unlikely to welcome any attempt to augment Russian power, while at home the educated and politicized sector expressed bitter hatred for Russia's ancient rival. For example, in 1812 the first issue of *Syn Otechestvo* (Son of the Fatherland) contained a scathing attack on the Poles.[3]

Alexander acknowledged this sentiment when he informed Prince Adam Czartoryski that anti-Polish feeling in Russia impeded his efforts to restore Poland. The tsar wrote, "The sacking by Polish troops of Smolensk and Moscow, and the devastation of the whole country, has revived old hatreds."[4]

Moreover, Alexander's advisors urged him to treat the Poles harshly. In late 1812, Charles Nesselrode, then a promising young member of the Russian diplomatic corps and later Russian Foreign Minister under Alexander I and Nicholas I, drafted a memorandum sharply critical of any plan to revive Poland. With the notable exception of Czartoryski, the tsar's long time friend and advisor who was dedicated to re-establishing a Polish state with Russian help, the tsar's counselors endorsed and elaborated Nesselrode's memorandum during the next three years. Its principal arguments reverberated throughout the nineteenth century. First, Nesselrode suggested that Russia, like Napoleonic France, treat the Polish question as a means and not an end. As for Russian Poland, he assigned it in perpetuity to the Empire, noting: "We are the masters, to dispose of it." Admitting that the Polish partitions may have been morally and legally reprehensible, he observed that they served to reduce European tensions. Citing several vital reasons, he vigorously argued against reviving even a truncated Polish state. He warned that a reconstructed Poland would not only throw Austria into France's arms but would also create additional problems for Russia because the Poles would inevitably demand independence and enlarged boundaries. Furthermore, Nesselrode observed that any constitutional scheme for a resurrected Poland would place the Russian tsar in the untenable position of simultaneously functioning as an autocrat and a constitutional monarch. According to Nesselrode, this dual system would collapse in recriminations and war since it was impossible for these governmental principles to coexist in the same society. Finally, he remarked that Russians everywhere would regard any re-establishment of the Vistula state as a serious affront since they so despised the Poles and Poland.[5]

Nesselrode's memorandum came in response to Czartoryski's renewed attempts to advance his ideas for a Polish restoration. Adam Jerzy Czartoryski, scion of a magnate family tracing its lineage back to the ruling Lithuanian dynasty, was born in Warsaw on January 14, 1770.[6] Prince Adam inherited his father's and grandfather's political mantle as leader of Poland's most powerful aristocratic party.

The Czartoryskis, principal supporters of a Russian connection in pre-partition Polish politics, owned great estates in Lithuania, the Ukraine and Byelorussia as well as in Poland proper. After Kościuszko's unsuccessful 1794 revolt against the Russians, Catherine ordered young Czartoryski to reside in St. Petersburg as a guarantee against his family's encouragement of, or participation in, activities designed to throw off the Russian yoke. During his "confinement," Czartoryski became close friends with Grand Duke Alexander. Although Czartoryski was older than Alexander, they shared a common enthusiasm for liberal and enlightened ideas. Shortly after Tsar Paul's murder, Tsar Alexander invited Prince Adam to join his Secret Committee. Czartoryski also played a major role in shaping Russian foreign policy. Appointed Foreign Minister in 1804, he sought to achieve an Anglo-Russian understanding to counter Napoleon. Dismissed after Austerlitz, Czartoryski's fortunes ebbed in direct proportion to Napoleon's success. His anti-Napoleonic posture was now a distinct liability. Nevertheless, he managed to retain his position as Curator of the Wilno Educational District which included the Empire's western, and thus formerly Polish, provinces. His close personal friendship with the tsar also weathered the crisis.

As early as 1805, Czartoryski advocated a Russian-sponsored restoration of Poland. He envisioned a Polish state enjoying pre-partition frontiers and governed by the May Third Constitution.[7] Clinging to this proposal throughout the lean years of politically enforced absence from Alexander's side, he re-submitted it to the monarch at the height of Napoleon's power and popularity in the Duchy.[8] And when the fortunes of war began to run against Napoleon, Czartoryski again called for Poland's resurrection under Russian sponsorship.[9]

Alexander, however, moved with great caution, never revealing his true intentions. Certainly both the international situation and internal opposition among advisors, generals and court circles served to restrain him from formulating concrete proposals for Poland's future. In fact, at various times he gave contradictory signals on this important matter. On occasion he seemed to fall under Czartoryski's spell. Thus, in a January 31, 1811 (O.S.) letter to his former Foreign Minister, the tsar specifically accepted Czartoryski's proposals with some minor revisions. Most importantly, Alexander added the *sine qua non* that the new Poland be united forever to the Russian crown.[10] On another occasion, as his armies prepared to cross the Polish frontier, Alexander reportedly announced his intention to create a

Polish Kingdom with himself as ruler. Moreover, he proclaimed that his new kingdom would benefit from a separate administration and possess distinct national laws based on the May Third Constitution.[11]

At other times Alexander appeared to reject Czartoryski's plans. Judging from Czartoryski's spring 1813 correspondence, the tsar not only dismissed Prince Adam's projects but also sanctioned confiscations against members of the Polish army and imposed a punitive, plundering administration on the Empire's Polish *gubernii*.[12] Later, on June 27, 1813, he signed the Treaty of Reichenbach with Austria and Prussia which, among other things, provided for the destruction of the Duchy of Warsaw and indicated that yet another partition of Polish lands was in the offing.

In all probability, however, Alexander's well-known letter of January 13, 1813, to Czartoryski most accurately assessed the situation, and disclosed the tsar's true feelings. He reaffirmed hid dedication to the Polish cause and assured his friend that neither he nor his armies would take revenge on the Poles or their lands. But, echoing Count Nesselrode's recent memorandum, the tsar cited obstacles which prevented him from immediately "realiz[ing] my favorite idea as to Poland." He mentioned hostile opinion in Russia to any Polish reconciliation, and the certainty that a move on his part to reconstruct Poland would, "throw Austria and Prussia entirely into the arms of France." The tsar then asked for Polish trust, wisdom and prudence so that "your hopes will not be deceived." However, Alexander bluntly warned, "Do not forget that Lithuania, Podolia, and Volhynia are hitherto regarded as Russian provinces and that no possible reasoning could persuade Russia to see them under the rule of another sovereign than the one that rules Russia." He followed this caution with the cryptic remark that, "The name under which they continue to form a part of Russia is a difficulty that would be more easily overcome."[13]

During the early months of 1813, in the wake of Napoleon's disastrous Russian campaign, the Duchy collapsed. In March 1813, the Russians, having occupied a passive and demoralized Warsaw, replaced the Duchy's governing bodies with institutions of their own creation headed by the Supreme Provisional Council. This turn of events propelled the Polish question to the fore. While the outcome of the war still hung in the balance, the tsar had prudently refused to make firm commitments or propose border rectifications which might frighten his allies. Now, Alexander's military triumphs enabled him to drop his equivocal stance in favor of a Polish course more to his liking. To this end he summoned the eager Czartoryski to his side at Paris. Standing as Napoleon's conqueror and master of Europe, Alexander could develop his "*idée favorite*" and employ his most enthusiastic supporter on this matter with confidence and boldness. Victory freed Alexander from the fetters of unfavorable Russian public opinion as well as from his fear of antagonizing his allies.

In the Duchy, the Russian sponsored Supreme Provisional Council began to function as the civil authority in the spring of 1813. Widespread war damage, traditional Polish-Russian antipathy, Napoleon's presence in the field with a seemingly inexhaustible supply of soldiers and Poland's apprehensions about its fate combined to complicate the Council's task. Despite these obstacles, the Council succeeded in administering the Duchy fairly and efficiently for more than two years. Partial credit for this success must go to Alexander who not only provided for Polish membership on the Council and a Polish deputation to coordinate affairs with the Council, but also issued a proclamation legitimatizing the Duchy's civil administration, upholding its laws and retaining its officials unless replaced by the Council.[14] These measures reflected Alexander's grand Polish strategy which demanded a satisfied and even grateful Polish population. Credit must also go to the Russian, Count Vasili Lanskoi, who as chairman of the Supreme Provisional Council relieved Polish society with his mild rule and friendly attitude.[15] Furthermore, Czartoryski labored to safeguard the Kingdom's projected viability, and N.N. Novosil'tsov, Lanskoi's deputy, energetically and benevolently employed his undeniably superb administrative skills. In a reasonably short time, the Council restored order and set in motion the local administration and courts.

The Polish army, which loyally followed the French emperor to the end, received special attention. At Alexander's insistence, this army, which was interned in France, was permitted to return home with its ranks, arms, uniforms and Polish and French decorations.[16] The tsar also ordered those Polish soldiers held as prisoners-of-war released. In April 1814, the tsar consolidated these troops into a single corps and honored it by naming his brother, Grand Duke Constantine Pavlovich, as its commander-in-chief. This force soon swelled to more than 20,000 men.[17] Alexander's sympathetic treatment could not fail to impress the Poles who regarded it as a favorable harbinger for their continued national existence as well as a gracious nod to their military reputation, something the Poles have always valued greatly. Moreover, the preservation of the Polish army paid Alexander an extra dividend when he exploited it to disquiet his allies at the Vienna conference.

Alexander finally informed his allies of his Polish plans when he met with Lord Castlereagh, the British Foreign Secretary, during fall, 1814. He told the British statesman that he was determined to re-establish the Kingdom of Poland and grant it a liberal constitution. Furthermore, according to Alexander the new Poland would be tied to the Russian Empire in the person of the Russian tsar who would also serve as Polish king. Territorially, resurrected Poland would include the bulk of the Duchy of Warsaw.[19] For different reasons, both Great Britain and Austria rejected the tsar's scheme. Prussia, which was to receive Saxony as compensation for the loss of her Polish territories, supported Alexander.

Although he won Polish support for his plans, Russians were dismayed. In fact, the rumor spread through St. Petersburg that, "hating and despising Russia, Alexander intended to transfer his capital to Warsaw."[20] Furthermore, Lanskoi, Alexander's representative in the occupied Duchy of Warsaw, characterized the newly-created Polish army as "a serpent always ready to spit its venom at us," and cautioned that "it is impossible to count on the Poles in any case."[21] During Napoleon's Hundred Days, the influential Russian General Alexander I. Chernyshev warned Alexander that his proposals for Poland threatened to sap the nation's spirit and energy for the upcoming struggle.[22]

The more liberal elements in educated, politically literate Russian society also disapproved of Alexander's plan to create a Polish state. General Michael Orlov, the future Decembrist, believed that the Congress Kingdom would harm Russia's vital interests and weaken the Russian state itself. While he termed Alexander's Polish policy an "enormous mistake," he also applauded the tsar's constitutionalism:

> The setting up of the Kingdom of Poland is a matter of nothing other than constructing a new crucible of mutinies and seditions . . . . On the other hand, many hope that in granting a constitution to Poland, the Emperor will not neglect Russia.[23]

Czartoryski, well aware of the menace in such anti-Polish sentiment, wrote from Warsaw to inform his friend that a secret society composed in the main of military people had been formed in St. Petersburg "to frustrate Your Majesty's beneficent intentions in regard to Poland."[24]

Moreover, with the exception of Czartoryski, Alexander's principal advisors strenuously opposed the tsar's plan to restore Poland. At this time Alexander leaned heavily upon non-Russian counselors. In addition to the Pole, Czartoryski, these included the German, Baron vom Stein; the native of Corfu, Capo d'Istria; and the Corsican, Pozzo di Borgo. Each of the latter three drew up lengthy statements pointing out the inconsistencies and hazards of the emperor's Polish proposals. Reiterating Nesselrode's 1812 warning, they cautioned that Poland's re-establishment would create serious problems for Russia both at home and abroad. The most inclusive and incisive criticism came from Pozzo, who submitted a lengthy memorandum to Alexander in October 1814. Pozzo expressed fears that his master's plan would inadvertently plunge Russia forever into barbarism and convert her into an exclusively Asiatic nation behind a Polish barrier. Additionally, Pozzo cited the standard diplomatic argument that a new Poland would not only alienate Prussia and Austria but also result in Polish agitation for a reunion of all Poles. Pozzo then identified the linchpin of Russia's modern history as:

> the destruction of Poland as a political power...(in order to) ...secure to the Russian nation wider relations with the rest of Europe and to open to Russia a wider field and a nobler and better known arena in which she could develop her forces and talents, and satisfy her pride, her passions, and her interests.[26]

Certainly Alexander could not ignore that most fundamental consideration!

Furthermore, Pozzo seriously questioned whether Alexander could reign simultaneously as both an autocrat and a constitutional monarch:

> The title king of Poland would never harmonize with that of emperor and autocrat of all the Russians. These are two factors which never would coalesce: they imply such different functions that the same sovereign is not able to combine them without exposing himself to the discontent of one or the other nation, and, perhaps, to both.[27]

Finally, Pozzo argued that under no circumstances could the tsar safely contemplate detaching Russian Poland from the Empire. The former was now an integral part of the latter, and any attempt to sever it would generate a dangerous opposition. Pozzo then proposed several measures to settle the Polish question. Concerning the Vienna negotiations, he urged Alexander to treat the Polish problem as a matter of territorial adjustments, plain and simple. Following agreement on this point, he continued, Russia must not hesitate to annex the resultant Poland. Finally, Pozzo suggested that Russia then systematically and permanently Russify all her Polish lands.[28]

However, Alexander's frequently demonstrated propensity to act independently of his Foreign Ministers surfaced once again at the Vienna Congress.[29] At the pinnacle of his power and determined to force upon the assembled diplomats his own solution to the Polish problem, the tsar emerged as the only factor within the Russian delegation. His ministers simply served to execute his will. Under these circumstances it became an easy matter for Alexander to ignore von Stein's, Capo d'Istria's and Pozzo's cautionary advice, and to replace the recalcitrant Nesselrode with Czartoryski. While Prince Adam was certainly not more malleable than Nesselrode, he shared Alexander's Polish views and steadfastly supported him at Vienna.

The story of the protracted Polish negotiations is well known and need not be repeated here.[30] Suffice it to say that Alexander's schemes to continue Russia's westward expansion under the guise of a large Polish state with himself as its ruler ran afoul of British objections to the preponderance this would give Russia on the continent as well as French and Austrian reluctance to compensate Prussia with Saxony for its projected Polish losses. Diplomatic stalemate resulted until Prussia greedily pressed her claim to Saxony, thereby precipitating a war scare. This galvanized Great Britain, Austria and France into signing a secret treaty against Russia and Prussia on January 3, 1815. The terms of the treaty, which made definite provisions for war, were quickly leaked to Alexander and the crisis evaporated.

This armed alliance, coupled with opposition at home and within the Russian delegation, the Russian army's exhaustion and the continuing drain on Russia's meager resources, convinced Alexander to settle for what was available. The agreement reached on February 11, and published on June 9, provided for a small Kingdom of Poland. Including the Polish capital, Warsaw, Alexander's Poland consisted of 127,000 square kilometers with a population of 2,500,000. Carved from the major portion of Napoleon's Duchy, Poland was dynastically tied to Russia. Both Prussia and Austria received Duchy territories not included in the new Kingdom, while Cracow, still disputed, was made a free city.[31] Although the disappointment among the Poles with this settlement was considerable, it appears to have been magnified over the years. Contemporary Polish statements and actions indicate relief and genuine gratitude rather than despair and frustration.[32]

As a sop to the Poles, Alexander inserted the following clause in the general treaty:

> His Imperial Majesty reserves unto himself to give this State (Poland), enjoying a distinct administration, the interior extension which he shall judge suitable.[33]

While stimulating Polish hopes for a union of Russian Poland with the new kingdom, the emperor purposefully phrased this reservation obliquely in order not to provoke Russian opinion. In his first public address Alexander continued to appease his new Polish subjects:

> In taking the title King of Poland I wanted to gratify the wishes of the nation. The Polish Kingdom will be united with the Russian Empire by the terms of its own constitution on which I want to base the happiness of the country.
>
> If the great interest of general peace does not allow the union of all Poles under one sceptor, at least I tried to sweeten, as much as possible, the unpleasantness of partition and to secure for all peaceful exercise of their nationality.[34]

During a June 1815 performance at the Warsaw theater, Novosil'tsov leaped to his feet and shouted, "Vive le roi de Pologne."[35] In this dramatic manner, the Poles learned of the Duchy's fate and their new political-national destiny. A few weeks later, Czartoryski arrived from Vienna with "The Bases of the Polish Constitution" in hand.[36] Recently confirmed by Alexander, "The Bases" provided for a national constitution founded on the principles of order, justice and liberty, and adapted to the Polish character, the Polish language and local needs. Alexander intended that "The Bases" serve "as immutable rules and as instructions to the new provisional government."[37]

Poland Reborn, 1812-1815

Acting as Alexander's plenipotentiary, Prince Adam energetically worked to establish the new country's institutions and administration in accord with the tsar's wishes. On June 20, 1815, he presided over the transformation of the Supreme Provisional Council into the Provisional Government of the Kingdom of Poland. He then proceeded personally to direct the Provisional Government's activities for the next five months. During this hectic period the Kingdom's civilian infrastructure began to assume a definite shape: a state council was formed and its duties enumerated; ministries were established and state counselors assigned to them; a national executive branch emerged; and an attempt was made to place the new state on a sound financial footing. Simultaneously, one specially appointed committee began to draft the constitution while another committee composed organic statutes for the various government bodies.[38]

Except for one vital area, work on the Congress Kingdom's formation progressed satisfactorily. Almost from the start, Czartoryski and Grand Duke Constantine quarreled over the question of civilian control of the military. The Grand Duke not only claimed a free hand for himself in military matters, but also demanded funds for his army which the impoverished kingdom could ill afford. Czartoryski tried to place military affairs under the Provisional Government's jurisdiction until the creation of a war ministry. Constantine refused, and his determination to maintain control of the army and his insulting personal conduct compelled Czartoryski to complain to Alexander.[39]

This irritant was temporarily forgotten as the time drew near for Alexander's triumphal entry into Warsaw. The country anxiously awaited its new king. His arrival on November 12, 1815, dressed in a Polish uniform adorned with the Order of the White Eagle, touched off mass demonstrations and a frenzied round of festivities. Most Poles, especially those who had witnessed their country's obliteration from the European map a scant twenty years earlier, rejoiced at their extraordinary good fortune. After Napoleon's defeat they had anticipated a return to the *status quo ante bellum* at best. Most feared ruin and retribution for their collaboration with the French. Contacts with Russian officers during the dark days of 1813 had only served to increase their apprehensions Miraculously, however, Poland had been reborn, though under a Russian sovereign and much diminished in size. For the moment there was euphoria, relief and astonishment at the victor's unexpected generosity.

CHAPTER 2

THE CONSTITUTIONAL MONARCHY: TSAR ALEXANDER'S "LIBERAL" EXPERIMENT, 1815

On November 27, 1815, in the midst of the celebrations commemorating the emperor's visit to Warsaw, Alexander promulgated the Congress Kingdom's constitution.[1] A lengthy, French language document divided into seven sections containing 165 articles, the charter proclaimed Poland a constitutional monarchy (arts. 3, 4), "...united in perpetuity to the Russian Empire...." (art. 1) by the person of the king who is also the Russian tsar (art. 3). The constitution stipulated that Poland's foreign policy must conform to Russia's (art. 8) and her military forces must remain at the tsar's disposal (art. 9) with the condition that "The army of Poland shall never by employed outside Europe" (art. 10). A newly created post, Minister-Secretary of State for Poland would attend to Polish matters in St. Petersburg (art. 77). To manage affairs during his absence from Warsaw, Alexander appointed a Viceroy or Lord Lieutenant who served at the monarch's will and had to posses Polish citizenship unless he belonged to the royal family (arts. 5, 6).

The constitution's second section dealt with personal freedoms and citizens' rights. Its articles expressed decidly liberal principles and reflected Alexander's commitment to Enlightenment ideas about the individual. Thus, Poles gained freedom of the press (art. 16), equal protection under the law, (arts. 17, 18) the right of *habeas corpus*, (arts. 19, 20) the right to speedy trial, (arts. 21, 22) the right to judgment by law and sentence by courts (art. 23), the freedom to move self and property in accordance with legal procedure (art. 24), freedom from unlawful transportation (art. 25), and a declaration that property was sacred and inviolable (art. 26). The eleventh article granted freedom of religion. However, the affirmation that "...there shall be no distinction in the enjoyment of civil and political rights...." applied only the Christians. Moreover, article eleven noted that the Roman Catholic Church would "...receive the most careful attention from the government...."

Provisions requiring that all public administrative, judical and military business be conducted in the Polish language (art. 28) and declaring that public offices, military as well as civil, be occupied only by Poles (art. 29) helped to safeguard the new state's sovereignty against the legal and physical proximity of the Russian Empire.

At first glance, the constitution embodied the classic separation of powers among the executive, legislature and judiciary. But, in fact, the monarch's authority superseded all three governmental branches. In the executive sphere, Article 35 specified that "All executive or administrative authority can emanate from him" (the monarch). The following article proclaimed the person of the king sacred and inviolable. Moreover, the ruler reserved the right to dispose of the state's revenues in conformity with a budget which he would not only prepare, but also approve (art. 39). Alexander also enjoyed a preponderant position in legislative matters. He alone possessed the right to initiate legislation (art. 86), and to convoke, prorogue, or dissolve the Sejm (art. 87).[2] Additionally, the king wielded an absolute veto over the Sejm's resolutions (art. 105).

The constitution provided for a detailed administrative apparatus. Article 63 established a Council of State, *Rada Stanu*, presided over by the Lord Lieutenant and composed of the respective ministers, councilors of state, several other high ranking officials, and prominent individuals chosen by the king. The constitution charged the Council of State with direction of the Kingdom's public affairs in the sovereign's name and during his absence (art. 64).

However, actual administrative power resided with the Administrative Council, *Rada Administracyjna*. The Lord Lieutenant chaired this body which consisted of the principal officials of the five governmental departments, and "other persons especially summoned by the king" (art. 66). Alexander's Viceroy exercised great authority, having jurisdiction to draft laws and make decisions in lieu of the king as long as he did not contravene the constitution or existing law (art. 67). Almost two and one-half years after promulgating the constitution, Alexander finally enumerated the Lord Lieutenant's powers.[3] In ordering the Viceroy to defend the constitution and uphold the laws of the land, the royal rescript commanded him to maintain order and public safety, keep vigil over implementation of the laws, insure protection of the members of the government, guarantee respect for public authorities and magistrats, apply legal protection to all citizens and appoint officials except for those with life tenure.[4]

The constitution called for five ministries: Justice, War, Interior and Police, Finance and the Treasury and Religion and Instruction. A chief official appointed by the king headed each ministry (art. 76). The principle of ministerial responsibility was established by the articles which required the appropriate minister to countersign all acts or decisions published by the monarch or his Viceroy.

The fifth section took up the question of national representation, while several subsequent statutes further developed this area.[5] Article 87 called for a national Sejm to meet in the capital every two years for a thirty day period. It consisted of two chambers, a Senate and a House of Deputies, whose members could be neither arrested nor judged by a criminal court without permission of the member's own chamber (art. 89). Open sessions were required, although a vote by one-tenth of those members present was sufficient to close the sittings to the public (art. 95). In the upper house the president of the Senate presided, while in the lower chamber the monarch appointed a marshal each time he convoked this assembly. Alexander reserved for himself the right to appoint these presiding officers (arts. 126, 129, 134). Rights, privileges and duties accorded to the marshals were not strictly defined, a lapse which prompted vehement protests at a later date when representatives accused marshals of advancing the government's interests to the detriment of the constitution. The organic statute assigned control over the sessions to the respective chambers, granting them the right to impose house arrest on members guilty of committing misdemeanors at the sessions.

Four detailed articles spelled out the Sejm's responsibilities. Article 90 gave it the power to decide on all projects of civil, criminal or administrative law sent to it by the king or State Council. The next article extended the power of the purse. Article 92 provided for the right of petition by the representatives and deputies of the communes on behalf of the welfare and interests of their constituents. Finally, article 94 restricted the Sejm's activities to matters mentioned in the preceding articles or in the act of convocation. But the seemingly broad constitutional competence vested in the Sejm was severely limited by the monarch's privileged position as sole initiator of legislation, his power of absolute veto and his right to dissolve the legislative body.[6]

The Senate consisted of princes of the blood, bishops and the highest provincial officials (art. 108). Its total membership could not exceed one-half of the total number of deputies sitting in the lower house (art. 109). A senator, selected by the king from candidates recommended by the Senate and Viceroy, held that rank for life (art. 110). The constitution required senatorial candidates to be at least 35 years of age and to pay taxes totaling at least 2,000 *zlotys* per year. But princes of the blood secured the right to sit and vote in the Senate at age 18 (arts. 111, 112). Article 118 stated:

> The Chamber of Deputies is composed of: (a) one hundred representatives nominated by the districts or assemblies of the nobility, (*semiki*) one representative to a district; (b) sixty-seven deputies of the communes (*zgromadzenie gminne*)....

However, actual representation in the lower house was always less than the stipulated 167.[7] Representatives held a six year mandate with the right of re-election for an unlimited number of terms. One-third of the House stood for election every two years (art. 120). Candidates had to be at least 30 years of age and pay at least 100 *zlotys* per year taxation (art. 121). The organic statute on national representation forbade government officials to stand as candidates without the authorities' express permission. Moreover, they could not stand in the same district in which they fulfilled their duties. Elected deputies who subsequently accepted a government position lost their mandate.

A royal decree specifying both duration and agenda served as the basis for convoking the assemblies of the nobility and the commune assemblies. The right of participation in both assemblies depended upon the citizen being enrolled in either the administrative district's book of aristocratic citizens, or its book of commune citizens. Individuals possessing electoral privilege were entered in the appropriate book only after presenting documents attesting to their loyalty to the king, their residency within the district and their age.[8] Both assemblies occupied themselves exclusively with electing representatives to the Sejm's lower house, selecting members fo the district council—an elective institution charged with choosing the minor judiciary and promoting district interests as distinguished from the district commissions which were the government's provincial organs—and drawing up lists of candidates for offices in governmental departments (arts. 125, 130).

The royally appointed Sejm Senate exercised a great degree of direct control over the assemblies of the nobility and the commune assemblies, as well as an indirect control over the Sejm House of Deputies. For one thing, it monitored elections to the House. Moreover, it judged the validity of the assemblies' choices and supervised the entries in the citizenship books (art. 117). Furthermore, the organic statute gave to the Senate the right to investigate and rule on complaints arising from the assemblies' activities.

General suffrage in the assemblies of the nobility extended to landowning citizens of aristocratic rank (art. 125). As for the commune assemblies, the constitution bestowed the franchise on:

...(a) All non-noble citizen-proprietors who pay taxes on landed property; (b) All manufacturers and foremen; all merchants who own a business or shop valued at 10,000 zlotys; (c) All parish priests; (d) Professors, instructors, and other persons in charge of public instruction; (e) Every artist distinguished for his talent, his knowledge, or his services rendered to his profession or to the arts.... (art. 131).

Alexander's Polish constitution continued and significantly expanded liberal trends first discernable in the Duchy's constitution. Most importantly, perhaps, it increased society's participation in the country's political life. On the one hand the lower house's organization underwent marked streamlining while its competence in the legislative field was broadened. On the other hand, the number of electors increased in comparison with the Duchy even though the total population declined. Moreover, the new charter extended the suffrage to several heretofore disenfranchised segments of the population, the largest category being non-noble leaseholders on both crown and private lands.

One study determined that between 106,000 and 116,000 Polish citizens enjoyed the franchise under the 1815 constitution.[9] There were 37,000 *szlachta*, 30-35,000 burghers, 1,000 professors and teachers, 3,000 priests and 35-40,000 peasants. The total figure represents an unusually large proportion of the Congress Kingdom's two and one-half million population. Contemporary France, functioning under its 1814 Charter, granted suffrage to only 80,000 citizens although its total population was more than ten times that of Congress Poland.[10]

Despite the monarch's powers, the Polish constitution enumerated and protected "the rights of man and the citizen." For Poland, the document contained the assurance of that nation's political survival after its twenty year absence from the European map. The Kingdom's constitution—which enthroned Polish as the state's official language, allowed the Poles to participate in government, established Polish courts and instituted the Polish army—gave Poland a legalized national identity and considerable control over its own destiny.

However, constitutional theory and practical reality failed to coincide. Poland's constitution, laboriously constructed by Adam Czartoryski and Alexander after examples of the French Charter, the American Constitution, and the British system, contained in its articles the essential guarantees for a liberal, enlightened state. However, it also included specific provisions firmly tying the politically representative state of two and one-half million to the semi-feudal, absolutist Russian Empire of 45 million. Moreover, it contained numerous ambiguities and gaps which the Russian autocrat could employ to impose his will and to negate Poland's quasi-independence. In fact, the constitution was breached in substance and spirit even before its promulgation.

In November 1815, Alexander passed over the Polish hero, Kościuszko, for the post of commander-in-chief of Congress Poland's army. In his place he selected his brother, Grand Duke Constantine Pavlovich, a man disliked by the Poles due to his unbridled temper, his brutal nature and his Russian origins. Nevertheless, Constantine now took command of 22,000 veteran Polish troops as well as 7,000 Russian soldiers stationed in Poland. Alexander directed that he be granted complete control over "all that which belongs to the army," a vague authorization fraught with negative consequences for constitutional order.[11]

As temporary commander of the Polish army from 1814, Constantine had already aroused great uneasiness among influential Poles. After the Vienna negotiators acquiesced in part to Alexander's Polish designs, Czartoryski repeatedly called the emperor's attention to Constantine's transgressions even prior to the Grand Duke's appointment as permanent commander-in-chief. Czartoryski wrote:

> His Highness the Grand Duke has several times intimated to the Government that civil officials, magistrates, mayors, etc. should be brought before him, and the other day he placed the President

of the town of Warsaw under arrest. Some days ago, too, His Highness issued a decree by means of which he will have the power of trying any citizen by court martial.

The provisional government cannot but recognize that such proceedings are contrary to the rules established in all countries for the public peace and security, and that they are especially in direct opposition to the Constitution which Your Majesty has just granted to the country.... [12]

On July 29, he complained that Constantine found the constitution a matter of incessant sarcasms, "shouting down and covering with ridicule ...the rule of law." In this same letter Czartoryski included a proposal to transfer the tsesarevich to the Guards, and to create a Ministry of War conforming to constitutional requirements.[13] Czartoryski severely criticized the army's "state within a state" existence under Constantine:

The presence of Grand Duke Constantine in this country and the special powers with which he is invested, have precluded all relations between the provisional government and the military administration, which is placed under a separate committee. This total separation between the civil and military administration gives rise to the gravest difficulties.[14]

In conclusion, he called for a Ministry of War subject to constitutional control to replace the current independent military command.[15]

Apparently Alexander tried to steer a middle course. During the latter months of 1815, he bowed to Czartoryski's repeated requests to create a constitutionally responsible Ministry of War, but he also named Constantine permanent commander-in-chief, gave him the right to choose the new Minister of War and vested in him total control over day to day military affairs.

Within a short time, Alexander's imprecise delimitation of powers precipitated a major constitutional crisis. In early January 1816, the Administrative Council requested from General Wielhorski, Constantine's designated Minister of War, a report detailing his ministry's organization. At the Administrative Council's January 12 meeting, the secretary read two communiques from the Grand Duke. The first one was addressed to the Lord Lieutenant. Constantine referring to Alexander's decree of November 16, 1815, naming him commander-in-chief, noted that Alexander expressly stated that, "...the military authority is a branch absolutely separate, distinct, and independent of all the other administrative branches of the government...." On this basis he claimed sole control over military matters and demanded that the Administrative Council deal directly with him.[16] The second announcement was addressed to Wielhorski. Constantine, once again referring to Alexander's decree, forbade the War Minister to respond to the Council's interpellations. He then indicated that he would send the project for organizing the Ministry of War directly to the monarch and, furthermore, that he would not allow Wielhorski to present any project to the Council.[17]

These pronouncements stunned the Council and led to a serious public rift. Zajączek, the Lord Lieutenant supported Constantine's actions whereas the remainder of the Council, including Wielhorski, rejected the Grand Duke's position and called for strict adherence to the constitution.[18] Czartoryski, analyzing the situation, said:

...this is the first step, the first test in the attempt to violate the constitution. If it succeeds, subsequently article after article will be violated, the constitution will lose all its meaning, its entire strength, and will be a dead letter. Thus during this first attempt, the first step, although with proper respect, there must be opposition.[19]

The problem remained unresolved for several weeks. Czartoryski tried to move Alexander with an eloquent letter imploring the tsar to return Constantine's organizing project to the Administrative Council for its consideration as prescribed by the constitution, and urging him to support the constitution in the face of attacks which threatened its viability.[20] Alexander declined to reply.

The Polish Minister of War, General Michael Wielhorski, occupied the most precarious and uncomfortable position. Although handpicked by Constantine on the basis of his loyalty, courage and devotion to strict discipline, Wielhorski now came out in favor of resolving the crisis according to constitutional procedure. His decision enraged the tsesarevich and caused a total rupture between the two men. Consequently, Wielhorski petitioned Alexander for permission to retire. The tsar, however, refused to act. This unnatural condition persisted until early spring 1816, when Constantine's extra-constitutional actions once again prompted Wielhorski to ask for permission to retire. This time the king agreed, thereby giving his brother full freedom to select a more pliant candidate to fill Wielhorski's vacated office. Constantine did not make the same mistake twice. He picked General Maurycy Hauke who faithfully fulfilled the Grand Duke's every wish and command until lynched by a Warsaw mob during the first days of the November 1830 insurrection.[21]

Alexander's support of Constantine contained grave implications for the Kingdom's future. Essentially, the monarch now accepted Constantine's claim to exclusive control over military affairs within the Kingdom, in spite of all constitutional provisions to the contrary. The constitution suffered irreparable damage and the Grand Duke gained a supra-constitutional position in the military sphere which invited further encroachments into the civil sphere.

Why did Alexander consign his brother to Warsaw in the first place? Mystery surrounds the emperor's motives. As in so many other instances, Alexander never gave a definitive explanation for his action. Without question, he knew that Constantine evoked fear and loathing among the Poles. Depositing Constantine on the Vistula's banks would be an open affront to his new and traditionally anti-Russian subjects. Yet, for Alexander at least, the advantages of settling the Grand Duke there apparently outweighed any enmity or discontent on the part of the Poles. Historians have suggested several reasons for Alexander's decision. Many scholars believe that the tsar established his brother in Poland in order to remove him from the Russian capital where Constantine was very unpopular and where his presence as heir apparent might do fundamental harm to the autocratic system as well as the ruling dynasty.[22] Other students claim the childless Alexander foresaw a dangerous, opportunistic clique forming around Constantine if he returned to St. Petersburg.[23] Many historians consider Alexander's appointment of the tsesarevich to Warsaw as a device to keep the Poles under close surveillance.[24] One historian views the move as an attempt to mold the Napoleonic Polish army into a facsimile of the victorious Russian force, while another believes that Alexander wanted to expose the Grand Duke to constitutional rule in preparation for the day when Constantine would rule the Russian constitutional monarchy which Alexander intended to establish.[25] The respected authority Marian Kukiel, maintains that Alexander shipped Constantine to Warsaw in order to "make the existence of the Polish state more palatable to the Russians."[26] Far from being mutually exclusive, these explanations complement each other. By leaving Constantine in Warsaw, Alexander achieved several different purposes. Moreover, and perhaps most importantly, he retained for himself complete freedom of movement in matters involving Constantine's future status in both the Kingdom and the Empire.[27]

Constitutionalism also suffered when the ruler selected for high office a number of Poles who neither felt sympathy for the charter nor demonstrated any allegiance to it. The most notable example was the appointment of General Józef Zajączek as Viceroy, the most important and powerful constitutional post.[28] Born in 1752, in the present Ukraine, Zajączek spent a lifetime in military service. Fighting against the Russians in 1792, and again in 1794, he gained a reputation as one of Poland's most zealous and radical Jacobins. He emigrated to France in 1795, where he joined Dąbrowski's famous Polish Legions and later secured a command in Napoleon's imperial army, rising to the rank of general.

During Napoleon's Russian campaign, the tsar's troops captured him after he lost a leg in the retreat. In the course of his wanderings after leaving Poland, Zajączek's rabid Jacobinism had evolved into a deep-dyed conservatism, and after 1812 he quickly embraced the Russian cause. Nevertheless, his appointment as Lord Lieutenant instead of Czartoryski came as a shock to Russians and Poles alike.

Early on, Zajączek gave evidence of his lack of devotion to Alexander's constitution. At the stormy Administrative Council meeting of January 12, 1816, the Lord Lieutenant supported Constantine in his battle to maintain exclusive control over the Kingdom's military. Zajączek asserted that the Grand Duke's statements should be considered as issuing from the king himself.[29] In the face of continuing opposition, Zajączek lost his temper and shouted:

> Why do you remind me of this constitution? If the Grand Duke orders me, I will turn it upside down. What is the constitution, what is the country? Nothing!
> What did this country do for me? Emperor Napoleon gave me the goods which I have; today I owe my position to Emperor Alexander; but the country, what? To me the country is my forests and oaks. I will listen not to the constitution, but to Emperor Alexander, and I will do whatever his brother orders.[30]

In the weeks following this outburst, Czartoryski forcefully brought the matter of Zajączek's conduct to Alexander's attention on several separate occasions. He depicted Zajączek as lacking will power and sinking to servility before Constantine. He also accused him of failure to comprehend his duties under the constitutional system as well as ignorance regarding the essential points of legislation and administration. Czartoryski repeatedly begged Alexander to intervene, pleading with the tsar to instruct the Lord Lieutenant to respect the constitution and to defer to the ministers in matters not familiar to him. If this could not be arranged, Czartoryski apparently with tongue in cheek, advised Alexander to dismiss his current ministers and replace them with men more in accord with the Viceroy's views.[31] Once again Alexander ignored Czartoryski.

Alexander directed another blow at his own handiwork when, on December 1, 1815, he named N.N. Novosil'tsov, "delegate and plenipotentiary" to Poland. This position was not included in the constitution. Furthermore, there was a provision reserving all public offices for Poles alone. Patterned after Napoleon's "resident," Alexander's "Imperial Commissioner" exercised considerable power. The December 1 decree assigned him the task of ". . . easing the difficulties inseparable from establishing a new order and resolving the doubts which can unexpectedly happen, in Our absence, in the introduction of a new regime in Poland, as well as hastening the movement of events. . . ." The tsar also authorized him as confidential delegate ". . . to intervene in every instance where Our intentions are made known. . . ."[32] Appointed for "the first months of the introduction of the new organization," Novosil'tsov managed to remain a prominent and influential figure until the 1830 revolution forced him to flee. A contemporary described Novosil'tsov's function as, "promoter of the interests of the Empire in their relation to the business of the local government. . . ." Additionally, the observer credited Novosil'tsov with unofficial power over "all matters concerning the civil administration of the Kingdom and, in subordination to Constantine Pavlovich, the west, southwest, and White Russian provinces."[33] It appears Alexander singled out Novosil'tsov to fulfill two purposes beyond those noted in the official explanation for his presence in the Congress Kingdom. First, as the emperor's intelligent, observant, trusted henchman, he was to keep a wary eye on the Poles. Secondly, Novosil'tsov was to inform Alexander of Constantine's movements and activities, and to act as a check on the tsesarevich's behavior. In any event, his presence helped to circumvent the constitution. Through him Alexander could make his will known and press for its acceptance without resorting to constitutional methods. Reciprocally, Novosil'tsov fed Alexander a seemingly endless stream of reports which the latter came to rely on with increasing frequency to formulate policy for the Kingdom regardless of the desires expressed by the Sejm.

Nikolai Nikolaevich Novosil'tsov, the illegitimate son of Baroness Maria Stroganov, was born in 1761 at St. Petersburg.[34] Upon her death in 1764, her brother, the wealthy and socially prominent Count Alexander Stroganov, took the child under his care. Well tutored, thanks to his uncle, Novosil'tsov entered the army in 1783 with the rank of captain. He participated in Catherine's Swedish and Polish campaigns, taking part in the 1794 seige and capture of Warsaw and the subsequent negotiations over the third partition of the Polish Commonwealth. He remained in the army until 1795 when he resigned his commission. A year later he sailed to England where he remained for the duration of Tsar Paul's reign. In 1790, while still a member of the Russian army, Novosil'tsov traveled to Paris at his uncle's behest to retrieve his young cousin, the Count's son, Paul Stroganov, from the supposedly detrimental influence of the revolutionary Jacobin clubs. The ensuing friendship with young Stroganov brough Novosil'tsov into contact with Grand Duke Alexander. After Alexander ascended the throne, he named Novosil'tsov to his Secret Committee together with Stroganov, Czartoryski and V. Kochubei.

Before Alexander lifted him to prominence in 1801, the forty year old Novosil'tsov had failed to make his mark. Despite flashes of brilliance, he seemed destined for obscurity. Although contemporaries remarked favorably on his intelligence, erudition, energy and eloquence, he was generally considered dissolute, alcoholic and abnormally cynical. Unlike most of Russian society, Novosil'tsov lacked both means and social status. This twin shortcoming haunted him, and his determination to rectify the situation explains in part his later behavior in the Kingdom. At this time General Langeron characterized him as, "... this small, second-rate *chinovnik*—an underling—who through the friendship of Count Stroganov was raised even to friendship with the tsar himself, a man of the cabinet, excellent worker, cold, circumspect, well-informed about interests; I will not speak about his morality...."[35]

With Alexander's accession, however, Novosil'tsov was appointed to several powerful offices. Like all the members of Alexander's Secret Committee, he dabbled in various affairs of state without achieving much in the way of substantive results. Retaining his influence when the committee broke up in 1803, the emperor ordered him to England on a secret, diplomatic mission in the following year. The post-Austerlitz period saw a reversal of his fortunes. Dismissed from his positions as chamberlain, secret councilor and member of the legislative committe, he barely managed to hold his appointments as Senator and President of the Academy of Sciences. After Tilsit and the French alliance, Novosil'tsov's career suffered a complete eclipse. Unlike many of the ins now become outs, Novosil'tsov could not fall back on landed estates and a steady income. Uncomfortable in his status, Novosil'tsov remained at St. Petersburg, living off the kindness of friends, until 1810 when Alexander exiled him as punishment for his Anglophile sentiments. The next two years he spent in Vienna in destitute circumstances, probably surviving on handouts from Czartoryski.

This experience had a profound effect on Novosil'tsov. For one thing, he became even more drunken and debauched. More importantly, as he passed his fiftieth birthday he apparently began to analyze the emperor's character, concluding that his future well-being depended almost exclusively upon currying favor with Alexander. Realizing that the emperor frequently disregarded mere flatterers and sycophants, Novosil'tsov recognized that the most efficacious approach to gaining Alexander's confidence was to ascertain the monarch's position on matters of state and then to repeat it in a more polished and concrete form, embellished with a minor variation or two. If the emperor indicated displeasure, it would behoove Novosil'tsov to conform immediately to Alexander's wishes since intransigence or noncompliance on his part would only invite retribution later. Novosil'tsov perceived Alexander's basically authoritarian spirit and consciously opted to sacrifice principles for personal gain. From the depths of his Viennese exile Novosil'tsov foresaw little or no possibility to verify his analysis or implement his conclusions, but gathering war clouds presented him with a golden opportunity.[36]

In spring 1812, Novosil'tsov, quite unexpectedly, received orders to return to St. Petersburg and government service. His resurrection elicited sharply unfavorable comment from some Russians. Nesselrode's wife wrote to her husband on June 22:

> Despite the evil, which he had spoken, our Master of Novosil'tsov is here, once again in great favor; we learned from a certain source

that he has been received as an old friend, a man of surprising merit, while he is only a great nonentity.... They will send this pitiful person to England, to a country where they laugh at him.[37]

However, Britain was not his destination. Rather, for the remainder of 1812, the impecunious and unemployed Novosil'tsov resided in St. Petersburg. It seems that Czartoryski once again supported his old comrade. During these months Novosil'tsov made the rounds of St. Petersburg salons where he showed a great interest in Polish affairs, cultivated the St. Petersburg Polish colony and those few Russians sympathetic to the Poles, and gradually attained for himself a reputation as an expert on Polish matters. His continued close contact with Czartoryski persuaded Alexander to name him imperial intermediary with the Polish prince in the delicate matter of re-establishing Poland. His actions gained for him further enmity. Baron M.N. Korf attacked his dilettantism, sarcastically calling him, "... the universal man, the genius for any sort of work, the great man, the great minister, the supposed *philosophe*...."[38]

In May 1813, Alexander dispatched Novosil'tsov to occupied Warsaw. Named Vice-President of the Supreme Provisional Council of the Duchy of Warsaw under the presidency of V. Lanskoi, Novosil'tsov busied himself with governmental affairs including financial questions and police matters. Not yet positive of Alexander's intentions, he flattered the Poles and insinuated himself with the local population while at the same time he sent secret memoranda to St. Petersburg criticizing Russian leniency toward the Poles and proposing rigorous police surveillance.[39] His relations with Czartoryski, the chief power in Poland and one of the Tsar's key advisors, remained more than cordial. Czartoryski's lifelong inability to judge character manifested itself again. Prince Adam told the Polish poet and critic, Kajetan Koźmian, "I'm as sure of him (Novosil'tsov) as I am of myself; thank God that among Poles... they find such a well disposed and zealous supporter of Poland."[40] However, at least one Pole saw through Novosil'tsov and warned Czartoryski of the danger ahead. Ludwig Plater, government official and Czartoryski confidant, wrote, "Novosil'tsov does not appear to want the re-establishment of Poland. He is two-faced, that's for certain; but where is his sincere view and where is his mask?—it is up to you to decide... I have lost confidence in him."[41]

A few months after his appointment as imperial plenipotentiary, Novosil'tsov received a further boost in power and prestige. Zajączek, as he was destined to do many times over the next decade, acted as Novosil'tsov's witting or unwitting tool. The Lord Lieutenant informed the May 15, 1816, Administrative Council meeting that Novosil'tsov was displeased at having to learn about the Council's activities from newspapers or other indirect sources and not from the Council itself. Novosil'tsov judged that his position and the emperor's dignity called for a more direct method of communication.[42] Concurring with the Imperial Commissioner's observations, the Lord Lieutenant suggested that a suitable solution would be to permit Novosil'tsov to attend the Council's meetings. The Council, agreeing unanimously, sent an appropriate invitation to the Imperial Commissioner as well as a full report to the king.[43] But Novosil'tsov was not about to act without his master's explicit approval. On the following day, Novosil'tsov informed the Lord Lieutenant that although deeply honored by the Council's request, he could not accept without first securing Alexander's permission.[44] Saying this, however, Novosil'tsov knew full well that Alexander was not likely to veto a seemingly innocuous and even beneficial step taken at the Council's initiative and unanimously supported by its membership. A few weeks later, Novosil'tsov received royal permission to accept the Council's offer.[45] He put in his first appearance at the Administrative Council on July 11, and continued to attend its sessions until 1830.[46] Novosil'tsov thus gained access to the new kingdom's most influential body. Moreover, sitting as the monarch's representative, he carried great weight in the Council's deliberations. Surprisingly, perhaps, neither Novosil'tsov's extra-constitutional office nor his unconstitutional participation in the Administrative Council ever became an issue.

What motivated Alexander to subvert his own creation? Why did he foresake the constitutional and liberal principles which he had espoused with unusual frequency and gusto? The answer to this thorny problem lies in its semantics. Unquestionably, Alexander defined "constitutionalism" and "liberalism" quite differently than his European and American contemporaries. Despite La Harpe's instruction, the tsar never considered either constitutionalism or liberalism as catchwords signifying representative institutions, a strict limitation of the executive's power, governmental participation by legally defined and protected estates, or any other principle commonly associated with French, English, or American political thought. Alexander never intended to diminish the autocracy's powers. Rather he consistently exhibited a particular sensitivity toward and jealous concern for his autocratic prerogatives.

In this light it is inconceivable to believe that Alexander regarded a constitution as a means to limit the autocracy. Rather, he defined constitutionalism as an administrative reform of some magnitude designed to produce a more efficient, less cumbersome and more responsive autocracy. Alexander looked to a constitution to provide the rationalized system he deemed so vital for the task of reorganizing his empire on a modern basis. He believed constitutional and liberal institutions would eliminate caprice and arbitrary behavior by establishing an orderly government based on the rule of law. The tsar desired a comprehensive administrative ordering within the autocracy's framework and not a radical application of Anglo-Saxon governmental concepts.[47] In this context, Alexander's activities and appointments did not undermine the Polish constitution or destroy liberal principles. Rather, they were perfectly consistent with Alexander's peculiar "constitutional" and "liberal" philosophy.

Despite much obfuscation, on at least two separate occasions Alexander clearly described his autocratic position vis-à-vis the Polish constitution. During a protracted discussion with Lebzeltern, the Austrian representative in St. Petersburg, he said:

> There is a truth from which one can never depart without peril; and this is that together with constitutional or liberal principles that a sovereign feels obliged to adopt toward his people, he must establish proportionate means of repression.... I have felt obliged to give to the Poles a liberal constitution, but I have created together with this the means of repression of a kind to make them cognizant that they must not delude themselves, nor go beyond a certain line.[48]

In summer 1817, at a time when liberal constitutionalism seemed to be working well in the Congress Kingdom and before the first signs of either a parliamentary opposition or secret societies, the tsar, through the agency of the Minister-Secretary of State for Poland, Ignacy Sobolewski, wrote to Zajączek:

> ...by no means does His Majesty regard as irrevocable the benefits which he has showered upon the country; he believes his institutions obligatory for the nation, but not for him; in the agreement granted

to his subjects, he feels himself (to be) judge; he will fulfill the obligations only as long as in his wisdom he judges them conforming to the well-being of the nation.... His Majesty would believe himself obliged to dispense with all other considerations in order to fill the first duty of a good government, to attain the first object of all social harmony—that is to say—in order to maintain public order and general security.[49]

It would be incorrect to conclude that "Alexander knew liberal institutions only by name and not content, he loved them for vogue and not for real value."[50] Rather, it seems that he knew liberal institutions *as he defined them,* and loved them for their value in helping him maintain and more effectively administer his strictly autocratic Empire.

A careful study of both the tsar's constitutional concepts and his Polish activities serves to demolish the convention of dividing Alexander's reign into liberal and reactionary phases. As Professor M. Raeff suggests, this liberal-reactionary dichotomy is quite incorrect.[51] Once the smoke screen of lofty phrases and halting, seemingly timid gestures is penetrated, "the enigmatic tsar" emerges as a consistent and hardheaded ruler. Far from a weak, indecisive, and ineffectual dreamer dominated by strong-willed advisors, Alexander appears as a forceful realist, determined to the point of stubbornness and committed to reformist ideas *but only* within the well-defined context of the traditional autocracy. If Alexander did not consciously foster his public image as a "crowned Hamlet," he certainly took advantage of it to advance his objectives. He always showed a marked preference for subtle, indirect, even deceitful methods. This was an altogether natural result of his childhood experiences when he shuffled between his father's and grandmother's bitterly antagonistic coteries. Then, a quick-witted deviousness and evasiveness stood him in good stead with both courts. Endowed with an unusual gift for charming friend and foe alike, a talent which contributed to his sympathetic image, Alexander knew how to act ruthlessly, especially when he perceived a threat to his absolute power. Deeply suspicious of his advisors, he was as jealous of his powers as he was conscious of them. Throughout his entire reign Alexander never ceased to regard himself as an autocrat and to perform accordingly. Perhaps his most outstanding quality was an uncanny ability to leave himself a free and unfettered hand in every sphere. Never making irrevocable decisions, never prematurely foreclosing his options, he was the consummate diplomat-politician. More than anything this mastery explains his decision, for example, to remain silent about Constantine's abdication in favor of Nicholas. Up to the end, Alexander maintained for himself the unconditional right to reverse his direction and, in effect, personally select his successor.[52]

Addressing himself to the Polish question in 1814, Grand Duke Constantine demanded that a Russian governor and vice-governor be sent to the Vistula in order to "gouverner à la Russe."[53] This imperialistic statement accurately reflected Russian views on Poland during the Congress Kingdom's entire existence, and for that matter, during the hundred odd years or so still remaining for the Russian Empire itself. Alexander's proposal to re-establish a truncated Polish state on a liberal, constitutional basis— his *idée favorite* as he characterized it in correspondence with Czartoryski—elicited numerous negative responses. Never, perhaps, in his twenty-four year reign was the tsar so isolated as when he acted to revive Poland.

The vast conservative sector of Russian society which included politically literate landowners, high ranking members of the bureaucracy and military, intellectuals such as Karamzin and several members of the imperial family, rejected the emperor's program for several reasons. Psychologically, Russian conservatives found it difficult if not impossible to accept their autocratic ruler in his guise as constitutional monarch. To admit to this would challenge the Russian Empire's basic social structure which rested on a pyramiding of class obligations and privileges with the sacrosanct and omnipotent tsar occupying the apex. Russian state secretary A.M. Gribovskii described his feelings on viewing the tsar open a Sejm session:

> It is strange to see a despotic monarch, possessing 50 million people on one-third of the hemisphere, but speaking in a constitutional language and representing his government as limited in the presence of a puny nation, always an enemy of Russia, when in Russia itself an *ukaz* not only signed by him but only published in his name, decides without the least of ceremonies or forms about the lives and fortunes of the highest and lowest classes, and the smallest observation against the government on the part of a private person might entail the most terrible consequences.[54]

The great hostility with which Russian conservatives viewed Poland extended even to imperial officials assigned to serve in the Congress Kingdom.

Julius Schmidt, the Prussian consul at Warsaw, informed Berlin:

> When they (Russian officials serving in the Congress Kingdom) arrive at St. Petersburg... they are ill-received and treated as turncoats. They are called renegades and Polish counsels. General Arakcheev is one of their most obstinate enemies.[55]

One authority even suggests that the birth of Russian nationalism gave rise to the possibility of turning the perceived idea of the tsar against the reigning tsar. That is, Alexander, in his apparent liberalism, cosmopolitanism and "westernism," differed so radically from the preconceived, idealized and obligatory concept of "The Tsar," that he exposed himself to rumors questioning his very fitness to rule and his devotion to the country. Carried to its logical conclusion, this trend might eventually brand Alexander as the anti-tsar and even lead to his overthrow.[56]

Like the Russian conservatives, young Russian liberals, those educated members of Russian society who through either reading or first-hand experience or both had been infused with the ideas and ideals of the Enlightenment and the French Revolution, also passionately objected to Alexander's proposals. Although enthusiastically endorsing Alexander's progressive intentions, they demanded that he introduce them directly to the Empire without any Polish incubational period. The emperor dealt a crushing blow to their egos when he singled out the hated Poles for his imperial favor. The liberals considered the Russian nation infinitely more deserving. At this time General Michael Orlov, later prominent in the Northern Society, organized the secret "Order of the Knights of the Russian Cross" which called for "unconditional and permanent destruction of the Polish name and the kingdom of Poland, as well as turning all Poland, including the Prussian and Austrian sections, into a Russian *gubernia.*"[57]

Anti-Polish sentiment reached a fever pitch in late 1817. At that time a letter from Prince Sergi Trubetskoi, future chief of the St. Petersburg Decembrists, arrived in the Russian capital. Detailing Alexander's purported desire to unite the Russian Polish provinces to the Congress Kingdom and to move the imperial capital to Warsaw, the letter circulated among several members of the secret Union of Salvation including M.S. Lunin, I. Yakushkin and A. Murav'ev, all of whom were to be victims of the Decembrist purge. Gathering to discuss the matter, the alarmed conspirators finally decided to murder the tsar in retaliation for his Polish program. Yakushkin, a firebrand, took it upon himself to fulfill this duty. With the passage of time, however, tempers cooled and the planned tsaricide was abandoned.[58]

Opposition to Alexander's Polish policy was, it seems, the only area of agreement between such mutually hostile elements as the young Russian liberals, many of whom were to join the ranks of the Decembrists, and the conservatives, who figured prominently in court and gentry circles. Together they roundly condemned Poland's restoration and indicated their fierce displeasure at hints that the tsar would soon return the western provinces to Poland. Nevertheless, Alexander proceeded with his plans for Poland. He was not unaware of this opposition, but at the zenith of his power he was unlikely to appease his critics. However, a sovereign as shrewd as Alexander would hardly continue to ignore the discontent if it persisted. That a stubborn Alexander acted to satisfy himself on this occasion did not guarantee that he would repeat his performance at a later date under changed circumstances.

CHAPTER 3

AN AUSPICIOUS BEGINNING:
THE POLISH CONGRESS KINGDOM, 1815-1818

Despite the underhanded circumvention of the constitution and the appointment of high officials noted for their lack of devotion to the state and its governing charter, Polish affairs progressed satisfactorily throughout the initial years. Almost without exception, the Poles expressed surprise and relief at Russia's lenient treatment. In turn, this generated a genuine devotion and gratitude for the Russian monarch who had resurrected the Polish name. In the midst of general harmony and constructive undertakings only Constantine and his treatment of the army aroused discontent.

After Napoleon's defeat, the Duchy's troops were not dispersed as expected; instead they returned to Poland where they formed the Congress Kingdom's army. Originally numbering twenty-two thousand, the army quickly expanded into a thirty thousand man contingent. Constantine's despotic actions, his uncontrollable temper and his decision to introduce Prussian drill soon drove from the ranks many of the old cadre remaining from Kościuszko's and Napoleon's wars. By 1819 there had been an abnormally high turnover rate of about 35 percent. Constantine delighted in ousting the veteran campaigners whom he personally disliked and suspected of fostering improper sentiments if not open disloyalty. The remaining officers fell into two categories: either new additions loyal to the Grand Duke and committed to his views on military science, or timeservers who elected to accept the new if distasteful system rather than forfeit their numerous accrued benefits.[1]

Constantine's recruitment policy differed radically from the era's standards in that he revoked the accepted practice which allowed wealthy citizens to purchase a substitute soldier. Instead, exemptions from duty went to relatively few: teachers, priests and Jews, each of whom paid 700 *zlotys* per year for this dispensation. Artisans and manufacturing hands, formerly excused automatically, were now deffered only after

Grand Duke Constantine personally reviewed their cases.[2] Consequently, the Polish army included considerably more middle and upper class individuals than the norm. On the eve of the 1830 uprising one line infantry regiment drew more than one-third of its contingent from the middle and *szlachta* class, while the figure for another regiment reached above 25 percent.[3]

Only thirty-six years old when named permanent commander-in-chief of the Kingdom's military establishment, Constantine continued his disruptive activities which so upset Polish society when he held the post temporarily. Numerous diarists, contemporary observers and later historians have remarked upon the deleterious effect Constantine's savagery and brutality had on the army.[4] As early as 1815, he introduced corporal punishment into the Polish army. Combat veterans, schooled in the Napoleonic tradition, recoiled at the punishments inflicted by Constantine. Beatings and other public humiliations became commonplace at the infamous daily parade held at Warsaw's Saxon Square. Not infrequently, such treatment led to suicides within the officer corps and permanent disabilities among the ranks. In the first four years, the Grand Duke's harassment drove at least forty-nine officers to take their own lives.[5]

In describing military life under the Grand Duke one young officer wrote, "There now disappeared the prevalent merriment. Spying almost completely destroyed comradely relations. No one confided in anyone, everyone feared his own shadow."[6] Frequently, Constantine would not only degrade an officer before his troops but also order the chastened soldier to bear arms and march in the ranks. One account reports that he broke an officer discovered reading something other than a military manual. Despite his interest in the Polish army, he was not above publicly denigrating it before visiting Russians. On one occasion he remarked to a Russian general, "These villains (the Poles) wouldn't serve except for the money."[7] Detailed complaints about the tsesarevich's behavior regularly arrived at St. Petersburg. They barely elicited a response. Alexander, acknowledging the grievances, asserted that nothing could be done about Constantine at the time and advised patience in the hope that a quiet interlude would solve all problems.[8]

Perhaps the most accurate characterization of the Grand Duke is found in A.E. Koźmian's observation about Constantine's relationship to the military: "He loved the army like perverse children like toys, which occupy them, but which they break and smash; like they like dogs, cats, and birds with which they play, but which they torture mercilessly."[9]

Constantine's actions were rooted in two causes. In the first place, he was determined to remold the Polish army on the Prussian model. A strong partisan of military formalism and harsh discipline, the Grand Duke hated the Poles' freer military traditions and the progressive innovations of the Napoleonic period. In Constantine's view formal muster, uniforms, parades and garrison service decided an army's value. Obedience and submission were a soldier's highest duty. Constantine himself set a shining example. The Grand Duke lived a Spartan existence, never drank vodka and rose punctually at 4:00 A.M. every day in order to supervise pre-dawn drills. The only luxury he allowed himself was imported Cuban cigars which he defiantly charged to the Administrative Council.

Secondly, Constantine's own personality dictated the manner in which he would reshape the Polish army.[10] While not the "insane hyena" of Nicolson's *The Congress of Vienna*, the Grand Duke, nevertheless, possessed a frightening and repellent character. Born in 1779 and christened Constantine at his grandmother's insistence, the young Grand Duke never occupied the revived Byzantine throne Catherine intended for him. Although entrusted to the liberal Swiss tutor, LaHarpe, Constantine always preferred the military atmosphere at his father's residence. Constantine was not endowed with great intelligence and the Gatchina parade ground did little to enhance his education. At seventeen his grandmother married him to Princess Julia of Saxe-Coburg, a union which failed miserably due in great part to the Grand Duke's vile temper, rough behavior and abnormal devotion to military interests. Constantine's actual military career began with an appointment to Suvorov's command in 1799. Taking part in several battles, Constantine earned a reputation for courage. Apparently, however, combat experience also shocked and horrified him to such a degree that for the remainder of his life he expressed a strong distaste for bloodshed. In Constantine's view, an army was for show and not for war.

Over the years Constantine developed into a martinet with an ungovernable temper who antagonized almost everyone he encountered. His outbursts were legendary. Politically, he was uninformed. He disliked constitutions and equated liberalism with Jacobinism and revolution. He strongly endorsed an idyllic conservatism featuring a well-ordered society, adherence to treaties, maintenance of sworn oaths and fidelity to the sovereign. Considering blind obedience as the greatest honor and virtue, he practiced what he preached in his relations with Alexander as he slavishly discharged the tsar's every command. With time, he grew to despise civilians of every ilk, reserving particular opprobrium for the clergy and literary men. The tsesarevich claimed the lion's share of the country's revenues for the military. At no time during the Kingdom's fifteen year life did the army's portion of the budget dip below fifty percent of the total. The absolute amount spent on the army skyrocketed. In the five year period, 1817-1822, the official military budget increased from 20.7 million to 31.5 million *zlotys* while the number of men under arms remained constant.[11] The Kingdom's limited resources were further strained when Russia announced that it considered the nine million silver rubles it supplied to the Kingdom for its 1815-1817 military upkeep to be a loan and not a gift.[12] Concurrently, the Kingdom also supported seven thousand Russian troops stationed in Poland as well as the Russian armies passing through from western Europe on their return to the Empire.

Unfavorable trade agreements added another significant drain on Poland's meager financial resources. The December 19, 1818, St. Petersburg Convention with Prussia was especially burdensome. This treaty's provision which permitted the Prussians to levy high tariffs on all Polish raw materials passing through Prussian territory, crippled the Polish grain trade which relied on barge transportation down the Vistula to Danzig. Long term personal liabilities also aggravated the Congress Kingdom's financial woes. Individual Polish landowners labored under the handicap of exorbitant debts dating back before the partitions. One expert estimates the sum of these debts to equal more than 635 times all property values.[13]

Nevertheless, the immediate economic stituation was not perilous. In fact, certain indicators suggest that several sectors of the Polish economy experienced prosperous times during the years following 1815. In 1817, domestic prices for grains reached a fifteen year (1816-1830) high, while the 1816-1819 period witnessed yearly grain prices well above the Congress Kingdom's average. A substantial jump in wages for urban workers paralleled the rise in grain prices. During 1818-1820, masons reached a fifteen year peak for earnings, while carpenters also fared well.[14]

Despite the contention advanced by several authorities that serious economic difficulties crippled the Congress Kingdom from its inception, some evidence reveals that a mild prosperity of sorts characterized the state's first half decade.[15] Although economic disaster threatened in the early 1820s, the first years were good. However, for those who cared to look, the source of future trouble clearly revealed itself. Namely, inasmuch as the state's revenues could not hope to approach its expenditures, the yearly deficit grew by leaps and bounds. The chief culprit producing this dangerous state of affairs was Constantine's swollen military budget.

During the new Poland's first five years, the educational field witnessed unprecedented expansion. The authorities promoted steady growth in both types and numbers of educational facilities without draining the treasury or disrupting existing social patterns. One reason for their success was the great continuity which distinguished Poland's educational establishments. The Duchy's educational ministers and officials retained their positions and influence in the Kingdom. At its first session, the Administrative Council entrusted the newly created Department of Education to the former members of the Duchy's Headquarters of National Education.[16]

Stanisław Kostka Potocki (1752-1821), the Minister of Religion and Education, provided the impetus for education's universal development. Scion of one of Poland's wealthiest and most powerful families, Potocki enjoyed a considerable reputation as a man of great intellect and an enlightened freethinker of the Voltairian school. Actively participating in the forerunner of today's Polish Academy of Sciences, Potocki not only functioned as the Duchy's Education Minister but also served as President of its State Council. With the Congress Kingdom's advent, he retained his primacy in educational affairs and vigorously pursued an expansionist policy. Potocki also curbed the church's influence on instuctional matters, thereby earning for himself the enmity of the conservative Polish episcopate.[17]

Under Potocki's leadership, elementary schools, which heretofore had been almost nonexistent, began to appear in both the towns and countryside as exceptional growth took place. During Potocki's five year tenure, the number of elementary schools and pupils increased as indicated.[18]

Year	Schools	Pupils
1816	720	23,101
1818	969	32,355
1821	1222	37,623

Financial support for these schools came from an extraordinary tax levied on the peasants and collected by the school authorities. Nevertheless,

Potocki faced some serious problems. The difficulties involved in collecting this tax, as well as the peasantry's generally destitute situation, created problems which severely restricted elementary education's further growth. Moreover, Potocki's efforts to introduce compulsory education failed to generate much enthusiasm among the peasantry.

The growth rate for secondary schools, which prepared low ranking government clerks as well as students for the new university, also increased significantly. By 1820 Poland boasted thirty-four such schools with an enrollment totaling 6,444.[19] However, shortly after a clerical-conservative clique engineered Potocki's overthrow and reversed his education policies, (see Chapter 6), both figures began to decline.[20]

During Potocki's tenure, the Congress Kingdom gained a university. On November 19, 1816, Alexander announced his decision to expand the existing Warsaw institutes for law and medicine into a full-fledged university.[21] Shortly thereafter, the university's five departments—law, medicine, theology, philosophy-mathematics and science-fine arts—opened with great success. From fewer than 400 students, enrollment quickly swelled to 510 with a 44 man faculty.[22] By 1825, Warsaw University housed an impressive 115,763 volume library.[23] Unlike the Empire's universities, Warsaw did not bear responsibility for all education at every level within a delineated geographic area. In this respect it was unencumbered. Although the government exercised both direct and indirect control over the institution's fortunes, the university officials enjoyed a considerable degree of autonomy. Judging by the fact that more than sixty percent of the degrees granted during the 1817-1830 period were in law, it seems as though the university's chief function was to produce qualified persons to meet the bureaucracy's demands.[24]

In addition to the university, other schools of higher education appeared. They included the mining school at Kielce, the Warsaw forestry school, a first rate polytechnical institute, an agricultural institute, a school for training teachers and a rabbinical school. The government ignored women's education, although records for 1819 disclose that 1,257 girls attended private boarding schools.[25] Under Potocki, the Education Ministry also encouraged Sunday schools for the working artisans. Strong opposition from Jews as well as the Roman Catholic clergy scuttled plans to send Jews to the public elementary schools. As a result, in 1820 the ministry opened three lay elementary schools for Jewish children.[26]

The question of Poland's reunification hung over the Congress Kingdom during its entire existence and seemed to permeate every official and unofficial act. Alexander, for reasons of state, vaguely encouraged the Poles in their hopes for a unified country. The emperor often repeated his desire to unite the Lithuanian provinces with his new kingdom. However, he always expressed himself in obscure and ambiguous phrases and, as usual, never committed himself to a specific plan of action. Nevertheless, his nebulous hints about reunification served him extremely well in the Congress Kingdom where most Poles had never reconciled themselves to the partitions.

Alexander further endeared himself to patriotic Poles when he performed flawlessly at his Warsaw coronation. In mid-November 1815, a few days before his investiture, he received a delegation of Poles from Russia's western provinces headed by Michael Ogiński, Hetman of Lithuania, long-time supporter of a pro-Russian orientation, and the tsar's personal acquaintance. In a private audience with Ogiński, the emperor acknowledged the current absence of satisfactory relations between the western *gubernii* and Russia proper. Denying that he would ever detach these regions from the Empire, he informed Ogiński that he envisioned a union of all Poles with Russia under the aegis of a single, federated constitutional state. Constitutional Poland had to act as a model which, if successful, would enable Alexander to "carry out the rest." In closing, he counseled patience and warned Ogiński to refrain from any action which would place him (Alexander) in an embarrassing position.[27] Alexander never outlined his Lithuanian policy more clearly.

On November 26, 1815, Alexander granted the delegation a public audience. There Oginski read an address lavishly praising Alexander's military prowess and his mercy toward the Lithuanian Poles. In response, the ruler not only informed the deputation that their countrymen's welfare was the continual object of his attention and concern, but also testified that he persistently thought about means to improve their fortunes and to insure their peace and happiness. In conclusion he told his audience to assure their compatriots ". . . that I will do even more for them than they expect from me today, (. . .*je ferai pour eux bien plus même qu'ils ne peuvent s'y attendre audjourd'hui*)."[28] This speech left most Poles and many Russians with the distinct impression that the emperor was promising an eventual Polish-Lithuanian union. The ecstatic Poles chose to overlook completely the fact that whereas Oginski's deputation represented only Wilno, Grodno and Minsk *gubernii*, the Russian tsar forbade other deputations selected in Podolia and Volhynia *gubernii* to travel to Warsaw, and refused altogether to permit elections in Vitebsk and Moghilev *gubernii*.[29]

In the years immediately following his 1815 coronation as King of Poland, Alexander gave further evidence that he genuinely intended to unite the Congress Kingdom with the Lithuanian provinces. For one thing, the Polonization of the Wilno educational district under Czartoryski's directorship continued unabated. Moreover, clauses in the Vienna Treaty calling for free navigation and unhindered circulation of industrial and agricultural products in "all the extent of former Poland" facilitated commercial exchanges between the Congress Kingdom and the western provinces.[30] The 1818 St. Petersburg Convention which forced the Poles to turn eastward for markets stimulated trade relations. Finally, except for military governorships and the police apparatus, Poles occupied almost all the administrative positions within these *gubernii*. Thus, developments in the cultural-educational, economic and administrative spheres seemed to herald an impending unification. Nevertheless, in that part of Russian Poland seized in the first partition, i.e., Vitebsk and Moghilev *gubernii*, Russification advanced without pause.

The most significant development foreshadowing a Polish reunion occurred on July 13, 1817, when an imperial *ukaz* named Constantine to head a newly created Lithuanian corps. Supplemented by a second *ukaz* adding Volhynian and Podolian troops, Constantine now commanded forty thousand nominally Russian soldiers in addition to his thirty thousand man Polish army. Integration of the two forces appeared inevitable. St. Petersburg quickly transferred natives of the Lithuanian provinces into the new corps and issued orders that all recruits for the corps be drawn from Wilno, Grodno, Minsk, Volhynia and Podolia *gubernii*, and Białystok *oblast*. The Poles, as well as other interested parties, regarded these actions as the first tangible steps toward unification.[31]

In the course of Alexander's ten year reign as Polish king, he regularly dropped hints about a future Polish-Lithuanian merger. Despite the numerous permutations distinguishing both his tactical and strategical Polish plans, this ploy served him well, never failing to draw the desired response from Polish leaders. During the 1815-1819 period, it appears that Alexander genuinely intended to reunite the old Poland lands. In doing so, he apparently hoped to secure three advantages for the Russian state. First, he wanted to dispose of Polish irredentist claims against the Empire itself if not against the other partitioning powers. In fact, a union of Poles under Russian suzerainty would give Alexander the opportunity to manipulate these irredentist claims to further Russia's own diplomatic goals vis-à-vis Prussia and Austria. Secondly, he wanted to reinstate Peter the Great's old but successful policy of indirect control over Poland. A Polish-Lithuanian union, a magnanimous move designed to win Polish affections without relinquishing essential Russian control, represented real progress in that direction. Finally, he wanted to constitutionalize the Russian state. Toward this end Alexander proposed to extend his constitutional experiment first to the western provinces and then to Russia itself. Novosil'tsov's constitutional project (see Chapter 5) was the logical culmination of this policy as well as the high water mark of Alexander's constitutional plans for the Empire.

In the waning years of Alexander's reign, the Lithuanian gambit took on a different significance. Then it became the carrot in a carrot and stick maneuver aimed at restraining the unruly Poles. With the prospects of unification dangling before them, many influential Poles hesitated to voice criticism for fear that Alexander would rescind his "promise" to reunite Poland.

At the first Sejm (March 27-April 27, 1818), Alexander began to implement his long range plans. In his speeches opening and closing the deliberations, the emperor came as close as he ever did to publicly stating his intention to constitutionalize Russia and to amalgamate the Congress Kingdom with the western *gubernii*. Nevertheless, he carefully and purposely couched his designs in vague, ambiguous terminology defying precise definition. Moreover, apparently Alexander believed that his speeches were neither morally nor legally binding. In sum, Alexander committed himself to nothing.

In his brief opening speech the king alluded to his desire to extend the Polish constitution:

> The organization which was in force in your country has permitted the immediate establishment of what I have given to you, putting into practice the principles of those liberal institutions that have not ceased to be the object of my solicitude and whose salutary influence

I hope, with the aid of God, to extend to all the countries which Providence has confided to my care.

You have thus offered me the means of showing my fatherland what I have been preparing for it for a long time, and what it will obtain, as soon as the elements of so important a work will have reached the necessary development.[32]

In closing, Alexander turned, albeit abstractly, to the Lithuanian situation:

The results of your work in this first assembly will teach me what the fatherland is able to look forward to by your devotion to it, as well as your good feelings toward me; and if, faithful to my resolutions, I will be able to extend what I have already done for you.[33]

Eyewitness reports show that neither the opening nor closing speeches were spur of the moment pronouncements off-handedly concocted and lackadaisically delivered by a weak willed and unstable monarch drifting towards mysticism and black reaction. On the contrary, the evidence indicates that they proceeded from the emperor's painstaking efforts and careful calculations. Alexander knew precisely what the addresses conveyed to the Russians as well as the Poles. As early as February, Alexander asked his Foreign Minister, Capo d'Istria, to comment on the speech which the emperor had already prepared for the Sejm's opening. Capo d'Istria objected to both the comparison the sovereign drew between Poland and Russia, and his implied promise to return the Lithuanian provinces to Poland. Ignoring these objections, Alexander ordered Capo d'Istria to draw up his own project for the opening speech. Several days later, when the minister presented his work, Alexander simply set it aside with the remark that they would return to the question after their arrival in Warsaw. Capo d'Istria interpreted this as a rebuke.

Two days before the Sejm opened, Alexander handed Capo d'Istria the draft of a speech almost identical to the one given the Foreign Minister in St. Petersburg. He told Capo d'Istria, "I give you full authority to arrange phrases grammatically and to insert periods and commas, but do not make any other changes." However, Capo d'Istria could not remain silent. In addition to following the emperor's orders, the minister also composed a second draft in which he omitted or modified all references to potentially controversial subjects. When presented with this second work, the indignant tsar told Capo d'Istria, "You won't give an inch. This is more than perseverance. I am angry about the work which you took upon yourself. I thank you for it, but I prefer my rendition to yours."[34] On the next day Alexander delivered his unexpurgated speech to the Sejm.

If Alexander expended considerable time and energy composing the speeches and resolutely defending their contents in the face of repeated objections from his Foreign Minister he apparently devoted similar preparations to their delivery. A member of the imperial entourage present at the Sejm's closing described Alexander's bearing:

> The Emperor entered walking, went to the throne (in Polish uniform and with the order of the white eagle), bowed to all sides, and began to deliver this speech in French. He rendered it almost by heart and rarely glanced at the paper on which it was written. . . .
>
> We, the Russian adjutants, numbered seven: we stood by the side of the throne and from time to time shot glances at each other, in which were expressed that we hardly believed that which was taking place before our eyes. Only later did we agree that the Emperor, of course, repeatedly recited his speech before a mirror because he delivered it with such propriety and such stateliness as could have been achieved only by this.[35]

In this address Alexander praised the Sejm's working record and once again endorsed constitutionalism and the primacy of law. He also told the Poles:

> I will attentively consider your requests and you will learn, I hope, at your next session, that they will be satisfied as long as the circumstances permit it. The cares which I have for my country call me away from you; but your destinies will always be in my thoughts. I will return among you . . . to reap the new fruits of my solicitude. Poles! I hold to the accomplishment of my intentions.[36]

The evidence indicates that Alexander spoke sincerely when he hinted at extending the constitution and reuniting Poland with the western provinces. The care with which he wrote and delivered the speeches, the imperially sanctioned developments in Russian Poland, his continuing plans for administrative reform in the Empire and his unflagging interest in constitutions all give proof of Alexander's intentions. In this context his Sejm addresses seem to be yet another cautious, if more direct, step toward achieving his objectives.

Perhaps Alexander was about to realize his plans or perhaps he simply decided to sound out public opinion through provocative but non-obligatory declamations. In any event, public response was not long delayed. The Poles, naturally, reacted quickly and favorably. They interpreted the king's indistinct language as a definite promise to extend the Polish constitution to a Russian Poland legally joined to the Congress Kingdom.[37]

Russian reaction, just as swift, was almost uniformly negative. The avalanche of criticism took many forms. Count Mikhailovskii-Danilevskii observed:

> Russians finding themselves at Warsaw were all... occupied by the Emperor's speech at the opening of the national assembly in which it was said that the sovereign proposed to bring political freedom to Russia. Without a doubt it was curious to hear such words from the lips of an autocrat; it will be necessary to see, I think, the introduction of these principles into action. Peter the Great did not say that Russians were wild and that he intended to enlighten them; he shaped them without further ado....[38]

Other Russian military figures attending the tsar also reacted strongly. Ivan Paskevich, then a young general attached to Grand Duke Michael, grumbled that the opening speech was insulting to the Russians and detrimental to their self-esteem. Additionally, he contended that it heightened the Poles' arrogance, much to the distaste of the Russians who detested Alexander's attempts "to enlist the love of the Polish generals of Napoleon's army.[39] Count Osterman-Tolstoi, a minor hero as a corps commander during the 1812 campaign, prophesied to Paskevich that within the decade the latter, with his divisions, would storm Praga once again.[40] Osterman-Tolstoi miscalculated by only three years.[41] Others, such as General A.P. Ermolov, spewed forth unadulterated hate for the Poles as well as a shocked disbelief that the emperor would single out the "insolent, drunken, defeated Poles" as an example for the Russian Empire.[42] General A.A. Zakrevskii, then serving on the General Staff, foresaw horrifying consequences for Russia in Alexander's speech.[43] Count P.D. Kiselev, the emperor's aide-de-camp and later the author of a modest reform for state serfs, not only objected to the content of the speech, but also to its frankness. He also criticized the tsar's tendency to spring the unexpected.[44]

Although far removed from Warsaw, other influential Russians chimed in with their own critical comments. Count Rostopchin, the ultra-nationalist and self-proclaimed incendiary of Moscow wrote from Paris:

> It has been written, in confidence, from St. Petersburg that the emperor's speech at Warsaw, his distinct predilection for the Poles and the impudence of the latter have aroused people; the young people demand a constitution. All this will end with the removal of a dozen of the biggest chatters; they know how to shout but not how to revolt, and only tongues become rebellious. They consider as a constitution the freedom of the peasants, which is against the wishes of the nobility; but they do not want to restrict their power and bring it under the rule of justice and reason.[45]

Karamzin echoed Rostopchin's observations about the effects on Russian youth. Writing to I.I. Dimitriev, he noted that "The Warsaw speeches strongly reverberated in the hearts of the young," who now, "see a constitution in their sleep."[46]

Although true that the Russian youth generally reacted favorably to the tsar's pronouncements, they also expressed distinct and serious reservations. Young Russian liberals, including several future Decembrists, bitterly opposed unification of the western provinces with Poland. Moreover, they objected to what they viewed as Alexander's preferential treatment of the Poles. Regarding Alexander's Warsaw speech, the conspirator N.I. Turgenev commented in his *La Russie et les Russes*, "There were people, who, casting aside petty interests of *amour-propre* and ill-directed nationality, rejoiced freely in the intention of the emperor, although finding it little flattering that their country was less ready than Poland for liberty."[47] One of the causes for Turgenev's and other liberals' offense was a mistranslation of Alexander's speech. The translator, Prince P.A. Viazemskii, inadvertently substituted the word "education" for "organization," making it appear that Alexander praised the Poles traditional "educational" level rather than their "organizational" level. Concerned Russians drew an unfounded but not unnatural negative inference from these phrases.[48]

Alexander's former advisor and confidant, Michael Speranskii, also commented on the speeches. In a May 2 letter from Speranskii to his friend A.A. Stolypin, the exiled statesman cited the dangers inherent in the uproar surrounding Alexander's declarations. Speranskii maintained that the peril resulting from the address did not lie in Russia's vulnerability to the proposed reform, but rather in the fear beginning to grip the countryside. Rhetorically he asked:

> Is it possible to suppose that distrubed and uneasy feelings will remain in secret within the circle of landowners? Soon it will be perceived in the villages (an event very close) then there will come into being or, better to say, will be confirmed (for it already exists) the opinion, held by the serfs, that the government not only wants to grant freedom, but that it already has granted it, and that only the landlords do not permit it, or obscure its proclamation. What will result from this can be imagined with horror, but is quite understandable to all. This sorrowful prophecy is not founded on ideological presumption, but on all that which I have heard and seen during my seven years travel in Russia, based on a sound and experienced knowledge of all the contagion and indomitability of popular delusions.[49]

Speranskii once again clearly revealed himself to be a conservative reformer functioning well within narrow and fixed autocratic bounds. Even at this late date, Speranskii's fundamental political conceptions coincided with Alexander's, a fact adding credence to the supositions that the tsar dismissed his minister in 1812 for reasons of political expediency rather than for any essential divergence of opinions. Speranskii criticized the form and timing of the Warsaw pronouncements, but not their substance:

> ...you ask, or rather our short-sighted liberals ask, in what way, from two or three words of the Warsaw speech, might there occur very great and very foolish consequences? It may be that something has already resulted and been accomplished before our eyes. If the landowners, a class of people, without doubt, enlightened, saw nothing more in this speech than emancipation of the serfs, then it is possible to demand, what else may the common people see there? In all states few, but with us still fewer, people know the difference between political and civic freedom. In all probability, the meaning of the speech dealt with the former; the second might, or at least should be, the remote and gradual consequence. But attempt here

to assure minds already for a long time alarmed by fears or blinded by hopes. . . . Who sweeps the stairs from the bottom?[50]

Speranskii's oft-stated formula for reform did not differ substantially from Alexander's own concepts. Both statesmen envisioned nothing more than well-defined and gradually implemented administrative measures to cure the country's ills. At this time Speranskii offered a timetable for reform:

> (first) purify the administration. Then introduce constitutional (organic) laws: that is to say political liberty. Then gradually turn to the question of civil freedom, that is to say the liberty of the peasants. Here is the true nature of things.[51]

The criticism which Alexander's speeches evoked certainly penetrated to the throne room. However, neither the tsar's words nor his actions revealed any immediate inclination to modify his policies in order to mollify Russian court and gentry circles.

One important result of the speeches and the reactions they elicited was the tendency to overlook the day to day Sejm proceedings. Yet these sessions provide an excellent opportunity to measure the Sejm's depth of attachment to the king's person, the independence of the body's members and the national representation's relationship to the executive-administrative sector. Moreover, they clearly disclose the first signs of a Polish political opposition destined to plague Alexander until his death.

Although the larger towns elected several middle class deputies, the Sejm, as expected, possessed a decidedly aristocratic composition. Most delegates displayed a cautious attitude; and, at this point, it was impossible to discern any real political groupings. Rather, the 1818 Sejm resembled a congress of prominent individuals chosen by their peers without much regard for the business at hand. In such circumstances, the representatives usually voted their conscience on an issue by issue basis. Nevertheless, in the course of the sessions certain loose blocs or combinations emerged. However, they were undisciplined, amorphous and devoid of a mature political philosophy. On the right, an ultra-clerical clique consisting of the fourteen ecclesiastical representatives and several ardent Roman Catholic lay deputies surfaced under the leadership of Stanisław Grabowski and David Obszelwicz.[52] A second cluster numbering a dozen or

The Polish Congress Kingdom 51

so deputies with Wincenty Niemojowski and the Gawroński brothers at its head espoused the "liberal" cause. Despite these developments, the overwhelming majority of the delegates simply wished to follow the government's lead. They were quite content to declare their confidence in the king. Ironically, largely unaware of the seriousness of his rupture with Alexander, this grey mass looked to Czartoryski for leadership. A most unlikely deputy was Grand Duke Constantine, selected to represent the Warsaw suburb, Praga. Elected to this position in the hope that he would secure special privileges for his constituents, Constantine accepted the representative's mandate and attended the sessions in this capacity.[53] However, he disappointed his supporters. Instead of using his influence to aid Praga, he remained detached, viewing the Sejm itself as a ludicrous aberration and comparing it to a Russian stage comedy.[54]

The only battle of any significance during the Sejm took place over a government proposal to suspend the marriage law, i.e., to modify the fifth and sixth books of the Code Napoleon. The proposed project, a compromise which eliminated civil marriages in favor of a church monopoly but retained their secular court jurisdiction over marital affairs, drew fire from both the ultramontane elements and the liberal deputies.[55] The former attacked it for turning over vital church matters to lay authorities, an obvious infringement upon canon law. The latter saw in the project an unwarranted revival of ecclesiastical power as well as undisguised church interference in purely secular affairs. Although the Senate passed the measure, the two antagonistic forces together with a substantial number of "uncommitted" deputies combined to defeat the bill, eighty-two to thirty-six.[56]

The "liberals" also opposed a government project to reform the criminal code along Austrian lines. They attacked its foreign character, its inexactitude, and its length (586 articles).[57] Although the government's cosmetic additions and corrections failed to satisfy its opponents, the proposal passed anyway, sixty-four to forty-nine. Several deputies voting favorably noted that they deferred to the king's desires, not wishing to sadden Alexander's heart.[58]

More important for the Sejm's long term future than either the harmonious spirit then prevailing or the occasional resistance to a particular bill were the signs that an ideologically rooted opposition, dedicated to preserving the constitution in the face of government encroachments, might be forming. In an impassioned floor speech, W. Niemojowski sounded a harbinger of things to come when he warned his fellow lawmakers:

> The constitution is the consecrated fire of the people. We, representatives of the nation, are the guardians of this fire; woe betide the Sejm which permits it to be extinguished. The constitution is our political Gospel. The representatives of the nation should be vigilant so that its cardinal tenets are not impaired in the least.[59]

In the same speech he also reproached the executive on several counts: violating Sejm privileges, tolerating the government's anti-constitutional activities, assigning the Sejm a secondary and passive role in the Kingdom's affairs.[60] Here one finds a political philosophy completely at odds with Alexander's conceptions of constitutionalism and liberalism. In 1818, Niemojowski had no dedicated followers let alone a parliamentary faction or party, but his exposition fired imaginations and struck a responsive chord among younger, more cosmopolitan and better educated Poles.

Alexander's immediate concern, however, did not lie with fiery rumblings from an obscure deputy. Niemojowski's outburst seemed foolishly inappropriate in the face of the unrestrained adulation heaped on the tsar and the predominant spirit which Czartoryski described favorably as "the king with the nation, and the nation with the king."[61] What did upset Alexander, however, was the Sejm's official "Observations" in reply to the "Report on Government Activities presented to the Sejm by the Council of State."[62] Czartoryski, who composed the "Observations" in his capacity as Senator, employed it as a means to draw Alexander's attention once again to the lawlessness of the Kingdom's administration. Among other illegalities, he complained of lack of ministerial responsibility, the practice of introducing royal decrees into law without the appropriate minister's countersignature, occasional arbitrary censorship and blurring of the demarcation line between executive and legislative authority. The king took offense at the commentaries, seeing in them a direct challenge to his inviolable authority. Sending a response through the Minister-Secretary of State for Poland, he repeated his views on the Sejm and its relation to the government:

> According to article 154 of the constitution the Sejm does not have the right to indict the government or to make reproaches to it; it

must deliver its views only on those matters which the government communicates to it. So that its opinion might have real utility it should express concrete desires and not lose itself in general principles and theoretical examinations....[63]

Despite the liberal trappings and the repetitious mouthing of beautiful phrases, Alexander always remained a paternalistic autocrat at heart. An enlightened despot par excellence, he never relaxed his iron grip on the levers of power or yielded an iota of his immense authority. It must be reiterated that Alexander did not recognize in constitutionalism a political system to limit and define the sovereign's power and prerogatives. Nor did he perceive in a constitution a document of abstract political principles designed to guarantee the rights of the nation and its citizens through representative government. Rather, for Alexander constitutionalism explicitly signified a sweeping *administrative* reform. Under constitutionalism and liberalism, Alexander hoped to restructure the Empire's administrative institutions, to rationalize the government's apparatus and set it on a legal foundation, to eliminate caprice and to establish precise administrative and judicial procedures.

CHAPTER 4

STRAINED RELATIONS: THE AUTOCRATIC EMPIRE AND THE CONSTITUTIONAL MONARCHY, 1818-1820

During the 1818-1820 period, Alexander underwent a remarkable change of attitude toward Poland and the Poles. Commencing with personal displays of coolness and even disdain, Alexander eventually abandoned his long-standing reliance upon conciliation and cooperation. In its place he substituted authoritarian and autocratic control based on repression and retribution for those who refused to acquiesce in his wishes. Although many factors blended to dictate this striking reversal, two stand out. The most prominent was a wave of revolutionary activity in Europe. The Spanish, Portuguese and Neapolitan revolutions combined with the murders of August von Kotzebue and the Duc du Berry to undermine Alexander's faith in the moderate, even generous, means he had chosen. More enraged and apprehensive than disillusioned or crushed, the emperor became more willing to listen to Metternich's reactionary suggestions.

The second major consideration was the continuing hostility among many influential Russians to a Polish policy which seemed to them to border on treason. Opposition came from cosmopolitan liberals as well as provincial conservatives. Both future Decembrists and the Moscow-oriented nobility expressed distaste for the tsar's Polish policy. High ranking military officers criticized unwarranted leniency toward the Poles, and protested the Congress Kingdom's mere existence. The court itself was divided. The dowager empress, Maria Fedorovna, made little effort to hide her contempt for the Poles and her dissatisfaction with her son's course.[1]

During Alexander's reign the famous historian and man of letters, N.M. Karamzin, gradually turned his attention to the Polish question. Karamzin, a kind of self-appointed advisor to the tsar who did not shrink from expressing harsh or unfavorable opinions, first explored the Polish situation and Poland's position vis-à-vis Russia in his famous *Memoir on Ancient and Modern Russia*. Submitted to Alexander during the emperor's visit in 1811 to the Tver salon of his favorite sister, Grand Duchess Catherine Pavlovna, a politically ambitious woman who hoped "to play an important role at the court and to secure an influence over her older brother," Karamzin's *Memoir* defended the partitions as just and correct.[2] Defiantly he proclaimed, "Let foreigners condemn the partitions of Poland—we took what was ours."[3] After criticizing the Treaty of Tilsit for its failure to include a stipulation forbidding the resurrection of Poland, Karamzin outlined a policy of aggressive Russification for the former Polish lands.[4]

In political matters Karamzin exerted little real influence. However, as the Russian historian A.N. Pypin observes, his pronouncements are important in that they gave tangible life to the conservative majority's opinion.[5] This became evident once again in October 1819 when, in the wake of a long conversation with Alexander about Poland, the historian wrote his *Opinion of a Russian Citizen*. Karamzin, now residing in palace apartments at 'Tsarkoe' Selo, feared his blunt statements would anger the tsar and , perhaps, terminate their relationship. But, apparently, the tsar accepted Karamzin's candid remarks and the writer continued as a peripheral member of Alexander's entourage.[6]

In his *Opinion* Karamzin dealt first with Poland's restoration. Appealing to Alexander's sense of duty, patriotism and justice, he told the Emperor:

> ...Christian faith is a mysterious union between God and the human heart; it soars high above the world, over all physical, social, and national laws, but does not abolish them. Does Your Majesty want to restore the former Kingdom of Poland? Would such a restoration be consistent with the law of Russia's public weal? Is it consistent with your sacred duties, with our love for Russia and with justice itself? People may say that Catherine had lawlessly partitioned Poland! But your action would be still more lawless if you would try to redeem Catherine's injustice by partitioning the very land of Russia.[7]

Concluding this trend of thought with an abrupt *volte-face,* the historian justified Russia's role in the partitions saying, "We have taken Poland with the power of our sword. This was our right. All countries owe their existence to it, for they emerge out of conquest. In politics there are no old titles."[8]

As for merging the western provinces with the Congress Kingdom, Karamzin wrote:

> Either all, or nothing. Until now our national principle was not an inch of soil to either friend or foe. Napoleon might conquer Russia but you, Emperor, though being an autocrat, you had no right to cede to him by means of an agreement even a single Russian hut. Such is our character and such the spirit of our state.[9]

Karamzin then criticized Alexander's Polish intentions:

> ... Should, however, ancient Poland be restored ... and produce a worthy, sincere, impartial historian, he himself would condemn your magnanimity as harmful to your true country, good and powerful Russia. Such a historian would certainly not say what the Poles are telling you today. We will forgive them, but we, Russians, would never forgive you if, to win their applause, you would drive us to despair.[10]

In conclusion, Karamzin representing himself as qualified to speak for Russian society, warned that:

> ... the restoration of Poland would mean the downfall of Russia, or our sons would have again to shed their blood on Polish soil and again take Praga by storm.

> ... the Poles will never be to use either sincere brothers or faithful allies.... If you make them stronger, they will want to become independent and their first step towards independence will be separation from Russia.... The Poles, legally established as a distinct and sovereign nation, would be more dangerous to us than the Poles as subjects of Russia.[11]

Although his political opinions were neither original nor profound, Karamzin fulfilled his self-appointed role as counselor to the tsar and spokesman for Russia's powerful conservatives with some success.[12] In speaking of Karamzin's political writings, Baron M.N. Korf, Speranskii's biographer, accurately characterized them as "a skillful compilation of what he had heard around him."[13] The Polish historian, Jan Kucharzewski, citing this evidence, concluded that "one may therefore assert that the report on Poland (Karamzin's *Opinion*) expressed the opinion of all classes, from the court on to members of secret societies."[14] Nevertheless, despite alarming European events as well as Russian rumblings of discontent, Alexander at first not only continued to promote his Polish policy, but also took several more steps preparatory to introducing a constitutional regime in the Empire itself. Simultaneously, however, he approved certain measures which represented a distinct retreat from his implied goals for Poland as well as for Russia. These retrogressive steps were, in part, a direct reaction to current trends in the Empire and Europe and, in part, a practical manifestation of Alexander's philosophical views on the autocracy, Polish indepedence, government in general and constitutions in particular.

In most cases, Alexander appeared to be a shrewd and eminently practical politician. He felt no compunction about edging in two different directions at the same time. He strove to maintain his options, to insure himself the freedom to select the most efficacious path at the most opportune moment. In matters of his imperial authority, however, Alexander always set aside his cultivated pragmatism in favor of an uncompromising stance. Whenever he perceived an attack on his power base, he moved swiftly and forcefully to assert his omnipotence. It mattered not a whit to the monarch that the attack came under the guise of defending constitutional principles. In Alexander's scheme, the constitution existed for the emperor's (and state's) benefit, not as a cover for launching attacks on the autocracy.

In light of the foregoing, it would be incorrect to conclude that Alexander had already abandoned his goals or the means chosen to attain them. Most certainly it does not represent an end to his "liberal" period and the beginning of his "reactionary" phase. Rather, Alexander merely reacted to vastly different circumstances than had existed in the recent past. For one thing, Alexander was no longer the arbiter of Europe as he had been in 1815. Accordingly, his power to act unilaterally or to force compromises favorable to himself and to Russia diminished. Moreover, movements designed to undermine or topple legitimate authority frightened him. In part he blamed himself for fostering and encouraging tendencies which now seemed to pose a real threat to European stability. Finally, he found himself beseiged at home. Attacked from all sides because of his stated intentions, wearied by burdens of state which sapped his energies, and confronted by a growing realization that a succession crisis loomed on the horizon, the emperor hesitated and temporized before committing himself to any fundamental policy change.

During 1818 and 1819, Alexander significantly advanced his constitutional project for the Russian Empire when he directed Novosil'tsov to draw up a charter. The erstwhile Russian Senator handled this potentially dangerous chore in an exceptionally adroit manner, composing a constitution of 191 paragraphs which was an almost verbatim reproduction of the 1815 Polish constitution which Alexander himself had coauthored. In summer 1819, Novosil'tsov forwarded his draft to Alexander at St. Petersburg under care of young Prince P.A. Viazemskii, then assisting Novosil'tsov at Warsaw. In a lengthy audience, the tsar did more than express satisfaction with his Imperial Commissioner's work. He also detailed his plans to constitutionalize Russia, and informed Viazemskii that he would finish the project with Novosil'tsov during his coming visit to the Polish capital.[15]

When Alexander arrived in Warsaw in early October 1819 for a two week stay, he and Novosil'tsov added the final touches to "The Charter of the Fundamental Law of the Russian Empire."[16] In a revolutionary step for Russia, the proposed charter guaranteed basic civil liberties including *habeas corpus* and equality before the law. The charter also provided for a national Duma to meet every five years in either St. Petersburg or Moscow. However, the charter granted the Duma consultative powers only. Limited to discussion of issues presented by the tsar, the Duma could only make nonbinding recommendations. Moreover, the tsar reserved the right to choose all the members of the Duma's upper house and half the membership of its lower house. Finally, the charter specified that the sovereign represented "the sole source of all authority in the Empire."

The 1820 Russian constitution also envisioned a federated state. Novosil'tsov's draft called for division of the Empire into twelve autonomous governorships. Each new *gubernia* would have a consultative assembly elected by the landowning nobility and other citizens meeting education or property requirements. Real local power would rest with the imperially appointed governor. Under these provisions, Congress Poland could easily became a member province of a federated Russian Empire.

Nevertheless, Alexander never promulgated the charter. During his conversation with Viazemskii the tsar hinted that financial difficulties as well as opposition from his closest advisors threatened his constitutional plans.[17] Moreover, Alexander's alarm at revolutionary events in Europe and at home also acted to diminish his enthusiasm for any change in the *status quo*.

The entire project, kept secret even from Constantine, created a minor furor in 1831 when the Polish rebels printed two thousand copies of the document. A horrified Tsar Nicholas I commanded General Paskevich to confiscate it, writing, "...of one hundred of our young officers ninety...will not be stirred up or will hold it in contempt, but ten will keep it in mind, discuss it, and, most importantly, not forget it. This, most of all, upsets me." The Russians collected 1,578 copies and sent them to Moscow where they were burned on Nicholas' order.[18]

A tentative step toward Polish reunification also took place during this October sojourn when Novosil'tsov, at Alexander's request, prepared translations of the 1413 and 1501 acts strengthening the Polish union with Lithuania. In addition to translations, Novosil'tsov also included an analysis of the acts' basic provisions.[19] The two agreements enshrined the principle of a Polish-Lithuanian union. and called for the extension of various administrative uniformities to both states. They also confirmed the principle of a representative Sejm. In his explanatory note, Novosil'tsov emphasized the procedure which enabled the Polish king, Władysław, to yield *de facto* control of Lithuania to his brother which maintaining *de jure* overlordship for himself. It seems as though Alexander ordered the translations and analysis in order to supply legal and historical precedents to support his own unification scheme for Poland which provided for a gradual extension of the Congress Kingdom's political, judicial and administrative apparatus to the Lithuanian lands. In the blur of events, however, it is impossible to reject completely the thought that Alexander's desire to replace Constantine in the line of succession for the Russian throne prompted him to investigate the feasibility of awarding his brother *de facto* control over a quasi-independent Polish-Lithuanian state in which the reigning Russian tsar would retain *de jure*, hereditary suzerainty. This speculation gains some credence in light of the July 11, 1819 *ukaz* which extended Constantine's authority in the western provinces and gave him at least partial control of these *gubernii*. The Polish historian, S. Askenazy, asserts that after this *ukaz* was issued, the respective military governors of the western provinces looked directly to Warsaw and the Grand Duke for their orders.[20]

This series of projects, *ukazi*, and memoranda represents the high-water mark of Alexander's flirtation with constitutional rule for the Russian Empire. Moreover, the incident of the 1819-1820 Russian constitution also serve to illuminate Novosil'tsov's position. It reveals him to be a figure of limited power, dependent on Alexander's good will, and incapable of acting independently. Undeniably, the situation changed drastically over the next six years, but in 1819 the Imperial Commissioner played a clearly secondary role. In fact, in assigning Novosil'tsov the task of drafting a charter for the Russian Empire, the tsar placed him in an uncomfortable position. Given Alexander's previous treatment of his servants, Novosil'tsov had every right to feel apprehensive. Certainly, if he acted too independently he ran the risk of dismissal and banishment once again. Moreover, if for any reason the project failed, Novosil'tsov would be a convenient scapegoat. The Imperial Commissioner, however, handled his task skillfully. As a result he not only protected and stabilized his position in the Kingdom, but also gained a large estate at Słonim bringing in 125,000 *rubles*. Little wonder that Novosil'tsov referred to his constitution as "a masterpiece."[21]

Concurrent with his project for a Russian constitution, Alexander either endorsed or initiated procedures which conflicted with his previous moves to achieve a favorable relationship with the Poles. Alexander now began to retreat from constitutionalism and a modified rule of law. The most obvious reversal took place in the censorship field. Several unexpected and relatively trivial incidents prompted the Warsaw authorities to issue unconstitutional decrees without St. Petersburg's knowledge or direction. Nevertheless, when informed of this turn of events, Alexander, after careful consideration chose to support his appointees at the expense of his Polish policy and his high standing with the Polish population.

Before 1815, censorship played a minor role in the Polish lands. For one thing, it did not exist prior to its introduction by the Prussians after the partitions. Furthermore, the general cultural and educational level in eighteenth century Poland was so low as to make imposition of censorship superfluous for all practical purposes. The Russians contributed their share to Polish censorship when they extended Catherine the Great's 1796 preventive censorship law to their newly acquired Polish territories. After Alexander's early repeal of preventive censorship (*ukaz* of March 21, 1801, and July 9, 1802), the law of June 9, 1804, reinstated it.[22] The Duchy of Warsaw institutionalized censorship (article 40, Organization of the Ministries; April 20, 1808), parceling out its administration to both the Interior Ministry and the Police Ministry.[23] When the Provisional Government succeeded the defunct Duchy, it continued to enforce existing policy.

At this time censorship showed the pattern first established in Russia in 1804. Although comparatively mild and permissive, censorship was neither grounded in law nor governed by statutory principles, a defect permitting administrative caprice and excess. Preventive censorship aimed to forestall the publication and dissemination of all materials deemed harmful by the censors. Specifically, these officials guarded against the introduction of anything contrary to religion, government, morals and public order. To accomplish their assignment, they examined all books, periodicals, newspapers and even theatrical productions. Their scope extended to foreign language and imported works as well.[24] In addition to its preventive purpose, censorship also fulfilled an educational objective, placing before the nation works designed to inculcate and strengthen particular values and ideas judged suitable by the government. Responsibility for conducting censorship activities was never clearly delegated. At various times the universities, the Police Ministry, the Education Ministry, the Internal Affairs Ministry, administrative committees and select individuals enforced the law. The failure to delineate responsibility hampered censorship's efficacy and contributed to a beneficial laxness. Under less favorable circumstances, however, this uncertainty presented opportunities for baneful influences.[25]

Article 16 of the Congress Kingdom's constitution both guaranteed freedom of the press and called for the law to repress abuse of press freedom. In practice, the theoretical ambiguity resolved itself when the newly-created Ministry of Religion and Public Education assumed responsibility for observing and maintaining freedom of the press as well as checking its abuse. However, the Ministry of the Interior and Police was charged with insuring public safety, an assignment which included surveillance over the dissemination of printed materials.[26] As early as February 1816, the Education Ministry formulated a statute to resolve the conflicting aspects of the Kingdom's censorship. Potocki's project called for complete freedom of the press except in certain, strictly enumerated, instances. However, it failed to break cleanly with tradition in that it provided for "advisory" censors selected by the Education Ministry to "...protect freedom of the press, develop education in the people, and maintain peace and quiet both in public and in the home."[27] A third title dealt with abuses and incorporated the English principle that publishing may only be a medium of crime and not a crime per se.

The State Council occupied itself with lengthy and sometimes acrimonious debates on Potocki's proposal.[28] The Justice Minister, Walenty Sobolewski, speaking in favor of preventive censorship, demanded obligatory understandings between the author and the "advisory" censor before publication. J.K. Szaniawski, later chief of the censorship division, supported Sobolewski with the argument that, "discussion of works before their publication restrains only excesses, while never being contrary to spreading knowledge."[29] Others, such as L. Plater and Tadeusz Mostowski, Minister of the Interior, maintained that freedom of the press was a vital matter protected by the constitution. They argued that its restriction would fly in the face of reality and retard the Kingdom's intellectual growth. Moreover, they asserted, experience proved that censorship not only failed to prevent the spread of forbidden works, but only enhanced their desirability for potential readers. The State Council finally approved the Potocki project and forwarded it to the Administrative Council where it passed on March 16, 1816.[30] Sent to St. Petersburg for royal confirmation, however, the proposal languished and died there without explanation.

In practical terms, the failure to rationalize censorship seemed small cause for concern at this time. The Congress Kingdom, a poor, war-devastated rump, was populated by an illiterate peasantry subject to a gentry class devoid—for the most part—of all but a rudimentary education. However, more than a hint of change was in the air. The Napoleonic Wars once again brought the Polish lands into the main stream of European events. If their exposure to the cosmopolitan West excited Russian imaginations, one can picture the effect on the Poles with their Western traditions, their Roman Catholic religion and their close association with the French emperor. While Poland's re-establishment provided a major stimulus, advances in education and the university's establishment (see above, Chapter 3) also energized the population. By 1817 the country supported twenty-four publishers and ten booksellers.³¹ The international book trade flourished. Figures for 1816 and 1817 indicate a twenty-four percent increase in one year in the amount of money spent on imported books.³² During the first years after the abortive attempt to introduce precise censorship regulations, publication remained on an even keel. Despite Article 16, all writers submitted their works for prior censorship. Contenting themselves for their international coverage with excerpts from the *Hamburg Gazette* and Metternich's *Oesterreichische Beobachter*, the two existing newspapers, published twice weekly, made no waves.³³ On the domestic scene, the newspapers simply described social fetes and published various government communications. They deified Alexander and, on the rare occasions when they turned to contemporary Polish affairs, they expressed deep satisfaction with the *status quo*.

In 1819, however, two dramatically different newspapers appeared on the scene. *Tygodnik Polski i Zagraniczny (Polish and Foreign Weekly)* and *Gazeta Codzienna Narodowa i Obca (National and Foreign Daily Gazette)*, were both edited by the youthful Bruno, Count Kiciński, and the recent university graduate, Teodor Morawski. These young men turned to political affairs with a gusto both terrifying and ominous for the governing authorities. They published excerpts from foreign liberal papers on the most controversial issues of the day, including French constitutional struggles and Karl Sand's assassination of Kotzebue. Moreover, they frequently ran long articles on constitutional philosophy. Openly exercising the right of freedom of the press, the publishers antagonized the government.

Passions boiled over in May 1819. Earlier in that year, *Gazeta* had reprinted selections from Niemcewicz's new work, *Dzieje Panowania Zygmunta III (History of the Reign of Zygmunt III)*. In response the government, with Novosil'tsov taking the lead, denounced Niemcewicz's book, characterizing it as filed with "unbridled hatred for Russia" and "intense libels against Russia."³⁴ At the start of May the national theatre was the scene of rowdy behavior when the spectators hooted the actress Phillis, one of the Grand Duke's intimates. Constantine, reacting through the office of the Warsaw municipal president, issued an order calling for the immediate arrest of anyone expressing public displeasure with theatrical performances. In its issues from May 13 through May 19, *Gazeta* roundly attacked this order as unconstitutional. This charge infuriated

Zajączek who instructed the Education Ministry to bring *Gazeta* under the same preliminary censorship as the more docile newspapers. *Gazeta*, citing the constitution, refused. Consequently, on May 19, 1819, the Lord Lieutenant order the newspaper closed and its publishing house padlocked.[35] On the twenty-second Zajączek presented the Administrative Council with his decision to require all newspapers and periodicals, without exception, to submit to government censorship.[36] Potocki, in order to avoid a major constitutional crisis, reluctantly countersigned this arbitrary decree.

On June 12 the Viceroy permitted Kiciński's and Morawski's publishing house to reopen on the condition that it not distribute any periodical without first subjecting it to censorship. He assigned surveillance over the firm to the Interior Ministry.[37] The Minister, however, neglected to communicate Zajączek:s exact words and meaning to his police. Shortly thereafter, the publishing house began to issue *Kronika Drugiej Połowy Roku 1819* (*Chronicle of the Second Half of 1819*). It carried the same tone as its predecessor, i.e., adoration of the emperor, defense of the constitution, and a firm commitment to freedom of the press. In fact, *Kronika* differed from *Gazeta* only in that it did not appear periodically.[38]

At the stormy Administrative Council session on July 13, Zajączek expressed shock that Kiciński and Morawski had been allowed to publish scurrilous matter once again, and demanded an explanation for this outrage. Mostowski replied that surveillance over publishing did not fall within the purview of his police authority. Potocki then stated that he could not possibly enforce censorship without police assistance. Reacting to the Viceroy's anger at this ploy, Mostowski amended his declaration to read that a lack of specific regulations prevented his Ministry from implementing the Lord Lieutenant's decision. On this note an indignant Zajączek closed the meeting.[39]

The ministers fell in line at the next meeting on July 16. At this session the Lord Lieutenant issued a second rescript extending preventive censorship "...to all publications and to all the works of any kind which will appear in the kingdom...." even though these publications are not periodicals.[40] Moreover, the Viceroy specifically ordered the Interior Ministry to enforce the new regulations. Once again the weak-willed and basically subservient ministers acquiesced in Zajączek's actions and countersigned his manifestos.

The Warsaw authorities originated and imposed strict censorship without first consulting St. Petersburg. When news of Zajączek's May 22 decree reached the capital, however, Alexander confirmed his functionary's decision and called for a determination of whether or not an organic statute on censorship would be advisable.[41] The Viceroy turned this matter over to the Education Ministry for discussion in the State Council. In short order a project emerged which closely resembled Potocki's forgotten 1816 proposal.[42] This project, however, was pigeonholed.

Alexander expressed his sentiments on censorship in a December 13, 1819, letter in which he not only reconfirmed the Lord Lieutenant's decrees, but urged the appropriate bodies to formulate law projects on censorship for presentation to the 1820 Sejm.[43] He observed that if article 16 concerned suppression of abuse it might also be concerned with the means to prevent abuse. The emperor considered this as the most certain guarantee against arbitrary actions by public authorities operating in emergency situations where no regulations existed.[44] Although appearing to favor the rule of law, Alexander had, in fact, endorsed an unconstitutional, preventive censorship based on the Lord Lieutenant's arbitrary edicts.

At about the same time that Zajączek issued his censorship decrees, two similar but distinct socio-political movements began to make their presence known. One was the Liberal Opposition, a Polish political movement descended from the Enlightenment. It championed rationalism, constitutionalism and a parliamentary system in order to achieve a genuine rule of law in an independent Congress Kingdom. The other was the Polish secret society movement. It favored mystical rituals and conspiratorial action in order to revitalize the human spirit and to reunite all Poles under one national government. Although derived from divergent philosophies and advocating contradictory solutions to achieve dissimilar goals, both phenomena posed serious problems for the Congress Kingdom's administrators and Alexander's grand Polish designs as well. Starting from scratch, both movements attracted sufficent recruits from among the Kingdom's most intelligent citizens to challenge the *status quo*. Neither an isolated occurrence nor an indigenous Polish development, both movements formed an integral part of the widespread European discontent with the Vienna settlement and the legitimist restoration. Distressed by the administration's disregard for legal forms and its callousness towards reasonable Polish ambitions, both currents drifted into opposition after initial attempts to co-operate with the authorities had failed. However, they never joined together to face the common enemy. Even united, the opposition could have entertained little hope of success against the powerful and entrenched executive; as was the case, they faced certain defeat and extinction.

Although secret societies flourished among both the student population and military circles, there was little interaction between the two groups. The young cadets and officers, because of their part in igniting the November Revolution, have attracted more attention than their academic counterparts.[45] Nevertheless, the secret societies of Polish students fundamentally shaped and influenced that era's Romantic political movement.

German student associations and European Freemasonry served as the chief examples for young Poles. Beginning with the *Tugenbund*, both open and clandestine societies thrived in Germany. Student unions reached the height of their power and popularity in the years following the Congress of Vienna when Karl Follen forged the *Burschenschaft*, an amalgamated national student alliance.[46] During the *Burschenschaft's* heyday, numerous Polish students in attendance at German universities experienced on a firsthand basis both the philosophy and the day to day activities which distinguished the German members. In fact, as early as 1816 Polish scholars at Berlin and Breslau, inspired by the German example, formed their own societies called "Polonia."[47]

Strong Masonic organizations also existed throughout Europe, and Poland was no exception. Warsaw alone boasted several lodges. Not only Alexander, who gained wide notoriety for his support of the Masons, but also Poland's chief administrators including Constantine, Novosil'tsov and Zajączek, maintained their ties to Freemasonry. Many students simultaneously belonged to the Masons and to student secret societies. Almost without exception, Polish secret societies adopted Masonic ritual for their meetings.[48]

A strong desire to strengthen internal life and to search for moral harmony in mutual coexistence characterized the first Polish student societies. Guided by ideas of moral excellence, humanitarianism, sentimentalism and comradeship, their members found nobility in study and learning. At a later date they fused these ideals with more practical plans for national regeneration and independence from foreign domination.[49]

After familiarizing themselves with such Enlightenment sages as Voltaire and Montesquieu, the students quickly turned to early Romantic writers such as Byron and Scott. In their eyes, however, J.J. Rousseau towered over all the rest. They wildly applauded his distrust of pseudo-civilization, his attacks on the modern system's injustices, his frankness and his determination to glorify the individual. The students drew two guiding principles from their attachment to Rousseau: an admiration for human individuality and a love of liberty. In somewhat more practical terms these highly abstract concepts translated into internationalism and cosmopolitanism.[50] The students, sympathetic to unfolding revolutionary movements in western Europe, hungered for details of events in Spain, Naples and Paris. On the domestic scene, they lent moral and vocal support to those Polish elements defending the nation's laws against the government's arbitrary and capricious actions. Following Rousseau's principles, the students developed a hatred for tyranny, oppression and intolerance. In turn, this provoked loathing for reactionary Russia and esteem for opponents of despotic and iniquitous rule. As love of liberty matured into love of nationality, the students became ardent patriots.[51]

In most cases, the early student societies operated at two levels. On the surface they appear as legal associations engaging in public and permissible activities. At their weekly meetings the members read poetry, translated foreign works, presented their own original contributions and occupied themselves with self-education. The larger societies engaged in more general activities, and, in one instance, the largest association at Warsaw University rented a hotel suite where it established a reading room and library in a club-like atmosphere.[52] This appearance, however, occasionally served to shield conspiratorial designs pursued by a small, activist minority. Nevertheless, in the initial years at least, even if secrecy was not unusual, plotting was.

One early literary-social circle, displaying a nascent patriotism, pledged themselves not to speak French and to combat the incursion of French words and sayings into the Polish language. They also gave up French styles in favor of national dress and sewed likenesses of Kościuszko onto their student caps. The founders of this circle included Kiciński and Morawski whose *Gazeta* precipitated the Lord Lieutenant's censorship decrees.[53]

Through the medium of well-placed spies, the government kept abreast of student activity. Their most valuable conduit was H. Mackrott, a Warsaw

University medical student and member of several student societies.[54] After his university career he continued to spy for the authorities until apprehended and executed by the Polish rebels. Mackrott, among other things, informed about the students' favorite meeting places, the demonstrations provoked by the student leader Chometowski's expulsion from Warsaw, and the May 3, 1820, manifestation at Bielany Woods commemorating the May Third Constitution.[55] This last morsel of information inspired police raids on "Gospoda Akademicka" (The Students' Inn), the largest and most public student society at Warsaw University. The secret police dossier containing Mackrott's biographical sketch reported, "He exposed to superior authorities all the contacts among academic students, their secret societies, their designs prejudicial to the public tranquility, and he has given the means to the government to prevent in time the expansion of the abuses of these students."[56]

Perhaps the most representative society of the early Warsaw organizations was "Panta Koina," (All United). Founded in December 1817 by Ludwik Mauersberger, a doctor's son, it was the oldest society at Warsaw University. Mauersberger epitomized the best qualities of his generation of Polish university youth. The following statement indicates his deep love of country and devotion to high-minded principles:

> In Berlin I was at a Polish tavern and became convinced of the good spirit of my companions. There they sang the patriotic song, "Beloved Fatherland," which touched me. I found out there, something I didn't know: that the Posen people (students from the Prussian controlled Grand Duchy of Posen) purely preserved the national spirit, that they were good Poles, and that they formed a Polish section of the *Landsmannschaft*. Here I discovered the difference between the *Burschenschaft* and the *Landsmannschaft*. I prefer the former since its tendencies seem to be liberal: Freedom and Fatherland, whereas the latter has only student prerogatives as its aim.[57]

Originally a strictly literary society, Panta Koina quickly expanded to include philosophical topics such as the study of ethics in a social context. When Mauersberger formulated the association's bylaws he enumerated three goals for its members: (1) friendship, (2) mutual help and (3) entertainment. Mutual help meant both material support and moral support. To accomplish the former, Panta Koina held special collections to aid indigent colleagues. The students understood the latter to mean that a brotherly hand was always extended. Entertainment consisted of meetings devoted to literature and philosophy where the participants read and discussed their own papers and translations.[58] The society encompassed university men of a like age and character. Meetings held over a two-year period usually attracted a few dozen students. Mauersberger wrote in 1819 that "we are so close among ourselves that it would be difficult to disassociate ourselves. We speak little of friendship, but we feel it strongly."[59] Members paid two *zlotys* dues per month. The society was secret and every member swore an oath to maintain this condition. Mauersberger detailed his familiarity with secrecy as practiced by the Masons and considered it necessary and useful for his society to follow their example. This anonymity served several purposes. For one thing, it created an attractive element of mystery. It also guaranteed a more careful selection of members in which to produce a uniform moral atmosphere. Finally, it acted to shield possibly illegal activities. Panta Koina revered Rousseau and frequently drew upon his works for inspiration and moral conviction. Mauersberger's speeches to the brotherhood sometimes paraphrased Rousseau's *Social Contract*.[60] In true Romantic fashion, the society's members worshipped the principles of national freedom and personal liberty.[61]

Panta Koina's story ended tragically when the police discovered its existence in early 1822. Although its headquarters had been disbanded for more than a year, the police, under Novosil'tsov's personal guidance, arrested the former members and carried out a lengthy investigation. The accused, as they had broken no law on the books at the time of Panta Koina's activities, were finally released. However, Mauersberger contracted tuberculosis while in prison and died in January 1823.[62]

During the Congress Kingdom's first decade, two important developments gradually effected radical changes within Polish student societies. The first was the drift away from abstract, moral-philosophical pursuits towards more concrete, political activity. Revolutionary events in Europe as well as official attacks on the Kingdom's liberal leaders and institutions elicited a strong response from the students. With increasing frequency they assigned a secondary role to mutual self-help and esoteric literary discussions. In their place they substituted passionate manifestations of patriotism and nationalism. The second development featured a move from open, legal activities to conspiratorial, illegal ones. Warsaw University's July 15, 1819, decree forbidding its students to associate, and the government's November 6, 1821, proclamation outlawing all secret societies forced Polish students into clandestine arrangements.[63]

In addition to secret societies, a political Liberal Opposition questioning Alexander's policy and his concepts of government, law and the monarchy, also appeared on the scene. This loosely organized group, consisting primarily of educated petty and middle *szlachta* from the country's western regions, occupied a narrow chronological middle ground. Too old to know and understand the forces of Romanticism now activating the continent's youth, they were too young to satisfy themselves with the dated political structures and methods whose lingering effects determined and restricted the political conduct of such grandees as Czartoryskii and S.K. Potocki. Rather, born and bred in an atmosphere of rationalism, they were true children of the Enlightenment. In truth, the Liberal Opposition could find no antecedents in Polish history and operated from a limited power base within the Kingdom. The quintessence of an imported political movement, the Liberal Opposition assumed a doctrinaire stance and relied on an ideology conceived of and developed outside Poland. Despite these handicaps, the Liberal Opposition served to illuminate the complex problem of the Russian autocrat's relationship to the Polish constitutional monarchy.[64]

Relying on France and to a lesser extent Great Britain for examples, the Liberal Opposition tried to erect contemporary European liberal theories on the Polish constitution's foundation. In pursuing a doctrinaire and legalistic course they adopted Benjamin Constant's political philosophy in its entirety. The Liberal Opposition maintained that representative monarchy must observe sacrosanct constitutional principles which form an immutable base for the entire political-social system. The constitution applies to all citizens including the ruler, and it must be implemented to the fullest extent since it is nothing more than the sum of its parts. Under this arrangement, four autonomous sources of authority continually interact while preserving a clearly defined balance among themselves. Public opinion is the first, and most important, source. Independent of the monarch and guaranteed by the constitution, public opinion participates in society and government through freedom of the press, sworn law courts and a parliamentary system whose main features include a parliamentary opposition, public legislative sessions, ministerial responsibility and the right of petition. Moreover, authority also flows from the monarch, the immaculate personification of the nation in whom

The Autocratic Empire and the Constitutional Monarchy   71

the people and the state merge to produce one semi-deified being representing perfection and sovereignty. Although he embodies grace and moral inviolability, the head of state is an irresponsible figure, strictly detached from the third, or executive-administrative, authority. While the person of the king remains above the fray, responsibility rests with the government and the ministers. To indicate that government actions derive from their advice, the appropriate ministers must countersign all orders and decrees. If these edicts violate the rights guaranteed in the constitution, the signatory bears the responsibility and the consequences. Independent courts impartially applying the law without interference from the three other sources represent the fourth authority.

In less abstract terms, the Liberal Opposition simply sought to defend the Congress Kingdom's constitution. To achieve this goal they intended to employ legalistic methods at the national Sejm where they envisioned themselves as fulfilling the role of "His Majesty's Loyal Opposition." Believing the constitution to be the inalienable property of the people and not subject to change or revocation from above, the Liberal Opposition proposed to serve as its guardians. They celebrated the Polish constitution's excellence in guaranteeing national survival, safeguarding public and individual freedom and answering society's needs. They felt no need to expand it or modify it in a more democratic direction. Moreover, despite strong national sentiment to the contrary, they reconciled themselves to the loss of the eastern lands including Lithuania. However, unlike their mentors, the French constitutionalists, the Polish Liberal Opposition consciously struggled for something more than political rights. According to the Liberal Opposition, France was secure in its sovereignty whereas Poland depended entirely on its constitution to maintain its national political existence. Consequently, they believed that the charter's destruction would be tantamount to abolishing the Polish state, and they labored to avoid this catastrophe.

In the course of events, the government's adversaries supplemented their Sejm opposition with a second tactic. Utilizing the liberal Western European newspapers, *Minerve Française* and *Le Vrai Libéral,* they began to inform Europe about the Polish government's repressive and illegal activities. Their immediate purpose was twofold: rally liberal Western European forces to their side; and unmask Alexander before the West, thereby forcing the self-styled liberal either to admit his illiberal nature or adhere to his constitution.

The prosperous Kalisz landowner, Wincenty Niemojowski, ably assisted by his younger brother, Bonawentura, led the Liberal Opposition. Both brothers had completed their educations in France where they fell under the influence of French liberal thought. Wincenty, thirty-six at the time of the 1820 Sejm, suffered from partial deafness which caused him to bellow his speeches. This condition, as well as the addresses' inflammatory content and the speaker's blustering style, combined to contribute significantly to that Sejm's tumultuous atmosphere. A contemporary observer who supported the government and was convinced that the Niemojowskis' defense of the constitution was simply a self-serving device to disguise their personal vendetta against Zajączek, described Wincenty:

> Deaf, and with tin horn in ear, lame, unpleasant of form, rough, brave to the point of impudence; the most difficult to fight was his deafness which prevented him from hearing defenses and (thereby) convinced him (of his correctness). Thus his stubborness... was founded in this deafness.[65]

The Niemojowskis went out of their way to assail literary as well as political Romanticism. Refusing to budge from an almost fanatical faith in Enlightenment precepts, W. Niemojowski equated his principles vis-à-vis Romanticism as reason versus feeling, fact versus sentiment, legalism versus revolution. The Niemojowskis viewed a secret, conspiratorial society with as much distaste as they viewed a reactionary, arbitrary government.

Throughout the Kingdom's lifetime the Niemojowski brothers remained popular figures with the vast majority of middle and petty *szlachta*. Despite the government's obvious aversion for them, they maintained their high standing with their peers because they conducted themselves in the traditional *szlachta* style of unlimited hospitality, camaraderie, food and drink. At election time, they dispensed free vodka with the same openhandedness as any sixteenth century Polish nobleman. Occasionally their personal popularity enabled them to carry their ideas; almost always it sufficied to permit a full airing of their views. However in proselytizing for a new and foreign doctrine, they found little support in a society tired of war and grateful to Alexander for restoring their country. Nevertheless, in adapting their ideals to practical situations and exploiting traditional Polish political behavior they enjoyed fair success. Never aspiring to or achieving more than an imperfect organization, the Niemojowskis and their allies continued to rely on the unrestrained individualism and the junto politics which had characterized the defunct Commonwealth's political life. Although they lacked large numbers of committed followers, the Liberal Opposition always devoted much time and effort to shaping public opinion and continually battled to preserve their popularity without sacrificing their principles.[66] Saturated with French liberal theories and determined to graft effective western parliamentarianism onto the Polish body politic, the Liberal Opposition stepped forward to challenge Alexander and his government.

Seemingly unimportant skirmishes at the 1818 Sejm not only disclosed the Liberal Opposition's opinions about the constitution, but also indicated the tenacity with which the Niemojowskis intended to sustain them. When the lower chamber's marshal rejected W. Niemojowski's request to append his critical minority report to the House Commission on Organization and Administrative Laws' favorable majority report, the Kalisz delegate brought the matter before the full House in a rousing speech. However, at Constantine's and Zajączek's request the *Dyariusz*, or published record of the Sejm, was censored, and Niemojowski's speeches were merely summarized and his general observations completely omitted. In retaliation, W. Niemojowski took it upon himself to publish his speeches and observations given at the 1818 Sejm.[67] When the government imposed censorship in 1819, the Niemojowskis were among the first to raise their voices in protest.

Despite Alexander's presence, the 1820 Sejm witnessed bitter clashes between the Liberal Opposition and the government. On November 15, 1819, Alexander had authorized a national congress, and on July 20 of the following year he set its opening for September 13. The Niemojowskis emboldened by that spring's stormy debates in the French assembly resolved to press their cause. In contrast to the first Sejm, the Liberal Opposition conducted caucuses before the initial session in order to sort out their positions.[68] Nevertheless, it would be erroneous to accord too much importance to these gatherings. For one thing, they attracted anywhere from twenty to forty participants, hardly indicative of an exclusive well-organized band. Moreover, General Rożniecki, head of the gendarmes and Constantine's underling, attended several of their meetings. Finally, deputies holding views diametrically opposite to those espoused by the

Kalisz circle also conducted pre-Sejm caucuses. Most likely, these meetings simply reflected a Polish awareness of and participation in that year's highly charged European political scene.

Despite an obvious lack of enthusiasm from their supporters, the Niemojowskis decided to introduce two specific measures at the Sejm. One called for the delegates to petition the king to suspend the censorship regulations for all speeches, reports and commentaries. The second tried to regulate the marshal's activities in the lower chamber and required him to read the minutes. Disapproval of their suggestions from within their own restricted circle indicated that the Niemojowskis could only count on eight to ten sure votes, hardly enough to challenge Alexander's monoploy on power. When the Sejm opened, the brothers abandoned their projects without even submitting them to the House.[69]

Nevertheless, the Liberal Opposition successfully repelled two government initiatives which threatened to circumvent the constitution. In the first initiative, a criminal procedure project, the government hoped to extend the public prosecutor's prerogatives and to introduce closed hearings.[70] The Liberal Opposition, attacking the project's unconstitutionality as well as its length and unwieldiness (535 articles), rallied the Sejm with an impassioned defense of public courts and the need for an independent, responsible judiciary. Wincenty Niemojowski cut to the heart of the Liberal Opposition's philosophy when he proclaimed, ". . . governments are for the people, and not people for the governments."[71] Even the docile Senate rebelled against this ill-considered project.[72] Not one representative spoke in favor of the project as it went down, 117 to 3.[73]

Sidetracking the second project, an organic statute for the Senate, proved to be a much more difficult assignment. After the upper chamber passed the bill, the lower house could only ratify or defeat it in its entirety. At first glance the bill seemed beneficial. In a clear and concise manner it restricted judicial and political activities to those senators not holding any official position. The project also prescribed procedures for the Senate when circumstances required it to function as the nation's highest court.[74] However, in discussing ministerial obligations, the project effectively substituted the State Council for the House as the accountable body. In practice such a step would destroy the principle of ministerial responsibility.

Alerted to this danger, W. Niemojowski, in his role as member of the Sejm Commission on Organization and Administrative Laws, attacked the project's constitutionality.[75] Failing to sway the Sejm Commission, he and his brother shifted their attack to the House's plenary sessions. Bitter and acrimonious floor debate resulted. B. Niemojowski, acclaiming ministerial responsibility as "the most certain right of the nation," demanded that the State Council not be permitted to intervene.[76] The government counterattacked: General Krasiński, marshal of the House, spread promises of an imminent reunion with Lithuania.[77] Other delegates emphasized the project's merits, while still others called upon the House to pass the project in order to prove to Alexander that the Poles properly appreciated his royal gift.[78] W. Niemojowski replied with a heated speech defending the constitution's inviolability:

> I know that there is but a step from the capitol to the Tarpeian rock, but nothing shall deter me from uttering the truth,—the charter is national property; the king has no right either to take it away, or to change it. We have lost the liberty of the press—individual liberty is gone—the right of property has been violated. Now they would abolish the responsibility of ministers. What will be left of the constitution?[79]

Ultimately, the House defeated the project by eight votes (61 to 53).[80] Nothing could be more misleading than the Russian historian Shilder's remark that, "...the Sejm rejected projects of laws presented by the government almost without discussion."[81]

The Niemojowskis pressed forward on another front when they introduced several petitions challenging recent ministerial acts and proclamations. Specifically criticizing the administration's unconstitutional activities, they demanded censorship's abolition, a budget submitted to and approved by parliament in accordance with the constitution and the institution of legal proceedings against Minister Potocki and his assistant, S. Staszic, for countersigning the censorship decrees. The Liberal Opposition felt obliged to attack Potocki despite his progressive achievements simply because he had acted unconstitutionally in countersigning obviously illegal decrees. According to their legalistic approach, he bore the responsibility and the consequences for his acts. Nevertheless, their complaint against Potocki failed by sixteen votes.[82]

The Liberal Opposition's performance at the Sejm insured defeat for the two government projects. More importantly, perhaps, their actions and speeches not only imparted practical meaning to their philosophical concepts, but also demolished their own assertions that the king stands above the political fray. Although they never dared to attack the ruler explicitly and, in fact, even made conspicuous efforts to exonerate him, it soon became evident that theory and reality could not coincide. Stripped of its verbiage, their critical thrusts struck at none other than Alexander himself.

The Niemojowskis' personal behavior and their leadership within the ranks of the opposition made them extremely unpopular with the Kingdom's administrators. Furthermore, the Niemojowskis made no effort to soften the government's hostility. In one incident Novosil'tsov privately admonished the Liberal Opposition, saying, "You will bear in mind gentlemen, that you have been granted the constitution and that it is possible to take it from you." W. Niemojowski imprudently replied, "Then we will become revolutionaries."[83] Such responses were not calculated to soothe the nerves of an apprehensive monarch who viewed with alarm and trepidation the wave of revolutionary activity then sweeping across Europe.

In the months leading up to the second Sejm, conflicting gestures reflecting Alexander's unsettled state characterized the tsar's behavior. Despite recent indications that Alexander, upset by European events, domestic criticism, the succession question and Polish ingratitude, intended to abandon his constitutional experiments, he moved swiftly to convene the Sejm within the period prescribed by law. Moreover, although he never retreated from his support for Zajączek's unconstitutional censorship decrees, he also announced before the Sejm opened that he would exclude its minutes and its record of daily events from the prevailing censorship regulations as a mark of his confidence in the national representation.[84]

However, a different tenor had appeared by the Sejm's end. Harsh words replaced conciliatory gestures as the emperor voiced deep displeasure with events in general. Pointing to "an evil spirit" which once again hovered over Europe threatening heinous crimes and catastrophes, the tsar asserted that this terrifying spectacle imposed on governments the obligation to preserve law and order from the fatal influence of agitated, deluded passions. This same obligation extended to the national assembly as well as the ruler. In closing, Alexander threatened to employ all necessary force to eradicate the embryo of anarchy and destroy the seeds of disorder as soon as they appeared.[85] Alexander's closing speech to the Sejm did not allow for any ambiguities. In blunt language Alexander called the Poles to account:

> Interrogate your consciences, and you may know if in the course of your discussions, you have accorded to Poland all the services that she expects of your wisdom, or if, to the contrary, carried away by the seductions so common to our days and giving up a hope that would have been realized by a foresighted confidence, you have not retarded in its progress the work of the restoration of your fatherland.[86]

In addition to this blast, Alexander also reneged on his promise to let the Sejm records appear free of censorship.[87] The Warsaw events angered Alexander and contributed to his slow evolution away from conciliatory tactics, including pseudo-constitutionalism, toward repression and harsh measures.

The uproar continued long after Alexander's closing speech. Prior to the Sejm's convocation, the State Council drew up its obligatory report on the government's activities for 1819. This document, citing the need to innoculate Poland against "the evil spirit" then engulfing Europe, included a vigorous defense of the new censorship regulations.[88] In turn, the government's position brought a storm of protests. The Sejm Commission responsible for examining the report strongly objected to the introduction of censorship. Equating publishing with thought and thought with man (I think, therefore I am), the Commission asked what possible reasons motivated the ministers to do such violence to the constitution.[89] The Senate's observations on the State Council's report sounded a similar note. Even this timid body bitterly complained about censorship, claiming that it stifled public opinion, a vital component of any constitutional government.[90] In its general comments the House minced few words. The deputies berated the government for its infringement upon the Sejm's sessions, the lack of ministerial responsibility, the failure to bring in a legal budget, the introduction of censorship and the dissemination of police and spies.[91]

These harsh observations brought a reply from the State Council defending its activities. Furthermore, Alexander himself wrote a long memorial from Troppau once again interpreting his relationship to the Polish constitution. Delving to the heart of the matter, he said:

...in disagreements over constitutional theories of representation as well as over results which derive from these theories and pertaining to the regulation of the Kingdom's Charter as well as any other acts flowing from this same source, (they) will conform as follows: if within the regulations there would be something dubious or in need of explanation, the Maker Himself [Alexander] would have the right to express Himself in this matter in as much as He alone really might know His own intentions.[92]

If the success of Alexander's Polish policy now demanded repressive measures to replace a constitutional facade left in shambles when too many of his subjects began to take his liberalism seriously, the emperor remained consistent in his conception of power; namely, that all power flowed directly from the emperor and resided in his person. Throughout his reign Alexander never waivered in this belief.

CHAPTER 5

THE SUCCESSION CRISIS: GRAND DUKE CONSTANTINE, RUSSIA AND POLAND, 1819-1823

As 1819 drew to a close, Alexander seriously began to contemplate radical changes in his fundamental Polish policy. Pressured by Russian court and gentry circles, deeply disturbed by European events and disappointed with what he deemed to be Polish ingratitude and intransigence, Alexander considered scrapping indirect control over Poland in favor of incorporating the Congress Kingdom into the Russian Empire as its westernmost *guberniia*. True to form, the tsar exhibited great reluctance to proceed resolutely or commit himself irrevocably to any one course. With Alexander taking halting and tentative steps at best, the various projects designed to effect the merger never bore fruit. This hesitancy, compounded by a lengthy and complex succession crisis, led to a certain aimlessness and vacillation which ended only when Alexander decided to maintain the structural *status quo* for Poland and bolster his direct authority with certain additions to the Polish charter.

A flurry of activity during the second Sejm (October, 1820) clearly demonstrated Alexander's departure from the conciliatory course he had pursued since 1815. Now, instead of vague pronouncements favoring constitutional extension and the reunion of the Polish nation, he questioned the Congress Kingdom's very existence. While journeying to the Troppau Congress, Alexander stopped at Warsaw in order to supervise the Sejm's sessions. There he heard Constantine denounce civilian subversion in Poland.[1] These accusations, coupled with the Sejm's unruly opposition and Novosil'tsov's insinuations, led the hostile and suspicious tsar to declare himself ready to abrogate the Polish constitution then and there. Cooler heads prevailed, and Capo d'Istria finally dissuaded the tsar from this precipitous action. Asking, "What will we say at Troppau? How to proclaim liberal ideas after such a scandal?,"[2] the Russian Foreign Minister posed the destruction of Alexander's European image as reason for restraint.

Nevertheless, Novosil'tsov prepared an *ukaz* incorporating the Polish state and its army into the Empire's administrative and military system. The proposal's brevity and bluntness, something very uncharacteristic of anything Novosil'tsov ever concocted, leads one to infer that he produced it hurriedly and without the customary drafting period. Most probably he drew up the proposal in response to an unexpected imperial request during Alexander's October visit. The project, assuming the existence of a general Russian constitution, noted that, "...two constitutions in the same (sic) Empire are unnecessary in that they are harmful for the unity of action necessary to all good government...." Novosil'tsov proposed that, "The Polish Kingdom, considered as a vice-regency united with our Empire, in the future will be organized, staffed, governed, and administered in compliance with the regulations of the Constitutional Charter of Our Empire, ..." Moveover, "The Polish army will preserve its organization, ...its eagles, colors and standards, under the title of Army of the West of Our Empire and under the command of...Constantine."[3] Although the projected *ukaz* never became law, it gave further evidence of the trend threatening Poland's independence which first surfaced in the 1819 censorship measures and the emperor's closing speech to the second Sejm.

Novosil'tsov followed up his proposal to incorporate the Kingdom into the Empire with a long memorial vividly detailing the evils inherent in constitutions. Though he directed his sharpest attacks against the Polish charter, Novosil'tsov denounced constitutions in general. He accused them of containing seeds of "democratic and revolutionary principles which infect the whole nation with gangrene and...summon forth fiery desires to change monarchical, even paternal, government for tyranny and violence, based on the autocracy of the people, that is, on republican government." Ridiculing the Polish constitution's physical arrangement which placed articles about "tsar" after articles about "government" and chapters on "political institutions" after chapters on "guarantees of political relations," he concluded that the document stimulated public interest in forms of government, a development quite contrary to the monarch's intentions. Novosil'tsov noted that their constitution permitted the Poles to demand a republican government of an autocratic people, an inadmissible request in that the Russian Empire's prosperity and its very existence depended upon its monarchial and despotic form.

Finally, Novosil'tsov pointed to the conflagration enveloping or threatening to envelop the European states and observed:

> ...to think that autocratic power will, with indifferent eyes, look on those members of the Sejm, those servile imitators of apostles of revolution, those worshippers and echoers of the most famous demagogues in Europe when they apeishly proclaim in their speeches the most pernicious doctrines based on the right that they, according to the constitution, are able to speak with boundless freedom? To be sure, No! No reasonable man will permit himself to nourish similar illusions; he can not make such a mistake and not be able to see the outcome, which should be expected, if the existence of the Kingdom's constitution serves only as a pretext and a means to demoralize the nation....[4]

It is unthinkable that so prudent and obedient a subordinate as Novosil'tsov would make such a criticism without his master's encouragement.

Another incident which not only testifies to Alexander's drastically altered relations with the Poles, but also may represent an initial concession in the abdication negotiations with the Grand Duke occurred after the Sejm closed. Accompanied by Constantine on the first leg of his journey to Troppau, Alexander gave him *care blanche* in the Kingdom. When the Grand Duke raised the question of the constitution, Alexander replied, "I take the constitution upon myself; act freely and don't worry about the rest, you have *carte blanche*."[5] Alexander repeated this pledge in May 1821, when he passed through Warsaw on his return from the Laibach Congress, and again in January 1822, when Constantine journeyed to St. Petersburg. Due to the verbal nature of Alexander's grant of power no documents exist to verify its authenticity; nevertheless, both Russian and Polish historians generally accept Professor Askenazy's description.[6] The tsesarevich later referred directly to this grant when he wrote to Alexander that "...I made use of oral authorization which Your Majesty deigned to give me in conversations before Your departure for Troppau, after Your return from Laibach, and most recently in St. Petersburg, although this Will expressed on Your part still has not been confirmed officially."[7]

Finally, the Congress Kingdom's right to an independent existence came under open attack in May 1821. Returning from Laibach, Alexander paid a two day call at Warsaw during which Novosil'tsov delivered a report detailing the Kingdom's general condition. Appealing now to "good order based on the principles of religion and morality" instead of justice and reason, Novosil'tsov painted a dark picture of revolutionary intrigue and subversion. In outlining the reasons for the second Sejm's "failure," he singled out an inflamed public spirit, the legislature's attitude and financial difficulties. Furthermore, he blamed secret societies, especially the Freemasons, for sabotaging Alexander's intentions.[8]

The anti-Polish agitation culminated in Alexander's well-known address to the State Council in which he remarked:

> ...matters have at length arrived at a point where the question no longer concerns the abolition of this or that office, the continuance or relinquishment of certain public works, but the ascertainment of whether the kingdom's resources be sufficient for the expenses of a separate government, or whether their inadequacy being proved, a new order of things shall be established.[9]

Luckily for Poland, Prince K. Drucki-Lubecki appeared on the scene at this time to manage the nation's financial affairs. Originally classified as one of Novosil'tsov's toadies, Lubecki proved to be both independent and competent. He revitalized Poland's treasury through a series of stringent fiscal measures not the least of which strictly limited Constantine's military expenditures and removed Novosil'tsov's grasping hand from the national coffers.

In the midst of this crisis, Poland once again turned to her most distinguished and influential citizen, Adam Czartoryski. Czartoryski responded in August 1821, with a personal appeal to the emperor. Lamenting the "extreme uncertainty and total discouragement" prevailing in the country, he said:

> It is feared, from certain phrases which have been uttered by those who are supposed to be the confidential interpreters of your views, that you regard the constitution as impracticable, useless, and involving too much expenditure, that the independence of courts of Justice is to cease, that public education is to be restricted, that the

The Succession Crisis 83

diets are inconvenient obstacles which should be abolished, and that the Kingdom is to be governed like the other Polish dominions of the Empire.[10]

Laying the kingdom's financial mess squarely at Constantine's feet, Czartoryski linked fiscal and national regeneration with expansion, i.e., a Polish-Lithuanian union. He also vigorously defended the constitution:

> It (the constitution) cannot be made responsible for the ill-directed or superfluous expenditure of the administration, for this expenditure has occurred because the constitution was not sufficiently obeyed.... The constitution prevents nothing that is necessary; unfortunately it does not prevent that which is superfluous and injurious to the state.[11]

Although it seems highly improbable that Czartoryski's letter convinced Alexander to spare the Congress Kingdom, it did alert the tsar to the feelings of a large and powerful segment of Polish society. Knowledge that Czartoryski and his supporters adamantly opposed any further measures to vitiate Poland's independence contributed to his decision to leave the Congress Kingdom intact. Moreover, cognizant of his great powers, the tsar began to realize that the constitution presented no real threat. Finally, Alexander recoiled from an act which would irredeemably compromise him in European eyes. Consequently, he retained Poland's quasi-independence and its constitutional facade in their entirety. However, he did satisfy himself with extra-constitutional procedures designed to break Poland's allegedly rebellious spirit.

Although generally overlooked by most historians, Alexandrian Russia experienced a succession crisis which played a major role in shaping Russo-Polish relations during the 1819-1823 period. Tsar Paul's 1797 succession law establishing primogeniture in the male line appeared to have solved an outstanding problem which had periodically disrupted the Russian state since Peter the Great abolished succession by primogeniture in 1722. But this solution proved to be momentary, and Paul's heir was the first to ignore it.

As Alexander's reign moved on, the childless tsar almost certainly began to realize that Russia might face a serious crisis upon his death.

Although Constantine was heir apparent, several important factors led Alexander to contemplate removing his brother from the line of succession. One was Constantine's own lukewarm to negative attitude toward assuming the throne. Alexander also weighed his brother's questionable capacities to rule. Furthermore, the tsar pondered the court aristocracy's deep-seated hostility toward Constantine who had antagonized this powerful element by his boorishness and his oft-repeated desire to punish his father's assassins. Moreover, his mother, the powerful dowager empress Maria Fedorovna, disliked Constantine and opposed his accession to the throne. Most importantly, perhaps, Alexander feared for the autocracy. A dynasty in which two of its last three reigning monarchs had been murdered could not be regarded as the unchallenged master of its own house. Quite possibly Alexander feared that Constantine on the throne would provoke the court aristocracy or praetorian guard to assert its now waning power and once again force a new ruler on Russia. Another regicide could not but severely damage autocratic institutions.

Alexander's apprehensions become even more understandable in light of the guilt and remorse he felt for his own part in his father's murder. Furthermore, the violent, revolutionary incidents then plaguing Europe added to the emperor's anxiety by injecting a new element, the oft-cited "evil spirit of the times," into the equation. Perhaps Alexander believed that the tsesarevich was more than likely to antagonize those Russians infected with the "evil spirit" and, possibly, to incite them to desperate measures. In sum, Alexander's resolution to remove his younger brother from the succession derived from reasons of state and not from any petty personal grievance or whim.[12]

In time the succession problem became an urgent matter. Apparently, concessions and compensations for Constantine in Poland, even if they harmed Alexander's original intention to treat the Poles with great care, seemed a small price to pay in return for the Grand Duke's abdication. Fortunately, and perhaps by design, the emperor's decision to act on the succession problem coincided with the shift in his Polish tactics away from leniency towards repression. However, that discussions over Constantine's abdication dragged on for more than three years only to end fortuitously not only demonstrates that the negotiations were long and arduous, but also counters the contention that the tsesarevich yearned to renounce his birthright.[13]

Veiled references to Constantine's possible renunciation appeared as early as 1817. Two years later, after the birth of Nicholas' son, the future Alexander II, they began to assume a more definite shape when Alexander broached the delicate subject to Nicholas.[14] During his October 1819, sojourn at Warsaw, Alexander consulted with Constantine about the succession question and proposed an arrangement whereby the latter would receive a divorce and permission for a morganatic marriage to his Polish paramour, Joanna Grudzińska, in return for waiving the succession rights for any children which might result from this union. The tsesarevich accepted, thereby clearing the path to the throne for Nicholas' son.[15] In April of the following year the promised divorce was granted and on May 24 Constantine remarried.

Further discussions aimed at securing Constantine's outright abdication occurred in October 1820, during Alexander's journey to the Troppau conference, and again in May 1821, during the tsar's return from the Laibach meeting.[16] In January 1822, during one of his rare excursions to St. Petersburg, Constantine finally signed a general abdication which read in part:

> Not finding in myself the genius, the talents, nor the force necessary to be elevated to the Sovereign dignity to which I would have the right by my birth, I beg Your Imperial Majesty to transfer this right to whom it would come after me, and thus to assure forever, the security of the empire. As to me, I will add by this renunciation a new guarantee and a new force to the engagement which I have voluntarily and solemnly contracted on the occasion of my divorce from my first wife.... Deign, Sire, to accept with good will my prayer; help me secure the consent of our Imperial Mother to this plan and sanction it with your Imperial assent.[17]

After an inexplicable delay of almost three weeks, Alexander replied on February 14, 1822:

> I have read your letter with all the attention that it merited. Having always fully appreciated the high sentiments of your heart, I found nothing in your letter to make me change my judgment.. It has given me proof of your sincere attachment to the Empire, and of your solicitude for its continued tranquility.[18]

This exchange hardly concluded the negotiations. A more comprehensive agreement in which the Grand Duke's abdication represented merely part of the whole was in the making. Apparently, Constantine demanded unlimited authority for himself in an autonomous Poland as well as full jurisdiction over the Empire's western *gubernii* as the *quid pro quo* for relinquishing his claim to the Russian throne. A series of proposals and imperial rescripts appearing over the nine months following the Grand Duke's visit to St. Petersburg strongly suggests that such were Constanine's objectives. Furthermore, subsequent events in the Congress Kingdom which reflect Constantine's strengthened position there tend to confirm this analysis, while Alexander's piecemeal concessions to his brother imply that no final agreement on the abdication question had been reached despite the tsesarevich's pledge.

In March and April 1822, several extraordinary communications passed between St. Petersburg and Warsaw which shed considerable light on the situation. In two projected decrees Alexander offered to cement the Grand Duke's position in the Kingdom. The first one, citing uncertain political conditions in Europe as well as the danger of revolution in Poland, vested dictatorial authority in Constantine:

> The state of minds in Europe since the restoration of general peace, and in particular since the events unexpectedly occurring during the last two years, more than ever before places on the government a new obligation to maintain general tranquility. Such a position demands every intelligent and prudent thought to prevent, as far as possible, the beginning of disorder and to extirpate its embryo...[19]

But this authority would only be temporary: "...to vest...for the present time as long as the jeopardy exists, a power...to put into practice precautionary measures...not soliciting royal approval beforehand."[20] In closing, Alexander reaffirmed his faith in the constitution, pledged to preserve it and showered praise on the Polish nation.[21] In the second rescript the king placed the army on a war footing and imparted full power to his assistant commander, Grand Duke Constantine.[22]

Constantine, not wishing to act hastily, received his brother's consent to solicit Zajączek's and Novosil'tsov's opinions on the issues raised by the proposed rescripts. All three men accepted the feasibility of settling dictatorial authority on the Grand Duke. In a like manner, but for different reasons, they unequivocally rejected the project's sections confirming the constitution's importance and discussing Alexander's relations to the country.[23] Novosil'tsov resoundingly defended the ruler's inviolable status:

> I have been detained by several expressions which appear contrary to the ideas of all governments, even representative government; and I have not been able to view without surprise that there can be any question about obligations which impose a suitable responsibility on the Emperor; as much as it is universally admitted that the Sovereign never is responsible except when he wishes to speak of his responsibility before God.[24]

In a long reply dated April 30, the Grand Duke issued a paragraph by paragraph rejection of the text. Constantine noted that he required dictatorial authority above and beyond the constitution in order to suppress revolutionary movements. Moreover, to achieve that goal, he would have to employ means which contravened the constitution's letter and spirit. However, the constitution's mere existence would vitiate any dictatorial power because it would stand as a parallel authority. In turn, this dichotomy would weaken and undermine the people's confidence in the unvarying firmness of their institutions, the vigorous execution of the law, and its equal application to all. In a blast directed at the constitution itself, the Grand Duke assailed it for providing refuge to culprits and scoundrels in matters of political offenses. Constantine demanded the constitution's revocation as a prerequisite for vesting him with dictatorial authority and he pointed out:

> In order that an existent force has the imposing character which suits it, it is necessary that it have the power to deploy itself without constraint and without hesitation, that it is able to overtake culprits in whom it should instill fear... without any institutions in contradiction with its existence coming to embarrass it, to paralyse it in its march, or to imprint upon it the outcast character of illegality ....To force to exist simultaneously two incompatible forms of government means to expose the rulers as well as the ruled to vacillation, unrest, and eternal blunders.[25]

With this response the Grand Duke rejected Alexander's offer of provisional dictatorial authority. This episode reveals the emperor's determination to fuse two antithetical concepts into one neat package. On the one hand, he hoped to satisfy Constantine with a temporary grant of ill-defined powers over the Congress Kingdom. On the other hand, by formally retaining Poland's legal-constitutional form, he hoped to pacify the Poles and to maintain his fading European image as a progressive monarch. This scheme's patent impossibility became apparent at the outset when the Congress Kingdom's three highest officials (Constantine, Zajączek and Novosil'tsov) agreed that the proposed decrees not only failed to enhance the Grand Duke's authority, but merely sanctioned an already existing state of affairs. Novosil'tsov summarized their observations when he wrote to Constantine that ". . . these laws do not offer anything new . . . ."[26] Doubtlessly, they fell woefully short of Constantine's demand for unlimited, autocratic power, a demand which required the constitution's destruction.

After Alexander's first attempt to accommodate Constantine failed to produce the desired results, the brothers again took up the matter when they met at the annual Wilno military review in May 1822. At that time, the Grand Duke apparently once more pressed his demands that the tsar legitimize his position and make it permanent, free him from constitutional restraints and extend his authority to the western provinces. Alexander reluctantly acquiesced to the last request. Returning to St. Petersburg, the tsar issued *ukazi* which made Constantine commander of the Active Army in the districts of Wilno, Grodno, Minsk, Volhynia, Podolia and Białystok. According to decrees promulgated on February 8, 1812, the commander of the Active Army exercised complete jurisdiction, including civil jurisdiction, over the designated areas.[27] This, together with the *ukaz* of July 11, 1819, on military matters (see above, Chapter 3), gave the tsesarevich a tenuous *de jure* as well as *de facto* control of Polish Russia.

Furthermore, a September 5, 1822, imperial rescript granted Constantine the right to establish his own diplomatic chancellery.[28] The issuance of this document indicates that the Grand Duke continued to advance his claims with some success. Superficially, it would appear that this new order moved Constantine perceptibly closer to the goal of an independent, autocratic state with himself at its head. But this proved to be deceptive since Alexander allowed his brother diplomatic relations only with Prussia, Austria, Saxony, France and the Holy See. More importantly, the emperor stipulated that diplomatic dispatches entering or leaving the Congress

Kingdom had first to pass through the chancellery in St. Petersburg. Finally, he forbade Constantine to assign his own ambassadors, specifying that Russia's diplomats would also serve Poland.[29] Nevertheless, a principle of sorts had been established.

Alexander's piecemeal concessions ceased when a wholly unexpected event intervened to undermine Constantine's position and threaten the Grand Duke with outright disaster. Constantine was placed on the defensive by the discovery of several Polish secret societies, a few of which had infiltrated his much prized army. Desperately he tried to conceal their existence from his brother. But Novosil'tsov fearful of dismissal if Constantine succeeded in instituting a second Romanov dynasty in Poland—a step which would end the *raison d'être* for the Imperial Commissioner's office—undercut Constantine's position by revealing the existence of a military secret society. In one of his periodic reports to the tsar written a few weeks after he discovered this secret society, Novosil'tsov attacked the Grand Duke for failing to act against the society, and for even doubting its existence. The Imperial Commissioner complained that Constantine's protective attitude toward the army crippled his investigation.[30] Only then, when Constantine could no longer suppress news of the conspiracies, did he reluctantly inform Alexander.

Although the Grand Duke belittled the associations and attributed them to a very few malcontents, their mere existence called into question his fitness to rule. How could Constantine aspire to more power and independence when he permitted that "evil spirit of the times" to penetrate his most sacred trust? With bombshells of information about uncovered secret societies in the Polish army exploding at every turn, Constantine found himself increasingly vulnerable to criticism from on high. Suddenly thrown on the defensive, he chose to suspend his demands rather than jeopardize his prerogatives. However, the matter of compensation for Constantine did not vanish. Rather, it was forced into the background where it remained until it reemerged after Alexander's death to exacerbate relations between Constantine and Nicholas.

Alexander only took steps to finalize Constantine's abdication in midsummer 1823 when he recognized that the revelations concerning secret societies had completely hamstrung his brother. On August 16, 1823, Alexander signed the manifesto appointing Nicholas heir. Refusing to publicize this act, Alexander ordered the document placed in a sealed envelope and hidden in Moscow's Uspenskii Cathedral. He also deposited copies in sealed envelopes with the State Council, the Senate and the Synod. Alexander's rationale for this secrecy, so instrumental in precipitating a major crisis upon his death, continues to puzzle historians. As one highly respected authority states, "It is still not known why this vital transaction, which affected the future and peace of the Empire, was kept in such secrecy as to create confusion at the crucial moment of Alexander's death."[31]

But in light of the foregoing it seems reasonable to infer that Alexander could not sign and distribute even a secret manifesto deposing his younger brother until he had first reached a firm agreement on the compensation question. In point of fact, the concerned parties never entered into a definitive and mutually satisfactory understanding.

However, even if by 1823 Alexander concluded that force of circumstances placed Constantine in such a precarious position that the matter was settled for all practical purposes, his disingenuous character, his Byzantine political methods and his absolutist political philosophy prevented him from publicizing the subsequent succession arrangements. To do so would have committed Alexander to an irrevocable course, something he always avoided whenever possible. However, if the transfer of power remained secret, then Alexander could retain for himself the maximum amount of freedom. Obtaining Constantine's abdication, yet keeping it secret, enabled the tsar to select the heir of his own choice and, consequently, represented a further concentration of power in his hands.

The succession crisis, occurring at roughly the same time as Alexander retreated from his commitment to constitutionalism and began to contemplate the Congress Kingdom's incorporation into the Russian Empire, impressed Novosil'tsov who proceeded to exploit these developments for his own interests. The Imperial Commissioner sent a lengthy series of reports directly to Alexander which supported the emperor's new course and confirmed his wisdom. Knowing his master's great uneasiness about general European conditions, Novosil'tsov played on Alexander's fears with a stream of revelations about secret societies and revolutionary manifestations in the Congress Kingdom as well as the western *gubernii*. Furthermore, correctly interpreting Alexander's current mood, he blamed constitutional government and progressive education for the prevalent restlessness.

Alexander's new course, moreover, offered Novosil'tsov a unique opportunity to increase his power. Although the tsar retained essential control, Constantine received several concessions which expanded his dominion in Poland and the western *gubernii.* Even though the tsesarevich's new authority extended to the civil as well as the military sphere, he concentrated his energies only on the latter, thereby creating a vacuum which Novosil'tsov quickly moved to fill. While Constantine immersed himself in army affairs, Novosil'tsov gained control over civil matters. Nevertheless, Novosil'tsov continued to show deference to Alexander's wishes even while he was manipulating Constantine. Indeed, Novosil'tsov used his reports to Alexander to maintain his ascendancy over Constantine.

The succession crisis and its aftermath softly reverberated throughout the nineteenth century down to 1917. In secretly replacing Constantine with Nicholas, Alexander fundamentally altered the course of both Polish and Russian history. The bloody events of December 14, 1825, precipitated in the main by Alexander's failure to divulge the new order of succession, are well known. Alexander must bear the major responsibility for that tragedy.

However, one must not lose sight of the fact that from Alexander's perspective at that time, he was accomplishing a political master stroke. His adroit maneuvering brought him the right to nominate his own successor without surrendering a great deal in return. The concessions the tsar made to his brother, although tangible, were chiefly window dressing. The Grand Duke acquired the trappings of power while Alexander retained real authority. In light of the tsesarevich's recognized devotion to Alexander, as well as his penchant for mindless obedience to the commander, it was not difficult for the emperor to prevail over his brother. With the abdication pledge in hand, Alexander easily warded off Constantine's more extravagant compensation claims. Although it seems unlikely that a clumsy martinet of Constantine's caliber ever stood much chance of extracting substantial concessions from the crafty tsar, the secret society scare provided Alexander with adequate means to bury the compensation question.

As it was, the brothers' mutually exclusive desires effectively foreclosed any possibility of satisfactorily settling the compensation question. Constantine demanded an autonomous, virtually independent Polish-Lithuanian state, sanctioned and legitimatized by the Russian Emperor, which he could rule autocratically and which his heirs could inherit. This step would furnish Constantine with his own domain and power base, provide him with a healthy measure of independence and perhaps pacify the Poles by serving as the sugar-coating enabling them to swallow the bitter pills of Constantine's permanency and their constitution's destruction.

But Alexander temporized, issued oral or exceptional decrees, used half measures and deceptions and ultimately refused to institutionalize a Polish-Lithuanian union on Constantine's terms because such a step would demolish his grand Polish strategy. Under no circumstances would Alexander surrender Russia's suzerainty over Poland. He adamantly opposed Poland's temporary separation from Russia, even with his own brother acting as regent. Despite Constantine's dependence on a Polish-Lithuanian union for his future security, Alexander never waivered in the pursuit of his original goal, i.e., continued Russian control over Poland.

CHAPTER 6

A NEW DEPARTURE:
NOVOSIL'TSOV'S RISE TO POWER,
1820-1825

During the last few months of 1820, revolutionary movements were sweeping over Europe, open opposition to Alexander was appearing in Poland and a military revolt was breaking out in Russia itself. It was in this atmosphere that the Emperor traveled to Troppau in Austrian Silesia for another of the periodic conferences which distinguished the post-Vienna era. There, in an interview with Metternich, he soberly told his onetime adversary that he was not what he had been before, and that he felt remorse for his previous activities and policies.[1] This speech, characterized by the cunning and dissimulation which Alexander employed from childhood, also contained a grain of truth. At Troppau, and again at Laibach and Verona, Alexander emerged as one of the foremost advocates of military intervention to secure "throne and alter."[2]

While at Troppau, Alexander received word of the Semenovskii mutiny, a particularly shocking event in light of the Russian soldier's proverbial submissiveness. Alexander attributed the revolt to Russian "radicals" who hoped to frighten him and force him to return to St. Petersburg, a strained conclusion even Metternich refused to share.[3] Nevertheless, in light of Alexander's statements to Metternich it seems that the Semenovskii mutiny further soured Alexander on liberalism and contributed to his decision to employ repressive measures in Poland.

In the Congress Kingdom, an acceleration and expansion of the trend toward authoritarianism reflected the shift in Alexander's Polish strategy. New developments in such areas as censorship, education, police and politics not only dramatized the constitution's ineffectiveness, but also threatened Poland's precarious national existence. Novosil'tsov teamed with Grand Duke Constantine, Zajączek and a number of pliant Poles to organize the reaction. However, St. Petersburg retained ultimate control, approving or vetoing plans originating in the Kingdom, suggesting various methods to achieve aims, and overseeing the entire operation. Alexander was no innocent bystander. Rather, possessing full knowledge of the general situation if not of every detail, he orchestrated events.

Among the most harmful actions was the decision to extend the censorship. In early 1820 the liberal newspaper, *Orzeł Biały* (*White Eagle*), followed its report on General Rożniecki's selection as delegate to the next Sejm with some doggerel about a soldier who disliked the smell of gunpowder. Rożniecki, Constantine's intimate, was reputed to be a coward, and nobody missed what the newspaper meant. Constantine, more concerned about damage to the army's reputation than to Rozniecki's vigorously complained to Novosil'tsov. In reply, the Imperial Commissioner informed the Grand Duke that at the next Administrative Council session he would raise the issue of the censorship's laxness and would propose an *ad hoc* committee to examine why censorship functioned so sluggishly.[4] Novosil'tsov followed through on this pledge with a statement to the Administrative Council reviewing the continuing abuse of freedom of the press and demanding to know who or what hindered the government's intentions to curb this abuse.[5] The Viceroy, supporting Novosil'tsov and noting that *Orzeł Biały* had elicted unfavorable comments from both the Grand Duke and the King, named a delegation to investigate the apparent slackness.[6] Novosil'tsov's and Zagączek's protests were the beginning of a skillful attack upon the Education Minister, Stanisław K. Potocki, who controlled the censorship. The objective was to wrest censorship management from him in favor of "more reliable" supervision.

Novosil'tsov explained all to Alexander in a report dated February 13, 1820. Assession the basic ill as "an evil spirit jealous of the calm and happiness reigning in Poland and desirous of troubling the peaceful order," Novosil'tsov identified its agent as "the most absurd ideas about freedom of the press." This, in turn, was nourished by "a rage of writing" which possessed several unconventional young men.[7] With the Sejm approaching, Novosil'tsov feared further abuses. This could be expected, he complained, since censorship responsibility reposed in the Ministry of Education, a department quite tolerant of "press stupidities." Next, detailing the *Orzeł Biały* scandal and his request for an *ad hoc* investigating committee, the Imperial Commissioner demanded a more alert and stringent censorship. To insure this, he suggested the appointment of T. Sumiński, chief of police, as censor for periodical and political works.[8] In this manner censorship would be transferred from the suspect Ministry of Education to reliable police authorities.

At month's end the *ad hoc* committee reported to the Administrative Council. After first observing that most published works conformed to prevailing standards of decorum, it criticized the Education Ministry for its failure to prod the censors once objectionable materials began to appear. It also decried the lack of precise censorship regulations. Among other recommendations, it called for the transfer of censorship over periodical and political publications from the Ministry of Education to the legislature would have rejected any censorship bill even if the divided government had miraculously manufactured one.

Both the Education and Interior Ministries submitted counterproposals. A compromise was reached and forwarded to the Administrative Council on March 4, 1820. There it gained acceptance with the added stipulation that the project must be held in abeyance until Alexander made known his will on the matter.[10] Despite apparent agreement, several days later the Lord Lieutenant, citing "need," unilaterally implemented articles 7, 8 and 15 of the proposals. These provisions gave censorship authority over periodical and political works to the police, and extended censorship itself to all published items.[11] Shortly thereafter, Alexander rejected the compromise proposal and once again confirmed the Lord Lieutenant's decrees of May 22, and July 19, 1819. Moreover, the tsar authorized the Interior Ministry to assume censorship functions formerly exercised by the Education Ministry over periodical and political works.[12] Sumiński was named chief of the new censorship division. With the police engaged in extensive censoring and all works now subject to censorship, the skirmish ended in complete victory for the country's conservative administrators.

Alexander indicated, however, that he still envisioned a suitable legal project on censorship which he could submit to the next Sejm. Consequently, he ordered the Kingdom's authorities to draft an appropriate proposal.[13] To facilitate their work he instructed Capo d'Istria to draw up guidelines. Capo d'Istria's "Some Thoughts on Executing Article 16 of the Polish Kingdom's Charter" included a modified version of the censorship provisions promulgated in Metternich's Carlsbad Decrees.[14] Several departments issued vague and noncommittal observations on Capo d'Istria's work, while struggling to frame a project which would satisfy the government and still find Sejm approval. The task proved too difficult, and the Sejm met without considering any censorship project. In light of the Sejm's hostile disposition, the ministers' confusion and the monarch's reluctance to press the subject, it is almost certain that the legislature would have rejected any censorship bill if the divided government had miraculously manufactured one.

The Sejm's aftermath brought several changes which vitally affected the censorship question, the most important one being Potocki's ouster from the Education Ministry in favor of the arch-reactionary, Stanisław Grabowski (see below). This move eliminated a problem area in the higher administration and paved the way for a more rigorous censorship.

The state of mind prevailing in the Kingdom's executive branch and, apparently, subscribed to by the tsar, is evidenced in Novosil'tsov's memorial presented to Alexander in May 1821. Turning to the question of public spirit in Poland, the Imperial Commissioner alleged a widespread disaffection: foreign periodicals, English as well as French, expressing the most hostile opposition to their governments stimulated Polish opposition; political brochures from abroad, distinguished by their dangerous doctrines and their violent tone, were read with a remarkable avidity; Polish dailies, generally edited by very young men consciously imitating the foreign opposition, spread false information among the provincial readers, worked to detach the people from the monarchy, and failed to support the idea that a close union with Russia was Poland's best hope. To combat these harmful tendencies Novosil'tsov recommended extending censorship to all periodicals and pamphlets. Citing Berlin and Vienna as appropriate examples, he also suggested that the government establish a daily newspaper in order to serve its own interests and to contribute to the formation of a suitable public opinion and spirit.[15]

Responding to Novosil'tsov's concern, the government resorted to a series of administrative measures to reinforce the existing censorship. While additional censors holding reactionary and/or clerical views received appointments, funds earmarked for censorship activities suddenly materialized. The first attempt to subject foreign publications to Polish censorship occurred in 1821. Enraged by foreign press reports that the British government had ordered Napoleon and the Queen of England poisoned, Constantine demanded that the censors be rebuked for their inattentiveness, and that all items from selected foreign journals undergo censorship. Several weeks later, a decree extended censorship to foreign newspapers mailed to Polish subscribers. It instructed the postal authorities to seize any newspapers mentioning Poland and to turn them over to the police for further inspection.[16] Expanded censorship had a deleterious effect on Polish journalism. New enterprises ceased publication in record time, closed by government order. Other publications, determined to accommodate the censors, became barren and lifeless. Others, such as *Kurier Warszawski* or *Pielgrzym Nadwiślański*, turned from political and current events to less controversial subjects such as women's fashion and literature.[17]

Furthermore, Polish censorship began to reach out beyond the Congress Kingdom's borders. Unfavorable articles which appeared in *Krakus*, a Polish language periodical published in the Free City of Cracow, disturbed Constantine so greatly that he addressed a sharp letter to Zarzecki, the Russian consul there, for communication to the city council's presiding officer. The Grand Duke threatened that, "... publications of this kind can not fail to produce impressions most prejudicial to the interests of the Republic (Cracow)...." He urged the council president to "... take the most effective measures to prevent repetition of similar articles which indicate the evil spirit of those who publish and propagate this spirit among their readers."[18] Zarzecki, reporting back that he had raised the matter as instructed, declared that both *Krakus'* editor and the censor who permitted the offending items to pass were summoned to the police authorities where they received admonitions.[19] Shortly thereafter, *Krakus* discontinued publication.[20]

In May 1822, Novosil'tsov engineered another modification in the Kingdom's censorship structure. He outlined his position in a memorandum to Alexander dated May 3, 1822. Commencing with a synoptic history of the temporary censorship in which he pointed out that Potocki's lack of vigilance had resulted in the transfer of surveillance over newspapers to the Interior Ministry's police department, Novosil'tsov observed that this step had failed to bring about the desired results. Because Sumiński, the Senator's 1820 choice to direct the operation, either through indifference or fear, neglected to execute his duty with the requisite zeal, the situation had deteriorated to the point that the scurrilous *Constitutionnel* "continued to arrive and to be read in every coffee house and cafe." Novosil'tsov then remarked that Grabowski's arrival at the Education

Ministry had measurably benefited that bureau; "Grabowski demonstrated great zeal and ardor in all which is relative to the repression of press abuse." The current situation's unsatisfactory state impelled Novosil'tsov to recommend not only Sumiński's discharge, but also the restoration of all censorship duties to the Education Ministry. The Imperial Commissioner had already transmitted this proposal to Zajączek who planned to introduce it at the next Administrative Council session. The proposal also designated J.K. Szaniawski, a bitter opponent of the Enlightenment's principles who was much beholden to Novosil'tsov, a censorship director. Discussing the feasibility of establishing a government operated newspaper, the Imperial Commissioner concluded that a better course would be for the government to purchase an existing journal and subtly redirect public opinion in this manner. Money for this purpose would be concealed in the budget as "Funds for Literary Encouragement."[21]

As with most, if not all, of Novosil'tsov's proposals, there was a personal interest behind this plan. In this case, while strengthening the censorship Novosil'tsov placed his own man at the head of the supervisory commission and thus assured himself a large voice in the Kingdom's censorship. Zajączek gave legal approval to Novosil'tsov's project at the Administrative Council's May 7 meeting.[22] After six years of confusion, overlap and blurred lines of command, sole responsibility for enforcing the censorship regulations now devolved upon one department. Szaniawski, like Zajączek a one-time Jacobin and ardent supporter of Napoleon, now directed the Kingdom's censorship in a manner designed to enhance the values held by the Polish episcopate and the country's rulers at the expense of the ideas and ideals of the Enlightenment and the French Revolution.

Almost at once, the effects of change were felt as the new censorship took over several previously exempt categories. On May 30, 1822, Zajączek prohibited the publication of local governments' manifestos without first submitting them to the censors. In December of the same year, the Viceroy placed all judicial proceedings, including such harmless items as announcements of sheriff sales, under censorship obligation. Moreover, the Lord Lieutenant decided to permit Szaniawski's bureau to pre-censor all theatrical presentations despite the fact that a municipal board for just such a purpose had been functioning to the government's apparent satisfaction since 1816.[23]

The Polish censorship stole a leaf from its Russian counterpart when it banned certain newspapers excluded from the Empire. Constantine, writing to Novosil'tsov, applauded this prohibition and commanded him to determine if there were additional newspapers forbidden in Russia which deserved a similar restriction in Poland.[24] Novosil'tsov, applying himself to the task with his customary zeal, sent to Zajączek the names of six additional publications banned in Russia. He cited Constantine's letter as reason to forbid their entry into Poland.[25]

These events served to revitalize earlier ambiguous and halfhearted attempts to co-ordinate Polish and Russian censorship. During Alexander's visit to Warsaw in January 1823, officials mulled over the measures needed to harmonize the two systems.[26] In response to Nesselrode's request, Novosil'tsov delivered a copy of the regulations guiding Polish censorship which he and Szaniawski had coauthored. A covering letter not only expressed hope that Nesselrode would utilize them to bring the two censorships into agreement, but also requested that the minister determine whether the enclosed regulations were sufficient.[27] Nothing further was heard on this score, perhaps due to an incident taking place several weeks later. At that time, Szaniawski complained bitterly to Novosil'tsov about a recent edition of *Sanktpeterburgskii Vedomosti* which carried an article on Napoleon's diaries.[28] Novosil'tsov, forwarding this complaint to Alexander, pointed out that according to Polish regulations "works of the type in question here can not circulate in the kingdom." With obvious pique he continued, "I supposed that the same course had been adopted in the Empire...."[29]

As with censorship, the field of education also experienced several major changes. The post-1820 period witnessed a philosophic turnabout which had the general effect of eradicating the rationality of the Enlightenment. The king deposed the incumbent school administrators and appointed obscurantists and opportunists in their places. The new authorities modeled Polish education after Russian and Austrian examples. The king himself suggested that Austrian textbooks supplant those now in use.[30] The new education authorities also established police surveillance over the schools. The net result was a perceptible decline in education.

The first step toward reorienting the Kingdom's education policy came with Potocki's ouster. In early 1820, Potocki, whose free-thinking had already won him the enmity of Polish reactionaries and much of Poland's Roman Catholic hierarchy, wrote *Journey to Darktown*, a novel in which he denounced the clergy for their ignorance and derided their claims to direct Polish education. Outraged, the Polish bishops launched a fierce counterattack. Approaching Alexander at the time of the second Sejm, they induced the tsar to order Zajączek to bring in a new organic statute for the Education Ministry which would specifically assure the rights and privileges of the Roman Catholic Church.[31] When Potocki's protests were ignored, he submitted his resignation. However, the Viceroy refused to accept it, fearing that such a move would be interpreted as a surrender to the Sejm's demands for Potocki's scalp over the censorship question. Finally, Zajączek relented and on December 9, 1820, Potocki yielded his portfolio.[32]

During the hectic days when he barely clung to his post, Potocki, who was obliged to comply with Alexander's order on the new organic statute, strived to salvage education in the Kingdom by appointing a group of moderates to prepare the Education Ministry's reorganization plan. However, Zajączek, on his own initiative, appointed a much more conservative delegation. To Potocki's disgust, it was this latter committee which produced the report which served as the basis for the reorganizing statute accepted by Alexander on August 14, 1821.[33]

Among other things, this statute legitimatized the prefect system. In November 1819, the Viceroy had established prefects at the Warsaw lyceum in order to exercise religious and moral surveillance over youth.[34] The new statute not only confirmed this action but also extended it to every Polish middle school, and instructed the prefects to initiate religious instruction.[35]

Stanisław Grabowski, Potocki's successor as Minister of Education, warmly endorsed the new statute. Grabowski, the wastrel, illegitimate son of Stanisław Augustus Poniatowski, Poland's last king, was a former Jacobin and defender of Napoleon. He had changed allegiances, however, and was now allied with reactionaries and fanatical clerics. Known for his weak character, mediocre intelligence and good humor, "Pan Stash" seemed an illogical choice for a ministerial appointment. But his support of throne and altar made him an acceptable, if unlikely, candidate. When Polish society charged him with slothfulness in his official capacity, the salon wit Niemcewicz defended Grabowski, saying, "It is not possible to accuse him of inactivity; he ordered pants for every crucifix."[36] Under his management, the Ministry of Education quickly gained the epithet "the Ministry of Darkness."

Ably assisting Grabowski was the energetic J.K. Szaniawski (see above), who stepped into the newly created position of Education Director on

October 16, 1821. An advocate of Metternich's school reforms, Szaniawski never ceased to emphasize the bond between religion and education. He proclaimed that, "Godliness is the beginning of wisdom."[37] "The science of religion," Szaniawski wrote, "is not only the leading, but is even the primary, necessary basis and predisposition to all other learning."[38] On another occasion he assigned to education the duty to entrench right principles and to promote religion, Christian morality, the monarchy, and the existing social order. Additionally, he stated that public education should lead youth to a love of God, a love of monarch and an obedient attachment to government and law.[39] According to the Education Director, the most urgent concern was "return of education and public instruction through the help of the clergy to the appropriate road of religious spirit and principles in order to establish conditions favorable to social order ...(and)...elimination of everything which might destroy or weaken the beneficial influences bettering educational principles...."[40]

It thus became obvious that by 1820, Alexander, in agreement with the rest of the continent's rulers, had come to regard the educational establishment as an indispensable tool for reinforcing the supremacy of throne and altar. Novosil'tsov expressed this view when he said, "If teaching of the Christian religion represents the first and essential fundamental of all education, the second is the attachment to the Sovereign and to his government."[41]

Considering education to be a major force to innoculate youth against contamination by liberal ideas and to preserve a laudatory spirit of submissiveness toward authority, restoration governments developed broad educational policies to achieve these goals. For lower and middle schools the authorities adopted a preventive course intended to shelter the pupil from dangerous influences and to inculcate a love of monarch and church. It was felt that the salutary results of this policy would become evident only at a later date. A different arrangement existed for the universities. Believing them to be thoroughly infiltrated by a revolutionary spirit, the authorities sought to destroy any vestiges of academic freedom and to terminate their independent status.[42]

A deep commitment to the post-Napoleonic reaction and a pathological fear of social change helped to engender these policies. The authorities were convinced that formal instruction must conform to social status. Thus, the Polish Bishop of Płock, Adam Prażmowski, explained that social tranquility depended upon class divisions in which each class not only fulfilled its class obligations but also expressed satisfaction with its fate. He warned that over-education of the lower classes would lead to social ferment and discord.[43] In this scheme of things, education served to reinforce class distinctions and stifle social mobility. If, however, education were to be extended to the lower classes, especially the peasants, it would have to be conducted in a Christian spirit and aim at instilling morality. To insure this, the authorities insisted that priests assume the teaching burden.[44]

In its drive to preserve the *status quo*, the government did not confine itself to reorganizing the Education Ministry and appointing more sympathetic officials. It also created an independent Educational Reform Committee charged with restructuring Poland's entire education system. The idea for an thorough reform first surfaced in early 1820, and Novosil'tsov brought it to Alexander's attention on several different occasions during the following year. Novosil'tsov realized that Grabowski's appointment as Education Minister had created a power vacuum, and he saw in his plan for education reform an opportunity to augment his personal authority and stature. Even though Novosil'tsov's project covered all branches of education, he singled out the university for special attention. He proposed to shake up its hierarchy, limit its jurisdiction and curb its independence.[45] Alexander enthusiastically endorsed Novosil'tsov's initiatives and anxiously awaited their results.[46] The emperor agreed that vices debilitated the education system and acknowledged the "necessity to heal them radically through general and effective measures." He believed that the most compelling necessity was:

> to fight the spirit of irreligion, immorality, and insubordination which seems to have corrupted these establishments (schools) and to outlaw the chimerical theories which only produce excitement in youth and inflame their passions; in a word it is to re-establish in the schools the moral purity, and the spirit of order and discipline which is necessary . . . .[47]

In late 1821 the Educational Reform Committee began to meet when Szaniawski, its nominal head, returned from an inspection tour of Austria. Despite Szaniawski's title, Novosil'tsov controlled the committee and gradually molded it into a vehicle for his own particular educational philosophy. Novosil'tsov had already outlined his pedagogic views in a long memorial for Alexander dated September 14, 1821. At the outset he reviewed the general history of European universities. The Imperial Commissioner concluded that their "state within a state" status presented an unchecked danger to legitimist order. The university's independence, he maintained, together with contemporary professors who advocated seductive theories and almost anything absurd, permitted and even encouraged wayward students to challenge the foundation upon which the current order rested. In order to combat this mischievous trend, Novosil'tsov recommended a total reordering of the educational establishment. According to Novosil'tsov, original thought was not required since a more than satisfactory model presented itself. Here Novosil'tsov referred to Napoleon's great education reform which placed French schooling on a quasi-military footing.[48]

Favorably citing Napoleon's example, he noted that:

> Bonaparte, at his accession to the Empire found a youth trained in all the republican fanaticism.... The old university system had been overthrown by the republic. He reconstructed it on new bases. In Paris he established a new university for all the Empire and he named its Grand Master.... In twenty-five principal French towns he instituted academies and he himself named their rectors, inspectors, and professors. The state paid all salaries.... Under the surveillance of these academies there were established...lyceums and he named the headmasters, the assistant headmasters and the bursars. The state paid all salaries. The private boarding schools were authorized and supervised by the government.[49]

Novosil'tsov added that Napoleon ordered all lyceum students to wear uniforms and distinctive hats, and to participate in daily military exercises in order to inspire military spirit, order and discipline. Novosil'tsov noted that Napoleon's reforms succeeded in exterminating republican ideas and paid an extra dividend in creating thousands of soldiers who proved the efficacy of his program on the battlefield. "This fortunate revolution in the students' spirits was accomplished in less than two years."[50] The Imperial Commissioner pointing to traditional Polish military *élan* as proof that the Kingdom would eagerly accept the suggested reforms, urged Alexander to implement them immediately in order to extinguish "revolutionary ideas which are held, sadly, by the best and the most brilliant of their age."[51]

Initially, both Grabowski and Szaniawski opposed the independent reform committee. They regarded it as too obvious a usurpation of the Education Ministry's power and prerogatives. But they proved no match for Novosil'tsov who had the emperor's support.[52] The committee, composed of Novosil'tsov, Stanisław Grabowski, Szaniawski, Generals Hauke and Mallet, Bishop Prażmowski, and Count Tarnowski, a prominent reactionary first assembled on December 18, 1821.[53] Setting out to draft reorganization schemes for elementary and middle schools, the university, and the planned polytechnic, the committee soon bogged down in deliberations over a proposed school police. Novosil'tsov dominated the sessions, turning them into a forum on his educational theories and, specifically, his projects for extending certain features of the Russian education system into Poland. Behind this activity lay Novosil'tsov's determination to entrench himself as Poland's master in the education field.

The Imperial Commissoner exhorted the committee "to suppress the teaching of all vain or idle theory, and to restrict it (education) to that which is solid . . . in order to form subjects who are able to serve equally with success and affection."[54] A few days later, he advanced several measures which hinted at Russification. Repeating Hauke's remark that Russian youths entering the military were, "more substantially instructed than those who come from the Polish lands," he recommended that the committee adopt the general public education plan recently introduced in Russia, as well as a supplementary plan calling for compulsory instruction in the Russian language. Pointing out the ease with which the committee could install a system already functioning successfully in the Empire, Novosil'tsov enumerated certain major benefits which would accrue to Polish students. This program, he said, would enable Polish youth to continue their education in the Empire and, consequently, to enlarge their career opportunities in Russia or with the Russian government. Moreover, he claimed that the Russification of Polish educational and cultural institutions would further "the amalgamation, so desirable, between the two nations."[55] Although the committee sidetracked these proposals, they frequently reappeared in piecemeal form under the Education Ministry's sponsorship.

After its initial sessions, the committee began to focus attention on the question of establishing a school police. Novosil'tsov led the way. Hoping to gain control over yet another spy operation, the Imperial Commissioner questioned the Education Ministry's ability to control Polish students. In private reports sent directly to Alexander, Novosil'tsov conducted a low-keyed, innuendo-filled campaign designed to win Alexander's approval for a school police independent of the normal education authorities. Mildly castigating Education Ministry officials sitting on the Educational Reform Committee for their inattentiveness to the surveillance matter, Novosil'tsov attempted to prejudice Alexander against those officials charged with overseeing Poland's education system. At the same time, he pictured himself as the vigilant and industrious defender of throne and altar.[56] Novosil'tsov's crusade succeeded when the Educational Reform Committee authorized the creation of the Curator General, a quasi-police body patterned after the Austrian school police.

When the Educational Reform Committee suspended operations in May 1822, it yielded only the Curator General for all its apparent labors. However, this meager result tends to obscure the committee's real importance. For one thing, its mere existence testified to Novosil'tsov's growing mastery over the Congress Kingdom's civil affairs. Moreover, it prepared several projects for curriculum modification and textbook alteration which the Education Ministry adopted independently (see below). Since these reforms were conservative in nature, Poland's educational program in 1825 bore little resemblance to the progressive one Potocki turned over to Grabowski in 1820.

The Curator General, proof positive of the government's obsessive concern with surveillance and discipline, enjoyed an existence independent of the state bureaucracy. Nevertheless, the chief of the newly created autonomous "police" hierarchy gained both a seat and a vote in the Education Ministry's councils. The Curator General directed the school police —the inspectors, deputy inspectors and sub-inspectors—as they fulfilled their duties at the universtiy and the middle schools.[57] The school police were assigned to "watch over discipline of students and over prescribed plans of instruction in schools, . . . to help families and teachers supervise school youth, always keeping a protective eye on the progress of classes in moral as well as educational terms."[58] At the university no student could attend classes until he received written permission from the inspector. The police then maintained surveillance over the student: recording his grades and noting his behavior; observing him in the classroom; monitoring his moves on campus; and inspecting his private living quarters. They also exercised the right to reprimand professors if their lectures or conduct deviated from required norms. In the middle schools, the police supervised teachers as well as pupils. They investigated private lives, visited living quarters, inspected books, and took precautions against undesirable friendships. The lower ranking sub-inspectors even escorted pupils to class and served as school disciplinarians.[59]

Despite Novosil'tsov's impatience, Alexander did not formally authorize the Curator General until more than a year after the Educational Reform Committee submitted its recommendations.[60] The delay can be attributed to Alexander's preoccupation with other matters and his retreat from day to day government business. It was also the result, however, of a determined rear guard action mounted by Lubecki and Stefan Grabowski, the Minister-Secretary of State for Poland. These two Poles criticized the project for creating unnecessary confusion and rivalry in the Education Ministry and for its potential cost.[61] Evidently, Alexander relied on Novosil'tsov for the final opinion on this question.[62] But the opponents won a victory of sorts when the tsar decided to establish the Curator General first in Warsaw and only later extend it throughout the country.[63]

In July 1823 the Curator General began to function in Warsaw after a special commission delineated and co-ordinated its activities with the ordinary police.[64] In September, Szaniawski, following Alexander's stipulation to spread it gradually throughout the country, ordered the Curator General to commence operations in Płock, Lublin and Kalisz.[65] In the next year, it was extended to every Polish province.[66] By 1826, the Curator General employed forty-seven agents and disbursed a yearly payroll exceeding 120,000 *zlotys.*[67]

In addition to the Curator General, the Education Ministry itself developed several innovations designed to align Poland's educational system with those of Russia and Austria. For middle schools Szaniawski recommended a reduction in the number of hours of instruction as well as strict limitations on the number of lecture subjects. To fill the resultant void, he increased the number of hours devoted to religious education and introduced mandatory instruction in "morality." He demanded that students attend daily Mass and confession and that teachers practice the same regimen.[68]

The officials also tampered extensively with the curricula. Regarding history as the ideal subject to influence student thought, they consciously omitted all facts which failed to meet the "demands of the time." This forced instructors to present versions of history favorable to political legitimacy and religious conventionality. Devoting special attention to ancient history, the authorities demanded that teachers emphasize the suicidal struggle among the Greek republics and the destructive Roman civil wars in order to demonstrate the catastrophic results of social upheavals.[69] The school officials either eliminated or drastically reduced courses in modern literature while they promoted the study of classical languages such as Greek and Latin. Although compulsory study of Russian was introduced at the pedagogical institute, attempts to extend it to the entire education system miscarried. In an effort to dampen enthusiasm for philosophy and law courses which, by their very nature, carried a latent threat to the *status quo*, Szaniawski ordered that their lectures be delivered in Latin.[70]

The authorities systematically harassed teachers. They subjected prospective educators to innumerable regulations pertaining to piety and moral fitness and surrounded these unhappy individuals with spies and underlings from the Curator General.[71] For those already accepted into the profession, the Education Ministry devised detailed rules to insure proper conduct. Furthermore, Szaniawski himself made frequent inspection trips to the provinces.[72]

The university, however, bore the brunt of the reactionaries' assault. Novosil'tsov repeatedly attacked its independence and demanded that henceforth the government appoint the rector and deans.[73] The Imperial Commissioner even assailed the word "university" as connoting ". . . old ideas of independence as well as new ideas of revolution and anarchy . . . . " He suggested changing the University of Warsaw's name to the Imperial, or Royal, Institute for Teaching of Sciences.[74]

While the university weathered these frontal assaults, the educational authorities developed another agency which relied on more subtle methods to retard Polish education. The September 14, 1821, Education Reorganization Statute provided for an Elementary Book Society to aid the Education Ministry. Not fully operative until July 1823, the Society was empowered to prepare elementary works and examine teacher candidates. Its membership reflected Novosil'tsov's powerful influence as well as Grabowski's and Szaniawski's commitment to reactionary and clerical precepts. The Ministry of Education awarded it forty-eight thousand *zlotys* per year to conduct its business.[75]

Despite its mandated obligations, the Society soon turned to other matters. Instead of writing elementary textbooks, the Elementary Book

Society, under Szaniawski's presidency, occupied itself with expurgating and revising current texts. The determining factor in all cases was not a book's intrinsic value, but whether or not it conformed to rigid religious and political preconceptions.[76] The Society also imported ideologically correct, if academically deficient, works from Austria and Russia. Likewise, materials authored by French Ultras who loathed liberalism and yearned to re-establish the *Ancien Régime* enjoyed great popularity among the Society's members.[77] In addition to manipulating youthful minds, the Society determined the composition of the university's student body by drawing up and administering the entrance examinations. On the one hand, the Society altered the examination's format, adding numerous questions on the catechism and morality. On the other hand, it graded the exams more subjectively than ever.[78] Perhaps its interference in the university's selection process helps to explain the dramatic decrease in the number of university activists after 1823-1824.

Several other individuals and agencies joined in mounting a general campaign to denigrate education and to belittle students as a class. As early as April 4, 1820, Zajączek, in the name of decorum, prohibited students from frequenting sweet shops, coffee shops or other public places.[79] Shortly thereafter, a royal decree prescribed distinctive uniforms for student and teacher alike.[80] In addition to the Curator General's servants, Constantine's secret police also hounded students. They not only kept tabs on their every movement, but also titillated and infuriated the tsesarevich with gossip about students patronizing brothels or dashing around town without the proper uniform.[81] Finally, fearing the proliferation of student secret societies and pointing to the adequacy of Poland's own educational institutions, the Lord Lieutenant issued a decree on May 25, 1822, prohibiting student travel abroad or study at foreign universities without the government's written permission.[82]

Quite possibly, the step most harmful for Poland's future educational development occurred in summer 1821, when the government discontinued collection of compulsory school taxes from the peasantry.[83] This decision effectively eliminated the sole means of support for rural elementary schools, shattered Potocki's educational reforms and ended the ambitious attempt to instruct the Kingdom's peasant population. This huge mass now sank back in ignorance. Statistics tell a striking story. In 1819 there were 846 country schools with an enrollment totaling 21,091;

ten years later, the number of schools had declined to 329 while enrollment dropped as low as 7,958.[84] The destruction of Poland's progressive education system was paralleled by an unprecedented growth in spy and police networks. Both developments added to the Kingdom's growing demoralization. Proliferating at an astonishing rate, the police and spy organizations contributed to the drain on the Treasury and perceptibly inhibited normal life in the Kingdom. The Polish conspirator, Major Walerian Łukasiński, wrote that "Spying and denunciations grew so frequent, that no one was at peace among his family."[85]

At least eleven distinct police and spy establishments, some consisting of a few individuals others employing dozens, operated during the Congress Kingdom's brief lifetime. On October 12, 1816, the Polish-born Russian General A. Rożniecki persuaded Alexander to establish a gendarme corps for Poland. Its initial outlay totaled 400,000 *zlotys*.[86] Under its commanding officer, Rożniecki, the gendarmes imitated Napoleonic examples and served as the prototype for the Russian gendarmerie which flourished during Nicholas' reign.[87] The Polish gendarmerie blanketed the Kingdom with more than 280 individuals of "good morals": literate, healthy and between thirty and fifty years of age.[88] Although ordered to maintain close liaison with civilian authorities, they were forbidden to follow civilian orders or allow themselves to be placed under civilian control.[89]

A first-rate gendarme unit commanded by Baron Sass, a Russian Colonel serving on Constantine's staff, was detailed for the Grand Duke's private use. In addition to his gendarme duties, Sass directed an independent spy unit assigned to collect information from foreign sources as well. At Constantine's command, for example, he maintained surveillance over Nicholas during the then Grand Duke's occasionally lengthy visits to Berlin. When Nicholas ascended the throne, Sass secretly began to inform St. Petersburg about Constantine's activities. Two other Russian officers serving the Grand Duke, Generals Fanshawe and Gendre, spied on Russian officers stationed in Poland.[90]

The military secret police, commanded by the Russian Colonel Iuri Kempen until his death in 1822, was the largest police operation if not the most efficient. Rożniecki, who succeeded Kempen as head of the military secret police, chiefly relied on a Warsaw carpenter, M. Schley, and the student informer, H. Mackrott, for his information.[91] Unbeknown to Rożniecki, his two principal subordinates organized and controlled the so-called "counter-police," Constantine's private spy network assigned to ferret out information about the administration's most important officials including Novosil'tsov and Rożniecki himself.[92] As with all the spies, they freely resorted to bribery, robbery, blackmail and extortion to complete their tasks. Many police figures, including Schley and Mackrott, were killed in action, executed or lynched during the 1830-1831 insurrection.[93]

There were other important instances of spying. The Prussian consul, Schmidt and his Austrian counterpart, DuChet, organized and directed their own intelligence services.[94] Novosil'tsov's private spy network, consuming more than 100,000 zlotys per year, gained an unsavory reputation. The legally constituted national police, operating on a comparatively minuscule budget of 58,000 zlotys, answered to the Interior Ministry. The Warsaw municipal police, superintended by Novosil'tsov's tool, M. Lubowidzi, played a more important role than its title indicates. Finally, Don Cossacks under Russian command performed frontier guard duties. One expert conservatively set the yearly total expenditure for secret police work at more than 500,000 zlotys.[95]

Luckily for Poland, the numerous police-spy establishments were plagued by intrigue and rivalries which crippled their effectiveness. Moreover, their agents, unable to uncover much subversion in a basically docile society, denounced each other with monotonous regularity.[96] Novosil'tsov, attempting to bring order out of this choas as well as increase his own power, proposed a Central Police Bureau to subordinate all the police to one authority. In Novosil'tsov's scheme, control over the Bureau would rest, naturally, with himself. Exaggerating a student secret society scare in order to justify further the need for centralizing police operations, he gained Alexander's approval in August, 1821.[97]

In calling for measures to revitalize the police apparatus, Novosil'tsov cited two negative factors which made centralization imperative. First, the division of responsibility among so many disconnected units caused both overlaps and lacunae which paralyzed the police. Secondly, the revolutionary ferment in countries bordering Poland not only threatened public order there, but also exerted a baneful influence on the Kingdom. In order to solve these problems, Novosil'tsov outlined a fifteen point program establishing a Central Police Bureau at Warsaw to oversee and coordinate security operations throughout the Kingdom. Under Novosil'-tsov's proposal, the headquarters of the Central Police Bureau would consist of the gendarme chief (who would also report directly to Constantine), the Warsaw fortress commandant, the superintendent of Warsaw's municipal police and the director of the national police. They would gather twice daily to receive reports and issue directives and, if conditions warranted, hold extraordinary sessions.[98]

Shortly after Alexander approved Novosil'tsov's project, the Imperial Commissioner crippled the national police when he lobbied successfully for a significant increase in both funds and jurisdiction for Lubowidzki's municipal police. The Imperial Commissioner distrusted the Interior Minister, T. Mostowski, whom he regarded as "soft" on vital security matters and he labeled the national police director, Sumiński, incompetent. Lubowidzki, on the other hand, faithfully executed Novosil'tsov's commands. Any growth in his power represented a growth in Novosil'tsov's power.

With the Congress Kingdom's tenth anniversary fast approaching, its future as an independent, progressive state seemed more in doubt than ever before. In addition to political and dynastic problems, Poland also experienced a concerted drive, officially sanctioned at the highest level, to impose a rigid, reactionary ideology over all aspects of its national life.

Censorship continued to function as it had since 1819—arbitrarily and oppressively. However, it had become more pervasive. It now extended its tentacles to grasp every work: political or non-political; Polish or foreign; book or newspaper. Lacking defined legal principles and regulations, the censorship's reorganized superstructure tended to bestow undue power on Novosil'tsov, who was no friend of either a free press or the Poles. Similarly in the education field, conservative forces gained control and embarked upon a course designed to subject instruction to clerical influences and reactionary doctrines. Abandoning Potocki's plans for quantitative and qualitative improvements, the authorities funneled much-needed funds to quasi-police agencies charged with hounding students and faculty. As he did with the censorship, Novosil'tsov advanced his own ambitions through endless reports to the emperor which played on Alexander's animosity toward real or imagined challenges to his authority and exploited the tsar's aversion for all movements which appeared to threaten the socio-political *status quo*. The Imperial Commissioner also insinuated himself into a leading role in the complex police apparatus. There was little effective opposition to Novosil'tsov's rise to power. Having already lost Alexander's confidence, Polish men of stature such as Czartoryski could not successfully confront the Russian representative. Moreover, Novosil'tsov retained enough Polish henchmen in high positions to deflect any complaints about Russian domination in the Kingdom. Constantine, of course, enjoyed greater theoretical powers than Novosil'tsov. But the Grand Duke, except for periodic temper tantrums, happily confined himself to military matters. Whenever he did turn to civil affairs, Novosil'tsov, confident that Constantine would soon re-immerse himself in army affairs, always moved quickly to manipulate the tsesarevich for his own purposes. Although airing his ultra-monarchist views in private discussions, the lightly regarded Zajączek faithfully and mindlessly executed every order.

Despite Novosil'tsov's apparent preponderance on the Vistula, Alexander remained the authentic master of Polish affairs. The emperor, cognizant of all that transpired, approved and supported the decisions which placed Poland on a reactionary course. Consequently, he bears heavy responsibility for the injury done to Poland's cultural, educational and social institutions during the 1819-1825 period. Nevertheless, Alexander was very reluctant to destroy the forms which gave the Congress Kingdom a liberal constitutional facade. This was only good politics. It reflected his not unreasonable desire to avoid further antagonizing the Poles, and to preserve even a tattered shred of his former reputation. Moreover, in maintaining appearances he provided himself with an escape hatch. If at any time he decided to reverse his field, it would be a relatively easy matter for him to reaffirm his faith in the forms he had created and to dismiss the rascals guilty of ignoring and perverting them.

CHAPTER 7

REACTION TRIUMPHANT:
THE FINAL PHASE OF TSAR ALEXANDER'S POLISH POLICY, 1820-1825

The reaction in the cultural, educational and social fields also extended to politics. Angered by the second Sejm's conduct, Alexander wanted the message conveyed in his closing Sejm speech firmly implanted in Polish minds. This task, however, required a subtle touch in order to avoid provoking a Polish or, even worse, a European controversy. Alexander made the first move when, shortly before he left for Troppau, he sent Zzjączek two unofficial communications designed to publicize his disappointment with the Sejm and to draw critical attention to the Liberal Opposition. Striving to avoid any adverse reaction and to evoke a favorable response, the tsar played the Lithuanian card once again. Alexander's first letter, sent under Minister-Secretary of State Sobolewski's signature, reminded the Poles that the Emperor represented the best hope for their future. It also suggested that Alexander, despite difficulties, still intended to reunite Russia's Polish provinces with the Kingdom. However, it warned against displays of opposition and noted that the "current dangerous spirit of imitation, and malicious exaggerations" were instrumental in turning him from his goal.[1]

The second message spelled out the measures which the Lord Lieutenant must employ to transmit the king's views to the nation. Alexander ordered him to forward the first note to the presidents of the Provincial Commissions along with instructions to read it to the Commissions, the Provincial Councils and the provinces leading citizens. Next, the Commission presidents were to induce the Provincial Councils to send addresses to the throne condemning the Sejm opposition and expressing deep regret for its insolent actions.[2]

After Zajączek carried out his orders, seven of the eight Provincial Councils bowed to the government's wishes and sent "addresses for His Majesty with expressions of regret that their representatives' conduct at the Sejm provoked the displeasure of His Majesty...."[3] Only Kalisz demurred. It chose to remain silent in the face of what it considered deceitful and illegal pressure.

On August 12, 1821, Alexander dispatched a rejoinder to the addresses in which he affirmed his belief in the nation's affection for him and reiterated his desire to safeguard Polish happiness, to unify the Poles and to preserve Poland from Europe's fate, i.e., "the evil spirit." The Poles, he said, would aid their cause by conducting themselves in "a spirit of peacefulness and submission to government authority." But the king also indicated that he would not tolerate any opposition. He threatened "to suppress by the most effective means all undertakings tending to disturb order or give reason for scandal."[4] Shortly thereafter, Alexander carried out this threat when his subordinates in Poland launched an attack on the Liberal Opposition's leader.

From the moment W. Niemojowski berated the administration at the 1820 Sejm, he became the target of a government campaign to discredit and destroy him. Police, hoping to incriminate Niemojowski, constantly spied on him both at Warsaw and Kalisz.[5] The government also slandered him. It spread rumors linking Niemojowski to the *Carbonari* and also suggested that "his" Liberal Opposition depended upon European revolutionary movements for its support. In early 1822, the Niemojowski brother's election to the Kalisz Provincial Council further infuriated the authorities.

At this time, the acrimonious conflict arising from the government's arrest of a certain Major Radoński complicated matters. Radoński, a former officer in the Polish army, was arrested while inspecting his Kalisz estates and charged with membership in the *Carbonari* and the intention to enter into a military revolt. Hauled to the Kalisz jail, he managed to contact W. Niemojowski who shortly thereafter arrived on the scene. Together the two men protested the arrest, and censured the government for violating the constitutional guarantees against illegal seizure. Niemojowski promised to raise the matter at the next Sejm. After the authorities dispatched Radoński to Warsaw, Niemojowski and his circle decided to notify foreign journals in hopes of attracting publicity.[6]

This incident served as grist for the government's mill. Novosil'tsov took great care to report the events to the tsar, emphasizing the principals' anti-government remarks. He also urged Constantine to summon the gendarme officers who witnessed the outbursts in order to detail Niemojowski's offensive behavior and, on this basis, to order the deputy to Warsaw to account for himself.[7]

In the meantime, Niemojowski wrote a long letter to Constantine in which he cited the constitution as sufficient defense for his activities. Furthermore, he took this occasion to elucidate his political credo and his parliamentary theory and to brand the government's behavior toward the Sejm as unconstitutional.[8] When Novosil'tsov reported this turn of events to Alexander, he lashed out at Niemojowski for "an act of usurpation as dangerous as it was reprehensible." Novosil'tsov claimed that "in his capacity as Sejm representative . . . (Niemojowski) believes himself able to set himself as judge between government acts and the individual the acts concerned."[9] Condemning Niemojowski's arrogant tone and false pretensions, Novosil'tsov launched into a complicated discourse defending the government and refuting Niemojowski's accusations. Novosil'tsov finally concluded that the Kalisz representative was guilty of a "state crime," but would never be punished because the Polish courts were too lenient. To remedy this miscarriage, Novosil'tsov urged "a special commission with the character, authority, and attributes of a High Court of Criminal Justice" to try Niemojowski—a solution he advocated for student members of secret societies as well. In closing, he asked if the monarch would at least consider an *ukaz* removing the offender from the deputies' list. The Imperial Commissioner assured Alexander that such a step would make a profoundly favorable impression upon the Poles.[10]

Two days later, Constantine submitted a pair of detailed, albeit illegal, projects to "annul and paralyze Niemojowski's factious influence." One, citing the representative's "illegal provocation" before the Emperor, called for a manifesto depriving Niemojowski of his representative's mandate and providing for a new election. The other envisioned a decree prohibiting him from being in the Emperor's presence, a more subtle if no less effective device to bar Niemojowski from the next Sejm.[11] Although Alexander was upset by the deputy's conduct, he did not wish to associate himself openly with illegal measures. Thus, Constantine's proposals served a valuable purpose. In allowing Constantine a free hand, the emperor knew that whichever course his brother followed would bring the desired results without overtly straining his own reputation.[12]

Novosil'tsov, meanwhile, clamored for his "High National Court" to adjudicate crimes of state. He pointed to the criminal codes's inability to distinguish between crimes of state and ordinary offenses, and cited its failure to establish a proper gradation between criminal preparation and criminal accomplishment. According to Novosil'tsov these oversights allowed crimes of state to go unpunished until executed, a situation beneficial only to rebels. The Imperial Commissioner claimed that a High National Court, plugging these loopholes, would not only buttress law and order, but would also insure public tranquility in turbulent times through harsh prosecution of potential as well as actual troublemakers. Novosil'tsov concluded with a careful explanation of how the sovereign possessed the inalienable right to introduce this tribunal without consulting the Sejm much less obtaining its consent.[13]

Several ministers objected to Novosil'tsov's plans for a new state tribunal. Consequently, when Novosil'tsov balked at sending Niemojowski through normal judicial channels, Constantine resorted to extraordinary measures. On January 8, 1822, the Grand Duke summoned Niemojowski to Belvedere where, in the presence of Zajączek and the ministers, he read to him the royal order forbidding him to appear in the tsar's presence because of his lèse majesté. Niemojowski was shocked but Novosil'tsov took perverse delight in informing Alexander that the opposition leader was socially shunned during his short stay in Warsaw.[14]

The authorities next turned on the Kalisz Provincial Council to which the Niemojowski brothers had been elected. Discovering procedural irregularities, they hoped to induce the Senate, the adjudicating body for disputes arising from elections to Provincial Councils, to annul the Niemojowskis' selection. However, even though the Senate was the ruler's handpicked body, the officials feared that they could not muster the fifty percent vote necessary to invalidate the election results. Consequently, they hesitated to press the case. Moreover, they suspected that if the Senate nullified the election, the Kalisz Council would use a new vote to select the Niemojowskis once again. At this juncture, Zajączek suggested suspension of the Kalisz Council as the most efficacious method to negate the Niemojowskis' influence.[15]

Disregarding the Lord Lieutenant's advice, the government brought the matter before the Senate which did indeed throw out the election results. When Alexander then delayed setting a date for a new election, the Kalisz Council simply appointed the brothers to fill the vacant seats. The government appealed. When the Senate rejected the government's appeal and declared the Council's action constitutional, Alexander dissolved the Council for an indefinite period and proclaimed all its operations illegal.[16] The Kalisz Council remained in limbo for the remainder of Alexander's reign as the tsar refused to lift the suspension.[17]

Concurrent with W. Niemojowski's Belvedere interview and the elections to the Kalisz Provincial Council, the government convoked the assemblies of the nobility and the commune assemblies in order to elect delegates to the Sejm scheduled for 1822. The authorities, viewing these elections as a fine opportunity to smash the Liberal Opposition, planned to dominate the electoral process and to hound individual opponents into oblivion. The government initiated several different measures to attain its goal. For one, it packed the Senate, thereby imparting to this chamber an even more bureaucratic and aristocratic character than it already possessed. Packing the Senate proved to be a relatively uncomplicated task since the executive authority controlled nominations to the upper chamber.

Because a simple packing of the House exceeded the executive's power, the government turned to more devious methods. It began by choosing men known for their obedience to the government to serve as marshals at the assemblies of the nobility and the commune assemblies. At Novosil'tsov's urging, Alexander approved a plan for the government to "reimburse" the marshals for expenses incurred.[18] Warsaw also ordered provincial officals to participate actively in the assemblies of the nobility and the commune assemblies in order to influence their proceedings. Finally, the government prepared to submit its own slate of "safe" candidates and Zajączek ordered the Provincial Councils to add to their electoral lists a number of officials not carried on the Council's rollbooks.[19]

The pressure did not cease with these measures. The proclamation convoking the assemblies of the nobility and the commune assemblies bade the delegates remember the recent experience of the second Sejm and instructed them to select "men loving public order, attentive, circumspect, and unshaken in moderate aims...."[20] Further, the government issued several supplementary proclamations serving to dampen public interest, to inhibit the meetings' freedom and to diminish their significance. Banquets, traditional in Polish politics from the Republic's earliest time, were prohibited, while sessions were moved from their usual location in churches to town halls or other government buildings. Zajączek, in his instructions to the marshals, placed primary emphasis on maintaining law and order, and commanded the marshals to suspend the meetings in case of difficulties.[21]

Despite these precautions, the government's heavy-handed interference provoked several incidents. At the Włocławek *sejmik* the pro-government marshal burned the ballots and dissolved the session when the delegates rejected the government candidate. The angry delegates rioted, prompting the marshal to call in the gendarmes to restore order.[22] At the Piotrków *sejmik,* the national police chief, Sumiński, was named as Sejm representative against the delegates wishes. They also reacted violently.[23] Ultimately, the authorities chose to exaggerate these incidents and to use them as an excuse to cancel the scheduled Sejm.

The collapse of the government's efforts to elect its own candidates also helped to convince the authorities of the need to cancel the Sejm. The opposition exhibited surprising strength and frequently swamped "offical" candidates with the result that the next Sejm promised to be even more shrill and recalcitrant than the previous one. For the government's benefit, however, the electoral events gave it needed experience in control techniques. Subsequently, it applied these lessons during the next elections to produce a pliant majority at the 1825 Sejm.[24]

The government's fiasco at the assemblies of the nobility and the commune assemblies prompted Zajączek to demand once again that the scheduled Sejm be postponed. In a March 7, 1822, memorandum to Alexander he complained:

> . . . the spirit reigning among the Polish nobility is perfectly contrary to the government's views. I am able to assure Your Majesty that this spirit is general and that the provinces can not be differentiated between those a little more audacious and those a little less.[25]

Three weeks later he wrote, ". . .it would be better to postpone the Sejm than to convoke it this year."[26] In support of his recommendation he cited a host of negative factors including the government's failure to influence the elections, the unruliness at the sessions, the recent discovery of secret Polish student societies and the discontent over Niemojowski's treatment. Claiming that these reflected the malicious mood guiding the Poles, he forecast division and strife at the Sejm.[27]

Grand Duke Constantine, at this time deeply enmeshed in the succession problem, anxiously wanted to portray himself as master of an orderly house. Consequently, he took sharp exception to the Lord Lieutenant's "unwarranted generalizations." He attacked Zajączek for his "alarmist views," and advised his brother to convoke the Sejm as planned. In a remarkable turn of events, it was Constantine who called for strict adherence to the constitution. He also warned that:

...postponement of the Sejm will be considered by this opposition ...as a sign of weakness, as a kind of silent recognition form the government's side that it is not in a condition to battle successfully with its enemies and abusers, and that it is seeking...to avoid attacks...; it seems to me that it is in the interests of the government to destroy this supposition.[28]

Novosil'tsov supplied the decisive opinion. Realizing that Alexander had no desire to re-enact the second Sejm's unpleasant scenes, the Imperial Commissioner counseled postponement of the national gathering for a wholly unanticipated but not entirely specious reason: namely, Tsar Alexander's great preoccupation with the European political situation which precluded his active involvement in any Sejm at this time.[29] Alexander accepted Novosil'tsov's excuse. However, not wanting to agitate the Poles further, he decided to postpone the Sejm only until spring 1823. At one point he even ordered the Kingdom's officials to commence preparations for a Sejm "the next Spring (1823) or somewhat later."[30] But this Sejm never met and Poland's national representative body gathered again only in 1825.

The government regarded the public character of the Sejms' sessions as their most dangerous and damaging feature. With some justification apparently several officials complained that opposition orators played to the public galleries which, in turn, egged on the speakers. Moreover, the Sejm's openness not only gave the opposition a public forum to rebuke the executive branch, but the publicity attending such behavior exploded the carefully cultivated myth of harmony between Poland and Russia. Alexander feared this disclosure would impair Russia's ability to influence European councils. Consequently, imperial officials concluded that the Sejm's openness posed a threat to fundamental state policy. Beginning in March 1822, Constantine suggested destroying the Sejm's open character in order to insure harmony and tranquility at the biennial meetings.[31] Novosil'tsov supported Constantine, proposing diminished but "loyal" galleries, censored Sejm minutes and daily reports, and a carefully prepared and strictly followed agenda.[32] Rejecting Novosil'tsov's proposals if not the spirit in which he offered them, the tsar formulated an alternative. He drew up a projected petition which the House would be induced to convey to the throne. This appeal beseeched Alexander to introduce changes in the constitution and organic statutes in order to suppress the dangerous "demagogic spirit" and preserve the country's independence and liberal constitution.[33] While this plan might have solved Alexander's problem, quite obviously the Sejm would never approve it. This fact convinced Alexander to follow Novosil'tsov's recommendations. In June 1824, the Imperial Commissioner forwarded his draft project destroying the Sejm's openness. The sovereign, accepting Novosil'tsov's work with only minor corrections, promulgated it on February 13, 1825, as the so-called Additional Article to the Polish Constitution. Henceforth, public meetings of the Sejm would take place only for the opening and closing sessions and for solemn occasions; all ordinary sessions would take place behind closed doors. Moreover, no minutes or daily bulletins would be published.[34] In promulgating the article as a simple addition to the constitution, Alexander explained that it came directly from the highest authority, i.e., the constitution's "father" and, therefore, did not require any ministerial countersignatures. In a real sense this was the first constitutional change achieved through a *direct* expression of the imperial will. However, Alexander's endorsements of the Viceroy's and Constantine's unconstitutional actions clearly indicated that his restraint had not been predicated upon any deep commitment to the charter.

As with almost all of the tsar's major projects, the Additional Article was preceded by false starts and indecision. Nevertheless, Alexander's long-standing desire to eliminate the Sejm's public character ended his vacillation. The Additional Article was not, as one historian claimed, a sinister plot on Novosil'tsov's part to keep Alexander in ignorance of the Sejm events, thereby forcing him to rely on the Imperial Commissioner for information about the legislature's proceedings.[35] Nor was it a manifestation of Alexander's desire, stemming from emotional instability and confused spiritual life, to strangle the constitution.[36]

The next Polish Sejm, finally convoked in late spring 1825, proved to be anticlimactic. The active opposition numbered less than ten deputies.

Their leaders and most dynamic speakers found themselves barred from participation and, in some cases, placed under house arrest. Moreover, as the king intended, the Additional Article smothered the Sejm in a cloak of secrecy and discouraged a considerable segment of articulate Polish society from even casual participation in politics.

Despite the Additional Article, the opposition once again resolved to protest against the government's arbitrary conduct. Since receiving the 1822 order forcing him to absent himself from the tsar's presence, W. Niemojowski repeatedly had made inquiries as to whether this prohibition extended to the Sejm sessions. Not receiving a satisfactory response, he announced as the time for the 1825 Sejm drew near that his constitutional mandate superseded any royal order and rode to the Warsaw suburbs. There, he made known his intention to attend the Sejm as Kalisz's duly elected representative. However, as he approached the city gate, gendarmes seized him and whisked him back to Kalisz where he remained under house arrest until the 1830 insurrection.[37]

The authorities hit upon a new and quite successful tactic to dispose of other opposition leaders. Embroiling them in spurious and trumped up court proceedings, the government produced a situation which enabled the Senate to expel the deputies from the House.[38] In Bonawentura Niemojowski's case the gendarmes gave him twenty-four hours to vacate Warsaw just minutes after the Senate formally barred him from taking his seat. Thus, not only did the government frequently elect its own representatives, it also managed to oust several key opposition deputies on technical points.

The opposition's disappointments continued during the unusually placid Sejm sessions. Its ranks decimated and scattered, the Liberal Opposition could only present its views in the Sejm reports and private petitions. The latter, containing several explosive complaints, were deftly turned aside by House marshal Piwnicki, a faithful government servitor and master of parliamentary procedure. The frustrated Liberal Opposition was reduced to boycotting the post-Sejm round of balls and festivities.[39]

Besides the Additional Article and the rout of the opposition, several other factors contributed to the Sejm's relative quiescence. Alexander, attaching considerable propaganda value to this Sejm, demanded submissiveness. Unlike the first two Sejms, he planned carefully in order to achieve his goal of a tame legislature. Only after the 1824 elections for

Sejm representatives assured him that the body's composition would not be hostile and the Additional Article guaranteed the absence of publicity, did he consent to call the legislature. Then, to insure tranquility, he instructed the government not to introduce any controversial bills. Furthermore, both before and during the Sejm, hordes of spies closely monitored the representatives in order to permit the government to head off any trouble. Finally, individuals sympathetic to Alexander constantly urged restraint and conciliation.[40] These factors combined to stifle any enthusiasm and render the Sejm more dead than alive.

During the Sejm's sessions the Poles behaved cautiously, thereby meeting the king's demand for meekness. Many Poles interpreted the Additional Article as a clear warning that disobedience would result in the constitution's abrogation and the Kingdom's absorption into the Empire. Even more Poles preferred to believe Alexander's new hints about uniting Lithuania and Poland.[41]

That the emperor would play the Lithuanian card once again was to be expected; that numerous influential Poles would choose to give credence to this tired ploy only indicates the overwhelming importance they attached to regaining "ancient Polish lands." Arriving in Warsaw in high spirits, Alexander radiated his legendary warmth and charm to good effect. Impressed by Alexander's favors and promises, Polish society once again prostrated itself at the tsar's feet. One can only speculate on the reasons for the emperor's striking reversal of form. Beginning with his October 1819 visit, Alexander had distinguished himself by his hostile attitude toward the Poles, a rancor so evident that foreign diplomats freely commented on it.[42] Now he delighted and indulged the Poles. Perhaps this was the prelude to reinstating the suspended tactic of flattering the Poles into the Russian camp. Most likely it was a subterfuge, a pretense to cajole the Poles into behaving with proper decorum and civility in the presence of the "monarch-father." In any event, Alexander expressed unusual pleasure with the results. He wrote to Arakcheev, "Here, thank the Almighty, everything goes according to wish and I am excellently content with the general situation."[43] In his last public appearance in Poland, the sovereign praised the Poles for their moderation at the Sejm and vaguely promised to move forward on the Lithuanian question.[44]

Despite these conciliatory words, skepticism prevailed among the nation's students who had been figuratively, and sometimes literally, battered from pillar to post during the previous half decade. It comes as no surprise to discover that Novosil'tsov played a leading role in persecuting the students. Understanding the emperor's growing disenchantment with secret societies, the Imperial Commissioner encouraged Alexander in order to further his personal aims. Shocked by the *Burschenschaft's* escapades including Karl Sand's assassination of Kotzebue, the *Carbonari's* growth and spread in western Europe and, perhaps most decisively, the Semenovskii mutiny which was widely attributed to an underground organization, Alexander anguished over secret societies and his former role as their promoter. In Poland, the tsar had encouraged secret societies, especially the Masons, as a means to support his efforts to enlighten Russian society and to break down traditional Russo-Polish barriers. Alexander's disillusionment with this course, most graphically reflected in his November 1821 decision to close the Masonic lodges, is yet another indication of his gradual withdrawal from a Polish strategy based upon conciliation.[45]

Wishing not only to ingratiate himself with the tsar but also to destroy a potentially powerful opponent, Novosil'tsov, at first obliquely but later more directly, denounced the Masonic order. After more than a year's innuendo and personal defamation, Novosil'tsov spoke openly against the Masons on May 24, 1821, when he told Alexander that "the pernicious obstinacy" and "the evil spirit" gripping the community resulted from secret societies. "Freemasonry," he continued, "is considered as the principal source and the matrix of the secret societies. It is on its forms that they (the secret societies) model themselves and under its cloak that they hide everything."[46] Several weeks later the Senator advised:

> ...they (Masonic lodges) have degenerated into genuine political clubs such as those which were observed in France preparing the revolution and directing it after it broke out...they try to disseminate and generalize in the country the ideas of the sovereignty of the people, the division of powers, the right of representation, etc. (I am) convinced in my conscience...that there is nothing so dangerous as such societies....[47]

At the same time, Novosil'tsov told Alexander wild tales of radical secret societies conspiring to raise the banners of revolution. Pressing to make mountains of molehills, Novosil'tsov cited a grossly inaccurate survey of student secret societies hastily drawn up for Constantine by Baron Mohrenheim, his future "foreign minister." In this fantastic document Mohrenheim purported to have unearthed a European-wide student movement consisting of twenty-thousand dedicated youths prepared "to sacrifice their lives for the revolution." Centered at Breslau, where "one could suppose the revolt to begin," the movement supposedly controlled students at Warsaw University as well as Cracow's ancient Jagiellonian University.[48] Novosil'tsov, after appending several suggestions for countering this threat, dutifully passed this report on to the nervous emperor.[49] Over the next few months the Imperial Commissioner hammered away at this subject.[50]

Fortunately for Novosil'tsov, in August 1821, the Cracow police arrested several students expelled from Warsaw University in March of the same year for their secret society activities. A search of their apartments revealed detailed plans to initiate *Burschenschaft* chapters at Cracow and the Kielce mining school under the auspices of a Warsaw *Burschenschaft*. Subsequent investigations proved that this Warsaw *Burschenschaft* enjoyed a purely fictional existence and that the accused students, although involved in secret society activity, had concocted a *Burschenschaft* from nothing more than their own experiences, reading and conversation with individuals attending German universities.[51]

Nevertheless, Novosil'tsov pounced upon their arrest and exaggerated its significance. Writing to Alexander, the Imperial Commissioner pointed to this case's special character and the dangerous circumstances which surrounded it as reason enough to strike another blow at Poland's judicial and national independence. He demanded "the formation of a mixed tribunal composed of judges from the Empire and judges from the Kingdom...."[52] When several investigations independently launched by Novosil'tsov failed to prove his allegations, he promptly inaugurated new investigations.

Although the king rejected Novosil'tsov's request for a new tribunal, the Imperial Commissioner continued to bombard Alexander with denunciations of the *Burschenschaft* "threat." Sometimes he forwarded testimony taken from the interrogation of arrested students, and on at least one occasion Novosil'tsov charged the *Burschenschaft* suspects with planning to arm the peasants.[53]

On May 3, 1822, Novosil'tsov summed up the results of his numerous investigations in a lengthy memorial sent to Alexander:

The results which we have obtained thus far in our investigations of secret societies prove that there reigns in the country a spirit of intrigue which tries to take possession of every class and whose tendency is, as I have proclaimed in several of my reports, to prepare the nation to seize the first occasion to shake off what they call the yoke of a foreign power, to reunite the different parts of Poland, and to form an independent state.[54]

It is hard to imagine phrases better calculated to justify the tsar's basic decision to persecute secret societies or to persuade him to continue and intensify this policy.

Certainly Novosil'tsov's deluge of denunciations reinforced Alexander's own growing antipathy toward secret societies and helped to bring about the monarch's November 6, 1821, proclamation forbidding all secret societies in the Kingdom. Shortly thereafter this prohibition was extended to the Empire itself.[55] Moreover, this ban further encouraged Novosil'tsov to arrest, interrogate and generally harass students suspected of secret society membership. When one suspect committed suicide in his cell Novosil'tsov commended this act for producing "a very salutary sensation."[56]

In characteristic fashion, the old Mason, Novosil'tsov, also took advantage of the proclamation outlawing secret societies to loot the order's treasury. Charged with cataloguing and liquidating the lodges' assests, the Imperial Commissioner pocketed significant sums. In this operation he was joined by his cronies, Lubowidzki of police fame and General Rożniecki, Polish Masonry's last Grand Master.[57]

Several months later, Alexander published Pope Pius VII's bull anathematizing secret associations in general and the Free Masons and the *Carbonari* in particular.[58] The spectacle of the Orthodox monarch disseminating a papal injuction indicates the seriousness with which the tsar viewed the secret society "menace." This period also witnessed the introduction of a rudimentary loyalty oath. On May 13, 1822, the Lord Lieutenant ordered the Interior Ministry to inform each state employee of the proscription against secret societies and to collect sworn statements from the employees to the effect that they no longer belonged to any society and would not join any society in the future.[59]

The Imperial Commissioner continued to press for major modifications in the Kingdom's judicial system. His projected changes were designed to wrest sovereignty from the constitutional courts and to establish special tribunals responsive to the king's and Novosil'tsov's, dictates. To justify his demands Novosil'tsov cited laxity in the Polish courts as well as the consitution's failure to define crimes against the state, let alone provide machinery to adjudicate such offenses. At various times he proposed a High National Court to try state crimes, a mixed Russian-Polish tribunal, and a permanent commission of inquiry to investigate not only all "crimes against the state" but also any act which conjectured about the existence of plots or conspiracies against the government.[60] Although the monarch refused to implement these proposals, Alexander did approve the use of mixed military-civilian commissions sitting *in camera* both to investigate and to judge accused students and military officers. The fact that the commissions occasionally number more Russian than Polish members apparently never disturbed Alexander.

During this time of increased repression, the composition, objectives and *modus operandi* of secret societies did not remain static. Polish student secret societies, like their western counterparts, metamorphosed from predominantly intellectual, self-help and/or literary organizations into politically active associations reflecting various degrees of political consciousness. Warsaw University's Union of Free Poles presents a fine example of a newly emerging student secret society structured along conspiratorial lines and committed to an active political course.

Founded by L. Piątkiewicz and W. Heltman in late 1819, the Free Poles pursued a clear political goal: revival of the fatherland and war with tyranny. The leaders aimed for Poland's re-unification in full independence as well as the "expansion and dissemination of liberal principles." To achieve their ambitions they considered it essential to seek "some kind of connection with foreign societies."[61] Copying Masonic forms, the Free Poles divided themselves into several lodges distinguished by an ascendancy of greater secrecy and fewer members. The highest circle, or chapter, headed by a Grand Master, numbered five members who were cognizant of the association's political nature and who directed the entire organization's activities. Ceremonial rituals, especially those relating to initiation, took on great significance. Typical activity in the lower level lodges consisted of writing and debating papers whose topic was the development of liberal programs within the context of a unified Poland.[62]

A determination to spread its influence and propagandize its philosophical beliefs characterized the Free Poles. Heltman confessed:

...our aim was to spread the society as much as possible, to send members abroad and to other Polish regions, in order to set up and form in these places similar societies and to unite with them to act towards the attainment of our goal—liberation of Poland.[63]

It is generally believed that the Free Poles, who numbered several dozen, sponsored those individuals whose arrest in August 1821 convinced Novosil'tsov of the *Burschenschaft's* existence at Warsaw University. In order to publicize the society's views, its leading members founded a periodical, *Dekada Polska* (*The Polish Decade*), devoted to political and cultural topics. First issued in early 1821, *Dekada* soon drew the government's wrath for airing such statements as, "without freedom—you have no fatherland." Although occasionally dealing with theoretical questions, *Dekada's* young editors—Heltman and Piątkiewicz— usually featured contemporary events: the Spanish, Portuguese and Neapolitan revolutions; German (*Burschenschaft*) and Italian (*Carbonari*) sects; Bentham's economic theories; judicial independence; and modern poetry. Sometimes they wrote original articles; more frequently they inserted selections from liberal French and German periodicals.[64] Disaster struck when the chapter decided to print, under *Dekada's* masthead, a thirtieth anniversary reproduction of the May Third constitution. Outraged by this development Constantine arrested the editors and brought them to Belvedere palace. There, after verbally and physically assaulting them, he deported the Galician, Piątkiewicz, to Austrian Poland and summarily dispatched the Lithuanian Pole, Heltman, to the Russian army as a common soldier.[65]

For all practical purposes, this episode terminated the Union of Free Poles' political activity. Fearing mass arrests, the organization's remaining spokesmen devoted their time and energy to destroying incriminating evidence and instructing lesser members on what to say and how to behave if arrested. The expected blow, falling only in summer 1823, when Heltman broke down under harsh conditions in the Russian army and confessed, found the society's members not unprepared. Despite the arrest of several leaders and a half year investigation conducted by the Grand Inquisitor, Novosil'tsov, no one else confessed and the government imposed no penalties. The unfortunate Heltman, however, received an additional sentence.[66]

The climax of the drive to eradicate student secret societies occurred in 1823-1824, when an aroused Constantine, goaded by Novosil'tsov and supported by the emperor, declared war on Wilno University. This vendetta began with an assault on the Filomats, a popular and high-principled secret society which counted the outstanding Polish Romantic poet, Adam Mickiewicz, among its founders. Inspired by earlier examples at Wilno, Mickiewicz, T. Zan, J. Jeżowski, and O. Pietraszkiewicz founded the Filomats in 1817. Originally apolitical, the society strove to develop mutual friendship and to promote moral self-improvement. Its formal activities consisted of reading and discussing scientific treatises and literary works. Conditions of admission to membership included authoring a learned article for the society. Through several superficial reorganizations the Filomats gradually evolved a vague patriotic and political consciousness. Nevertheless, moral perfection remained their principal goal. Adhering to a nonrevolutionary gradualism which envisioned global transformed public opinion and measured social reform, the Filomats examined problems concerning Polish national affairs, language and culture. They concluded that recovery of genuine Polish independence, a long term proposition, deserved the highest consideration. Although the Filomts. fashioned a net of subordinate societies among the Wilno educational district's middle schools, they maintained minimal contacts with foreign student secret societies. They specifically rejected any linkage with Warsaw's students whom they looked upon as not only deficient in the moral sense, but also adventurous to the point of recklessness.[67]

The Filomats remained undetected for an exceptionally long time. Only in late 1822 or early 1823, when the Russian spy, Karol de Chevegrois-Schweizer, informed Grand Duke Constantine about a secret student association at Wilno "maintaining relations with academic societies in the Kingdom and Germany" did the government receive its first indication that Wilno also harbored "the evil spirit of the times."[68] Then, on May 3, 1823, a sixth form student at the Wilno lyceum chalked on the blackboard, "Long live the constitution of May 3." This deed alarmed Constantine, who by now discerned conspiratorial designs behind any reference to the defunct Polish constitution. Arresting the university's rector, the official responsible for the lyceum, Constantine suspended an indifferent and desultory investigation of secret student unions then being conducted by Czartoryski, the Wilno educational district curator. In its place, he instituted a more vigorous and methodical probe under the direction of the local Russian police authorities. Shortly thereafter, Novosil'tsov persuaded Constantine to send him to Wilno in order direct the inquiry. Novosil'tsov informed Alexander that he intended ". . . to establish the degree of culpability of each of the students, as well as that of the university's rector and the professors who appear to have acted in this circumstance with a guilty slackness."[69]

Novosil'tsov saw more in this affair than simply another occasion to attack Polish students. He convinced Constantine to delegate him to Wilno, a region far removed from his Warsaw power base, because an investigation there presented him with two exceptional opportunities. One was the chance to extend his authority to a new geographical sphere. Having gained mastery over the Kingdom's cultural and educational policies—and to some degree over its entire civil existence—the Imperial Commissioner moved to bring the Empire's western provinces under his control. Secondly, he saw an opportunity to destroy the most influential Polish citizen and the only potential candidate to replace him as the chief imperial officer in Poland, Prince Adam Czartoryski.

Novosil'tsov achieved both objectives. His investigation, seemingly at a dead end due to the students' tightlipped responses, suddenly bore fruit when the Filomat, J. Jankowski, confessed. On the night of October 23/24 more than one hundred students were arrested in one of the largest mass arrests Europe had witnessed to date.[70]

Czartoryski fought back. Initially he tried to assure Constantine that the educational authorities had the situation well in hand and that they would not hesitate to pursue the matter with appropriate energy and severity.[71] Failing this, he sent the Grand Duke a detailed note rebutting the accusations leveled against the university by the Lithuanian governor-general, the Russian general Rimskii-Korsakov.[72] Later, in correspondence with Alexander, he pleaded for the opportunity to refute the charges in Novosil'tsov's report, stating:

> The manner in which Novosil'tsov, during his latest stay in Wilno has accounted for himself with regard to the university and the schools of its jurisdiction, makes me fear that, in his report relating to the events of the gymnasium, he has inserted grave accusations and conclusions most unfavorable to public instruction in the Polish provinces and to the institutions which are in charge.[73]

But his enemy triumphed. At their final meeting on October 30, 1823, Czartoryski asked Alexander for his dismissal, only to suffer yet another humiliation when the tsar postponed his request until after the investigation's completion.[74]

The scandal's denouement finally took place during spring and summer 1824.⁷⁵ After the emperor named Novosil'tsov to Czartoryski's old curator post, the Imperial Commissioner responded with a prolonged investigation of the district's middle schools which uncovered several Filomat sponsored societies and destroyed the district's educational infrastructure. The accused Filomats, thanks to their cohesiveness and some individual heroics, generally escaped unscathed. Of the more than two hundred unversity students interrogated, only twenty drew sentences. A few received prison terms, most, like Mickiewicz, were exiled to the Russian interior. The lyceum students did not fare so well. Hauled before military tribunals, they frequently received death sentences which were then commuted to hard fortress labor, hard labor at the Nerchinsk coal mines, or garrison services as common soldiers.⁷⁶ Novosil'tsov, continuing his riotous personal life, took advantage of the situation to extort money from parents and relatives of arrested students.⁷⁷

Alexander's August 14, 1824, *ukaz* confirmed the findings and recommendations of "The Committee to Examine the Causes of the Disorders Occurring at Wilno University" composed of Novosil'tsov, Arakcheev and the reactionary Minister of Education, Admiral Shishkov. Anticipating the Russification policy later practiced by Tsar Nicholas I and his Education Minister, Count Uvarov, the *ukaz* called for an increased emphasis on Greek, Latin and Russian linguistic training at the expense of law, natural science and politics. The *ukaz* eliminated these latter courses from the university's curriculum. Moreover, the *ukaz* provided for increased surveillance and new restrictions on the student body. It also ordered suspected books removed from the university and book imports strictly regulated. Academic freedom received a blow when the *ukaz* ordered professors to select assignments from an approved list instead of freely choosing topics.⁷⁸

Recently it has been re-argued that Novosil'tsov's actions at Wilno did not represent an early attempt at Russification, but only reflected his desire to weed out liberalism and crush anything smacking of revolution.⁷⁹ While it is true that both Alexander and Constantine despised revolution and wished to eradicate its signs in all lands under Russian domination, it seems more accurate to conclude that purely personal interests motivated Novosil'tsov. That Alexander and Constantine shared the same desire undoubtedly made Novosil'tsov's course that much smoother. Moreover, the evidence indicates that the two brothers encouraged and

Reaction Triumphant 131

applauded Novosil'tsov's efforts as an effective means to achieve their own goals. But in the final analysis, it seems that Novosil'tsov himself cared only about increasing his personal authority and solidifying his grip on a lucrative and powerful position.

Conventional wisdom holds that the proclamation outlawing secret societies and the subsequent persecution of Polish students eliminated any chance for open political expression and forced the students into clandestine, illegal associations. The theory concludes that the government's repressive tactics radicalized the students.[80] Those very few examples of secret societies active after the persecutions tend to confirm this hypothesis. However, the significant point is not that later student societies were more radical than their predecessors, but that there were significantly fewer such societies than before the government launched its campaign against them. Moreover, all available evidence indicates that these later student societies attracted fewer members, exerted less influence on students and non-students alike, and exhibited few signs of vitality. When the Polish insurrection broke out on November 30, 1830, student secret societies played a minor, barely perceptible, role. Neither their activity nor their importance increased during the course of the revolt.[81] This can only lead to the conclusion that the government enjoyed a signal triumph in its campaign against student secret societies. In the last few years of Alexander's reign the government ruthlessly smashed the students' organizations and they remained in shambles for the balance of the Congress Kingdom's lifetime.

EPILOGUE

1825-1830

Tsar Alexander's death at Taganrog in December 1825, came as a shock to both Poles and Russians. Unlike Russia, where the Decembrists attempted a coup d'etat, Poland remained remarkably calm. Perhaps this can be attributed to genuine pain at the departure of Alexander, a figure who never lost his popularity with the Poles; or to apprehension at the prospect of a new tsar who disliked the Poles; or to the harsh regime within Poland which had effectively silenced most critics. In any event, once the immediate confusion surrounding Nicholas' ascension to the throne had cleared up, Poland quickly settled back into its old ways. On the surface at least, the regnal change brought little change. The repressionary course introduced in 1820-1821 in the wake of general European unrest continued under the guidance of the same officials who initiated it.

The censorship clearly illustrates this point. It is impossible to establish a real division between the two reigns. Under both Alexander and Nicholas censorship played a central role in Polish life. Early in 1826 Grand Duke Constantine, after examining the Kingdom's censorship, ordered Novosil'tsov to tighten its regulations. Responding to this directive, Novosil'tsov demanded that henceforth Poland's censorship strictly conform to the censorship regulations then prevailing in Russia. Novosil'tsov's proposal not only struck yet another blow at Poland's independent status, it also promised to make a bad censorship situation even worse. Under Prince A.N. Golitsyn and his successor, Admiral A.S. Shishkov, Ministers of Public Instruction, Russia was carrying censorship to absurd lengths. Shishkov, for example, insisted that only "good matters" were worthy of publication, while the poet, F. Glinka, indicated that under Shishkov's censorship rules it would be possible to interpret "Our Father" as a call to revolution. Fortunately for Poland, Novosil'tsov's demands were ignored; but the Imperial Commissioner persevered.

He next transmitted a new comprehensive censorship plan to the tsar. This plan was almost identical to the one he had submitted in 1822 which Alexander refused to publish because it too obviously contravened the freedom of expression provisions in the Polish constitution. Nicholas endorsed Novosil'tsov's plan, but like his brother hesitated to promulgate it because of its constitutional implications. Rather, after congratulating Novosil'tsov for his effort, Nicholas informed him that he was sending the plan to the Kingdom's Administrative Council for approval. Apparently, Nicholas reasoned that it would be much less obtrusive to sign an unconstitutional measure emanating from the Kingdom's Administrative Council than to trample the constitution by royal fiat. The Administrative Council, however, would not lend its support. Recognizing the censorship proposal for the major constitutional issue it was, the Council procrastinated and effectively tabled the measure.

Nevertheless, this flurry of activity produced some practical results. Most importantly, the censorship budget received several substantial increases. Despite Treasury Minister Lubecki's protests, the amount allocated for the censorship more than doubled between 1826 and 1829. These funds went to hire new censors, to compensate the old censors and to expand and refurbish the censorship headquarters. Moreover, the operation itself underwent further centralization as greater authority was placed in the hands of the censorship bureau's director. This represented an important triumph for Novosil'tsov since the censorship's director was Szaniawski, the Imperial Commissioner's candidate for the post and Novosil'tsov's faithful lackey.

Continued attacks on real or imagined secret societies, especially among Polish students, paralleled the preoccupation with censorship. Once again Novosil'tsov figured prominently. Branding Polish youth as potential revolutionaries, the Imperial Commissioner repeatedly raised the specter of youthful conspiracies. His clamor served to focus the government's attention on the schools as hotbeds of secret revolutionary activity.

In the years following Alexander's death, schoolboy investigations took place with monotonous regularity. Not only were the university and the Warsaw secondary schools targeted, the inquisitors now extended their work to the provinces. For the most part, their efforts were in vain. Except for one insignificant circle of students, no new secret societies were uncovered. However, these investigations brought the arrest of several individuals who had been active in earlier and now defunct societies.

A few more were expelled from the university or cashiered from positions in the bureaucracy for their past transgressions. Virtually no civilians were arrested for current membership in secret societies simply because such civilian societies had ceased to exist. Frequent investigations also occurred in Lithuania. In the wake of the Wilno University affair, Novosil'tsov launched a campaign to root out any remnants of student secret societies in the western *gubernii.* Filomat influence had penetrated the Wilno Education District and a number of societies existed among the secondary school students. Novosil'tsov, having replaced Czartoryski as curator, attacked these offshoots with great ruthlessness. The punishments meted out were harsh—jail terms, exile to Siberia and impressment into the army. Novosil'tsov's campaign was successful; the old societies were eradicated and no new ones arose to take their place.

The ongoing secret society scare provided an ideal excuse for further tampering with the Congress Kingdom's public education system. While the Curator General's budget grew by leaps and bounds and its police functionaries took up their posts throughout the Kingdom, Novosil'tsov demanded yet another round of educational reform. Writing to Nicholas in November 1826, Novosil'tsov cited the immediate danger of student secret societies as reason to resurrect the lifeless Educational Reform Committee.

Novosil'tsov's suggestion was well received at St. Petersburg and the Educational Reform Committee was revived in early 1827. It continued to meet and set guidelines for Poland's schools well into 1828. Its composition was almost identical to the 1822 Educational Reform Committee and its assignment was the same: to reorganize Poland's public education system. Like its predecessor, however, the new committee failed to achieve its goal. Nevertheless, it acted to strengthen surveillance and to introduce certain important curriculum changes.

The curriculum changes are noteworthy in that they reflect both a fear of modernity and a desire to limit educational opportunities according to class. In their struggle to turn back the clock, the committee's clerical members repeatedly lashed out at the academic disciplines of mathematics and science, accusing them of "overthrowing religious principles and directing thought toward materialist doctrine." As a remedy they proposed to establish and teach these courses on the "solid foundation of Christian precepts." These same men also demanded that public education reflect and reinforce the existing social structure. The Bishop of Płock, Adam Prażmowski, summarized the committee's views on this matter when he said, "social tranquility, if it is to endure and be favorable, depends upon the division of classes so that each person is satisfied with his situation and fulfills his obligations. It is not necessary to prepare him for bitter discordent ferment through an ineffectual education system."

The post-1825 period also witnessed several tentative steps toward Russification of Poland's educational institutions. During Alexander's reign, Novosil'tsov's proposals to merge the Kingdom's educational system with the Empire's fell on deaf ears. Now, a less drastic approach gained the Education Ministry's approval. After first promising to reshape Poland's educational infrastructure along Russian lines, the ministry drafted a program to make study of the Russian language mandatory in Polish schools. Plans were laid to introduce obligatory Russian language and literature courses in all secondary schools and funds were allocated for this purpose. These plans were scuttled only when Lubecki vigorously opposed them. It is important to note, however, that Lubecki's opposition was grounded in fiscal consideration; he had no pedagogical or political objections to the proposals. Despite this setback, Russian language and literature did become a required course at the Pedagogical Institute, and the Elementary Textbook Society, charged with preparing school texts, conspicuously neglected its duties except to publish book on Russian history and literature for Polish students.

Warsaw University also fell on hard times. The cumulative effect of continuous police surveillance, frequent investigations and official hostility began to take its toll. Total student population dropped from 714 in 1826 to 608 in 1827 and 589 in 1828. Szaniawski's determination to limit the number of entering students accounts for at least part of the decline. At his insistence, the Elementary Textbook Society prepared a new entrance examination for the university which stressed "moral development" at the expense of intellectual growth. This tool allowed government authorities to regulate the number of entering students and to insure that those successful candidates would be docile and loyal.

The university's position was further weakened when the Education Ministry ordered that all lectures in the philosophy and law faculties, two disciplines deemed subject to subversive influence, be delivered in Latin. Despite the university council's protests that no one would show up for lectures in Latin, the order stood. As a result, enrollment in these two faculties declined significantly.

While public education in Poland languished, the fortunes of the Liberal Opposition also continued to ebb. After Alexander's death, the rulers of the Congress Kingdom viewed the Liberal Opposition with even greater disdain and alarm. One leading authority describes the post-1825 atmosphere in the following terms: "If up to now keeping of the constitution was damned as obstinancy and blind imitation of foreign examples, now it was treated as war against the monarchy and open revolution." This hostile attitude deepended perceptibly during the summer of 1830 when Nicholas expressed fears that the Niemojowski brothers would take advantage of the events in Paris to challenge openly his rule in Poland.

Despite this animosity, the Niemojowskis refused to compromise their liberal political beliefs. Sending a steady stream of appeals to the Senate, the Lord Lieutenant and Grand Duke Constantine, they and their dwindling band of supporters demanded genuine constitutional rule for Poland. Not unexpectedly, their pleas fell on deaf ears and the government, ignoring their defense of the constitution, took steps to intimidate and silence them. Their power base, the Kalisz Provincial Council which Alexander had suspended in 1822 because of its independent posture, was never reinstated. Bonawentura, the younger brother whom Nicholas delighted in calling Misadventura, was kept under house arrest until Nicholas' amnesty at the time of his 1829 coronation as King of Poland. The elder brother, Wincenty, was subjected to harassment in the form of trumped up legal proceedings and intense surveillance carried out by gendarmes and spies, several of whom successfully penetrated the Niemojowski household.*

Reliance upon police and spies was not limited to exceptional cases such as the Niemojowskis. Rather, their role in Polish life, already pronounced under Alexander, continued to grow after his death. Several different spy masters forwarded an unprecedented number of reports directly to Constantine; the Central Police Bureau expanded; more money was allotted for police operations; unsolicited denunciations continued to roll in; and the school prefect system, an ill disguised form of surveillance from its inauguration, was given new duties which finalized its transformation into yet another nation-wide spy network.

*The Niemojowskis played a prominent role during the November Revolution. Wincenty was a member of the National Government of 1831 and Boawentura served as the last president of the revolutionary National Council.

Epilogue

The apparent continuity in day to day Polish affairs which characterized the transition from Alexander's rule to that of his brother served to obscure and distort changed relationships and new perceptions which seriously weakened the already shaky foundation of Russo-Polish cooperation. Relatively quickly, it became evident that the Alexandrian legacy no longer satisfied either the new tsar or the Poles. Each struggled to alter the status quo without taking into account the others sensitivities. The resultant ill will paved the way for the November Revolution.

When constrasted with Alexander, Nicholas' personality alone was enough to generate serious problems. Unlike his enigmatic brother, Nicholas was, as one expert writes, "a round peg in a round hole." A rigid, doctrinaire type, the energetic but shortsighted tsar never experienced the instability, self-doubt and nervous agitation which distinguished Alexander. Furthermore, Alexander's cosmopolitanism, sophistication, and experimentalism were totally absent in Nicholas. Nicholas, who admired his Prussian in-laws and their militaristic system, was a traditional autocrat who clearly conveyed his belief that discipline, order, obedience and duty were the highest virtues.

If Nicholas, the man, disappointed the Poles, his attitude toward Poland in general and the Congress Kingdom in particular proved even more disturbing. Writing in 1827 about Alexander and Poland, Nicholas' police chief, Count A. Benckendorff, said, "The great Polish problem is the rock, the outrage, on which the love of Russia for Emperor Alexander shattered...." Nicholas was determined to avoid such a calamity. This was not a difficult task since Nicholas hated the Polish nation and distrusted the limited autonomy which his predecessor had bestowed upon it. Suspicious of the Poles whom he considered to be undisciplined, rebellious and permanently ill-disposed toward Russia, he viewed the Congress Kingdom as some sort of weird aberration. Nicholas preferred to think of Poland as nothing more than a conquered country, and ultimately he proved to be the executor of Karamzin's wish that Poland be treated as, "...a legitimate possession of Russia."

Although Nicholas made no effort to conceal his dislike of the Congress Kingdom, he did pledge to carry on Alexander's experiment and to maintain the institutions, including the constitution, which Alexander had given to the Poles. Apparently, Nicholas made this promise, one which must have been distasteful for him, out of a sense of loyalty to his charismatic late brother and a desire to remain on good terms with Constantine.

Perhaps most importantly, however, first the Decembrist revolt and then the Russo-Turkish War so monopolized his time that he could not devote himself to the Polish question.

Nevertheless, Nicholas broke completely with the Poles on the matter dearest to their hearts—the unification of Lithuania with the Congress Kingdom. Well aware of the importance the Poles attached to this matter, Alexander had masterfully played the Lithuanian card on several occasions. Dangling the prospect of unification before the Poles, he secured their cooperation and quiescence to say nothing of their good will. Over the first decade of the Kingdom's existence, the Poles, who considered Lithuania as indigenous Polish land, came to regard Alexander's oblique references to eventual unification as firm promises. Alexander did nothing to dispel this illusion, even after 1820 when the thrust of his Polish policy appeared to change. If fact, he continued to entice the Poles on this score until his death. Speaking of Alexander's last visit to Warsaw in 1825, Constantine informed Nicholas in February 1826, that the late emperor, "twice clearly proclaimed it (unification) to both of us (Constantine and his wife)... and repeated the same promises to other military and civilian persons."

Nicholas viewed the Lithuanian matter in an altogether different light. He was convinced Lithuania was Russian territory and he made clear from the start that his determination to integrate it into the Empire. Corresponding with Constantine, he wrote, "Lithuania... is a Russian province, it cannot be returned to Poland because that would strike at the Empire's integrity." Later, he said, "I would cease to be a Russian in my own eyes were I to believe it possible to separate Lithuania from Russia proper ..., I cannot permit any possibility, as long as I live, that these ideas of rejoining Lithuania to Poland should be encouraged because I regard the thing as impossible and the consequences for the Empire as disastrous."

Nicholas backed his words with deeds. Shortly after coming to power he embarked upon a series of measures designed to eradicate Polish influence in Lithuania and to bind those *gubernii* more closely to the Empire. His first important step was to destroy the Polish character of the Lithuanian Corps. Created by Alexander in 1817, the Lithuanian Corps seemed to be concrete evidence of the tsar's intention to unite Lithuania with the Congress Kingdom. Its 40,000 man contingent was recruited exclusively from the western provinces; its commander-in-chief was the Warsaw based Grand Duke; and its uniform was remarkably similar to that worn by the

Polish army. Nicholas, horrified by this state of affairs and scornful of his Polish subjects' desires, took action to deprive the Lithuanian Corps of its quasi-independent status. While Constantine was allowed to retain his command, the Corps was Russified. Its uniforms were changed to conform to the standard Russian army uniform; it now received recruits from the wholly Russian provinces of Pskov and Tver; and Nicholas ordered that the Corps be fully integrated into the Empire's army.

Nicholas also moved to Russify Lithuania's other institutions. The civil administration was systematically purged of Poles whose positions were filled by Russians. The Wilno Education District was stripped of its authority over schools in Moghilev, Vitebsk and Minsk *gubernii* and these provinces were transferred to the jurisdiction of the St. Petersburg education authorities. With Nicholas' approval, Orthodoxy began an aggressive campaign to win converts from Roman Catholicism and to absorb the Uniates.

While Nicholas' Lithuanian policy achieved its goal of drawing the western provinces closer to the Empire, it also devastated the Poles who felt betrayed and exploited on a matter of the utmost importance to them. Lithuania proved to be the rock against which any possible Polish affection for Nicholas shattered.

Bitter and disillusioned Poles, now convinced that Nicholas had no intention of fulfilling Alexander's vague promises, began to reconsider their relations with Russia. Persuaded that the Russian connection was a fruitless one, a number of influential Poles slowly started to contemplate a new course for their country under which Russian influence would be greatly diminished if not entirely eliminated. As in the past, they looked for leadership to Prince Adam Czartoryski. Czartoryski, for many years the foremost advocate of Russo-Polish cooperation, had faded into the background after 1815 rather than openly oppose his old friend, Alexander. Now he emerged from the shadows to resume an active role in Polish politics.

Czartoryski's decision was not a hasty one, nor was it a facile one. He was well aware of the consequences if he were to misread the situation. Nevertheless, he felt that the time was ripe to reappear on the national scene. Alexander's death, followed shortly by that of Empress Elizabeth, freed Czartoryski from old allegiances and emotional ties. Furthermore, Czartoryski fully realized that Nicholas, with whom he had abysmal personal relations, was no friend of the Poles, and that Alexander's death heralded the dawn of a new and forbidding era for Poland.

Czartoryski's decision to lead traditional Polish society away from the existing Russo-Polish relationship coincided with the appearance of Polish Romanticism, a movement openly opposed to the prevailing forces of reaction. Quite unlike Czartoryski's cautious approach and essentially conservative orientation, Polish Romanticism was adventurous and revolutionary. It envisioned an idyllic world reconstructed according to the principles of justice and liberty. While Czartoryski attracted the most prestigious and influential Poles, romanticism captivated the Polish youth and filled it with a spirit of patriotism and daring. Appearing in Poland chiefly as a literary mode, romanticism provided acceptable cover under which the young firebrands could contemplate, allegorically, an end to Russian domination and revolutionary action to restore Poland to its pre-Partition borders. Although Czartoryski's followers and the Polish romanticists never effected an alliance, their immediate goal was similar. Dissatisfied with the status quo, they both wanted to reshape the Congress Kingdom.

Caught in the middle of the growing rift between Nicholas and his Polish subjects was Grand Duke Constantine. His failure to legitimatize his position in Poland and Lithuania at the time of the succession crisis now returned to plague him. The Grand Duke considered his pre-eminent role at Warsaw and Wilno as permanent and unimpeachable, proper indemnification for surrendering his right to the Russian crown. But he had no legal standing in either locale, and Nicholas called into question his irregular control over both regions. Although Nicholas decided to continue Constantine's superintendence over Poland, he quickly moved to curtail the Grand Duke's powers in Lithuania. Constantine, despite his warning to Nicholas to "not change any of what our dear, excellent, adorable departed had done, either in the most important or in petty affairs," soon found himself losing control over Lithuania's civil administration as well as his beloved Lithuanian Corps.

Faced with the unpleasant realization that Lithuania was lost and that his hold on Poland was tenuous, Grand Duke Constantine underwent a metamorphosis. Once contemptuous of Poland's quasi-independent status, Constantine now became a staunch defender of Poland's (and his own) prerogatives against encroachment by Russia and his brother. Constantine, whose future was now inextricably bound up with that of the Congress Kingdom, led the fight for Polish autonomy at St. Petersburg. But the

Epilogue 141

very nature of this struggle, a dispute within the Imperial family, insured that it would be a private one.

Once the Grand Duke apprehended his changed circumstances, he also began to cast about for allies. Without hope of finding support among Russians, he set about wooing the Poles, particularly Czartoryski. But his clumsy efforts ended in failure. Rapprochement with Czartoryski collapsed when Constantine, unintentionally it seems, insulted and humiliated the prince during a private interview. On a grander scale, Constantine's offensive fizzled when he was unable or, more likely, unwilling to publicize his dispute with the tsar. Few, if any, had the slightest inkling that all was not harmonious between the brothers. This lack of publicity crippled Constantine's drive to win Polish backing for his position. Nevertheless, even if the Poles had been aware of the strained relations, there is some question whether they would have rallied to Constantine's cause. His brutal, insensitive, tyrannical conduct had so alienated Polish society that reconciliation was well-nigh impossible. For the vast majority of Poles, Constantine was an odious creature who had long ago worn out his welcome.

The final unraveling of Alexander's Polish policy, hastened by the changed relationships among the leading characters and the almost universal dissatisfaction with the existing state of affairs, took place between 1825 and 1830. During that half decade, a series of events vividly revealed both the deep cleavages separating Nicholas from his Polish subjects and Grand Duke Constantine's dubious position as upholder of a status quo no one wanted. The most obvious example of this general deterioration can be found in the bitter wrangling over the fate of the so-called Polish Decembrists.

In the course of interrogations following the abortive Decembrist revolt several Russian conspirators implicated Polish army officers. These Polish soldiers, remnants of the Patriotic Society which had been discovered and demolished in 1822-1824, now became the object of Nicholas' obsessive search for rebels. The tsar demanded a full scale investigation at Warsaw to determine Polish complicity in the attempted coup. Constantine, fearful that something would surface to damage the Polish army and his position as its commander-in-chief, tried to resist his brother. But the weight of evidence showing the existence of a conspiratorial group and its connivance with the Russian rebels was too strong. On

February 20, 1826, the Grand Duke reluctantly established an investigating committee to examine Polish collaboration with the Decembrists. The committee immediately outraged the Poles. They objected to its mixed composition—five Poles and five Russians; to its chief investigator —Novosil'tsov; and to the manner of inquiry—rough and arbitrary. The hostility which the committee engendered guaranteed that most Poles, including Czartoryski, would not support the crusade to punish the Polish Decembrists.

After sitting for almost a year, the investigating committee returned an indictment of sorts on January 3, 1827. Identifying a number of Poles who had had contact with the Decembrists, the investigators recommended that the nine who had been the most active be tried for a "remote attempt at high treason." Although Nicholas disapproved of this phraseology, Constantine endorsed it and reassured his brother that the miscreants would be dealt with harshly.

Almost immediately, however, a jurisdictional problem arose. Although Nicholas and Constantine felt that the trial should take place in Poland, they split over the question of what type of court should sit in judgment. Constantine proposed a special, secret military court. Nicholas suggested a criminal court applying Russian legal principles. This question was resolved when all parties agreed that the Polish Senate, sitting as a High National Court, would hear the case. The trial of the Polish Decembrists opened before the Senate in spring 1827.

Both Constantine and Nicholas expected the Senate to acquiesce in their demands for a speedy and harsh condemnation of the accused. Consequently, they were shocked and dismayed when the Senate rejected the investigating committee's report and embarked upon its own lengthy inquiry. This unexpected turn of events could be traced to Czartoryski, who provided leadership and guidance for the Senators. Czartoryski used the occasion of the Senate Court to demonstrate his displeasure with the status quo and to signal his intention to pursue a more independent policy for Poland. This was a development of some magnitude, not only because of Czartoryski's stature but also because he had been the major promoter of close Polish-Russian cooperation for many years.

Following Czartoryski's lead, the Senate ignored Nicholas and Constantine's wishes. On May 22, 1828, by a thirty to one vote, the Senate ruled that the Polish Patriotic Society was not in the least responsible for the

Decembrist Revolt, and except for a few minor infractions, found the accused virtually blameless.
Pandemonium reigned. Constantine, denouncing the Senate as stupid, disloyal, silly and wretched, quarantined the Senators and continued their internment at Warsaw for almost a year. Nicholas suggested that the Senate's president be tried for high treason. Knowing that such a course of action was impossible, the Grand Duke proposed several measures: a "mercuriale" for the Senate and its president; annulment of the sentences; and a retrial of the defendants by a specially constituted court. In turn, Nicholas rejected his brother's proposals and ordered the malleable Administrative Council to condemn the verdict. Specifically, he commanded the Administrative Council to determine whether the Senate verdict resulted from an imperfect understanding of the term high treason or from a feeling of solidarity on the part of the judges with the accused.
To everyone's astonishment, the Administrative Council, like the Senate, followed an independent course. Once again Czartoryski's influence proved decisive. Under his subtle direction the Administrative Council rejected both alternatives advanced by Nicholas to explain the Senate's actions. Instead, it declared that defects in the investigating committee's indictment forced the Senate to reach the verdict it arrived at despite its desire to fulfill the king's will. This was a devastating blow for Constantine and Novosil'tsov. In acting independently, the Administrative Council broke free from the Grand Duke's control. Furthermore, in citing the faulty indictment as reason for the Senate's verdict, the Administrative Council placed the blame for the failure to convict the Polish Decembrists squarely on the shoulders of Novosil'tsov, the investigating committee's presiding officer and the indictment's author.
The Administrative Council's findings offended Nicholas, but Russia's involvement in war against Turkey prevented him from pressing the matter further. Reluctantly, the tsar finally confirmed the Senate's verdict on March 26, 1829.
The significance of the Polish Decembrist affair was not lost on either the Poles or the Russians. Anti-Russian and anti-tsarist sentiments were heightened among the Poles, while the Russians saw insubordination and treason in the Polish action. More importantly, the incident represented a considerable departure from the recent past. By defying both Nicholas and Constantine, the Poles revealed their restlessness and their desire to

transform the Russo-Polish relationship. Alexander's goal of harmony between the two nations seemed further away then ever.

Another important manifestation of the bankruptcy of Alexander's Polish policy occurred in 1830 when the Polish Sejm met for the first time since 1825. Czartoryski used this legislative meeting as a vehicle to express the nation's deep dissatisfaction with the existing state of affairs. He outlined Poland's complaints in the Senate Observations, a written summary prepared by the upper house at the close of its thirty day session. On this occasion the Observation amounted to nothing less than a blanket condemnation of developments in the Kingdom since 1815. Placing particular emphasis upon the post-1825 period, Czartoryski, the author of the Observations, attacked the administration's lawlessness and the growth of a centralized bureaucracy which tended to usurp local rights. Czartoryski set greatest importance upon the restoration of the rule of law. Additionally, he urged the introduction of "necessary reforms" including changes in the regulations governing Jews, improved status for the peasantry, sweeping judicial reforms and submission of the budget to the Sejm as provided for in the constitution.

Czartoryski singled out the directors of public education and the censorship apparatus for special criticism. Attacking the hated school police as morally pernicious, Czartoryski also deplored the reduction of funds for public education, the decline in the number of schools and the number of pupils and the gradual disappearance of elementary schools in the countryside. As for the censorship, Czartoryski's Observations pointed out that its very existence contravened article 16 of the constitution. After pleading with Nicholas to observe the law, Czartoryski remarked that if the king decided to ignore the constitution on this score, the least he could do would be to appoint worthy officials to replace the knaves then holding sway. The Observations closed with a blunt reminder to Nicholas to fulfill his obligations to the Polish nation.

Coming at the end of fifteen years of unfulfilled hopes, seemingly broken promises and sometimes brutal lawlessness, the Observations not only gave expression to Polish frustrations, they also finished setting the stage for the November Revolution.

CONCLUSION

During the decade following the Congress of Vienna, Alexander pursued several Polish strategies. Although each strategy differed from its predecessor in content and emphasis, the tsar's goal remained constant. Alexander was determined to maintain Russian domination over Poland. In controlling as much Polish territory as possible, Alexander intended to eliminate any threat from Russia's ancient enemy and to insure for Russia a leading role in European councils.

Considering Polish acquiescence, if not enthusiastic support, as necessary for success, Alexander initially followed a strategy of reconciliation and friendship with the Poles. He sanctioned a Polish constitution, restored the Polish army, and turned his legendary charm on the Poles during his frequent visits to Poland. Characterizing the first three to five years of Alexander's reign as Polish king, this policy was most evident in 1818 when the tsar publicly alluded to a reunification of Congress Poland with the Russian Empire's western *gubernii,* and the extension of the Polish constitution to Russia itself.

By late 1820, however, revolutionary events in Europe and court and gentry opposition at home, prompted Alexander to abandon his attempts to placate the Poles. Instead, he turned to repression. The tsar subverted the constitution and devastated the parliamentary opposition. Moreover, he endorsed illegal acts by his officials in Poland, supported a baneful censorship, appointed men known for their hostility toward progressive education and encouraged the persecution of student secret societies. Finally, Alexander began to shun the Polish aristocracy, especially Czartoryski and those Poles who looked to Prince Adam as the nation's spokesman. Alexander's decision to ignore Czartoryski and to elevate obscure Poles without great standing in the country such as J. Zajączek, Stanisław Grabowski and J.K. Szaniawski, may have served to create an administration unquestionably loyal to and dependent upon the tsar, but it alienated the most powerful elements in Polish society and destroyed the rapport which Alexander, at one time, regarded as essential for the success of his Polish plans. Even worse, Alexander continued to make veiled references to a new Polish-Lithuanian union. Although after 1820 he "played the Lithuanian card" merely to keep an unruly people in line, the Poles chose to interpret the tsar's remarks as a firm commitment to act, With the tsar's encouragement, Polish expectations on this most sensitive point soared.

In the final analysis, Alexander's Polish policy pleased no one and upset many. At Vienna, his desire to create a large Poland under Russian control frightened Austria, France and Great Britain into an anti-Russian alliance. Furthermore, it alerted Europe to Russia's ambition to expand westward. As a result, the major European powers, including Alexander's closest ally, Prussia, watched Russia's behavior in Poland with suspicion and some trepidation.

On the home front, Alexander's creation of an independent, constitutional Polish state contradicted his advisors and exasperated his generals, while his friendly overtures to the Poles infuriated educated Russians who saw treason in his actions. Alexander's lenient treatment of the Poles served as a focal point for widespread Russian dissatisfaction and greatly stimulated the development of Russian conservative and nationalist thought. Led by N.M. Karamzin, Russian conservatives and nationalists advanced numerous excuses to justify Poland's extinction and to warn against its resurrection, especially on a constitutional basis. Although young Russian liberals praised Alexander's commitment to constitutionalism, they joined in the outcry against Poland's rebirth. Consequently, throughout the nineteenth century influential elements at court, and in the bureaucracy, the army, the gentry and the intelligentsia not only adopted these anti-Polish views, but amplified and perpetuated them.

Finally, when Alexander turned to repression in Poland he estranged many of the *szlachta* and the Polish intelligentsia who had formerly supported him. Without a doubt, Alexander's success in Poland depended to a large extent on his ability to capture sophisticated Polish society. On this score Alexander began auspiciously, but he lost ground steadily. Nevertheless, few if any Poles became openly hostile. This development awaited Alexander's less able and less popular successor. However, Alexander's decision to condone unconstitutional actions and to ignore legitimate Polish aspirations and expectations helped to foster an indigenous Polish opposition. Although both the Liberal Opposition and the student secret societies looked to western Europe for their inspiration and ideals, it is apparent that Alexander's peculiar understanding of constitutionalism and liberalism as well as his "mailed fist" approach to real or imagined challenges to his autocratic power stimulated the opposition and magnified its influence. A more evenhanded approach on Alexander's part probably would have defused the situation and vitiated the active opposition which had few adherents and little real support.

Instead, seeing ingratitude and betrayal in the Poles' conduct and perceiving a threat to his absolutist prerogatives, the tsar unleashed Constantine and Novosil'tsov. Motivated in part by base opportunism and in part by a sincere commitment to reactionary and clerical precepts, the high officials and their underlings trampled on the charter. Although the administrators effectively crushed the opposition, their self-seeking nature and their over-reaction to insignificant statements or actions earned for them the enmity of Polish society. This resentment, quite the opposite of what Alexander envisioned when he planned for a Russo-Polish *rapprochement,* contributed greatly to the deterioration of Russo-Polish relations.

Nevertheless, perhaps Alexander's concept of government and his views on the nature of power are the essential factors necessary to understand and to evaluate the tsar's relationship with the Congress Kingdom. Going beyond his complex and sometimes contradictory personality traits, Alexander, in politics at least, emerges as a reformist conservative who became more conservative and less reformist with the passage of time. Despite its constitution and its liberal institutions, Congress Poland was never a "liberal" state, just as Alexander was never a "liberal" ruler. Rather, the Congress Kingdom was simply the prototype of the rationalized state which Alexander hoped to introduce to Russia. Considering the Polish constitution as an exemplary vehicle for administrative reform, Alexander rejected any attempt to use it to dilute his autocratic authority. For Alexander, a pragmatic autocratic par excellence, power resided solely and indivisibly with the monarch; the government—be it constitutional or not—was subordinate and obliged to obey. When some Poles began to take the constitution and Alexander's liberal rhetoric seriously, the autocrat answered with unequivocal support for the unconstitutional and sometimes brutal actions of his servants in Poland. In Alexander's scheme of things, he could not have done otherwise.

The nearly unanimous dissatisfaction with Alexander's Polish strategies only helps to obscure and minimize his very real success in achieving his Polish goals. But this achievement lacked any permanency and, in fact, contained the seeds of its own destruction. In maintaining Russian supremacy over Poland, Alexander either created or fostered forces which collided explosively in 1830. Moreover, these forces gained a life of their own which soured Russo-Polish relations and nullified any possibility of Polish acquiescence in Russian domination.

NOTES

Notes to Chapter One

1. For the Duchy of Warsaw see: Marceli Handelsman, ed., *Instructions et depêches des résidents françaises à Varsovie, 1807-1813*, 2 vols. (Cracow, 1914); Edouard Bignon, *Souvenirs d'un diplomat. La Pologne, 1811-1813*. (Paris, 1864); Albert Sorel, *L'Europe et la revolution française*, 2nd ed., vols. 6-8 (Paris, 1887-1904); Albert Vandal, *Napoléon et Alexandre Ier*, 3rd ed., 3 vols. (Paris, 1896-1914); Emanuel Halicz, *Geneza Księstwa Warszawskiego* (Genesis of the Duchy of Warsaw) (Warsaw, 1962); Jan M. Chelmiński, *L'armée du Duché de Varsovie* (Paris, 1913); Marceli Handelsman, *Pod znakiem Napoleona* (Under Napoleon's Banner) (Warsaw, 1913).

2. J. Holland Rose, "Napoleon and Poland," *The Cambridge History of Poland*, W.F. Reddaway et al., eds. (Cambridge, 1941; reprint ed., New York, 1971), p. 219.

3. Michał Ogiński, *Mémoires de Michel Ogiński sur la Pologne et les Polonais depuis 1788 jusqu'a la fin de 1815*, 4 vols. (Paris, 1826-1827), 3:245.

4. Alexander to Czartoryski, January 13, 1813, Adam Czartoryski, *Memoirs of Prince Adam Czartoryski*, trans. and ed. Adam Gielgud, 2nd ed., 2 vols. (London, 1888), 2:234-235.

5. Count Charles Nesselrode, *Lettres et papiers du chancelier comte de Nesselrode*, 11 vols. (Paris, 1904-1905), 4:313-320.

6. Significant materials dealing with Czartoryski's life and activities exist at both Cracow and Paris. The former city offers the Biblioteka Czartoryskich w Krakowie (The Library of the Czartoryskis in Cracow), which survived World War II intact and houses most of the Czartoryski family papers. The Biblioteka Polska w Paryżu (The Polish Library in Paris) preserves important documents on Czartoryski and the Polish emigration after the collapse of the 1830-1831 insurrection. A fine English language biography has been contributed by Marian Kukiel, *Czartoryski and European Unity 1770-1861* (Princeton, 1955). Despite significant gaps of information, Marceli Handelsman, *Adam Czartoryski*, 3 vols. (Warsaw, 1948-1950), is an important source. Handelsman, an outstanding

Polish historian, had his work interrupted by World War II. Nevertheless, he persevered under the most arduous conditions until his arrest by the Gestapo. He died in a German concentration camp in early 1945, and his work was published posthumously.

7. Sparked by the shock of the First Partition and nurtured by Western European intellectual ferment, the May Third Constitution (1791) represented the political climax of Polish efforts at self-regeneration. Designed to strengthen the central government and to stop foreign intervention in Polish affairs, the May Third Constitution not only eliminated the elective kingship and the *Liberum Veto,* but also awarded considerable power to the minor nobility. In retaliation, dissident magnates formed the Confederation of Targowica, which called on Catherine the Great to restore their privileges. Russian intervention led to the Second Partition. In the nineteenth century, the May Third Constitution became the rallying cry for those Polish patriots determined to re-establish their country on a liberal, but not necessarily democratic, basis.

8. Czartoryski to Alexander, January 30, 1811, Czartoryski, *Memoirs of Czartoryski* 2:218-222.

9. Czartoryski to Alexander, December 27, 1812, *ibid.* 2:233-234.

10. Alexander to Czartoryski, January 31, 1811 (O.S.), *ibid.* 2:222-228.

11. Ogiński, *Mémores* 3:236-237.

12. Czartoryski to Alexander, May 4, April 27 (O.S.), 1813, Czartoryski, *Memoirs of Czartoryski* 2:237-239.

13. Alexander to Czartoryski, January 13, 1813, *ibid.* 2:234-237.

14. "Obrazovanie Verkhovnago Vremennago Sovieta, uchrezhdennago dlia upravleniia Varshavskim Gertsogstvom" (Formation of the Supreme Provisonal Council, established for governing the Duchy of Warsaw), *Russkii Arkhiv* 9 (1871): 1570-1578.

15. Józef Bojasiński, *Rządy tymczasowe w Królestwie Polskim, Majgrudzień 1815* (Provisional governments in the Polish Kingdom, May-December 1815) (Warsaw, 1902), pp. 28-29, 187. Unbeknown to the Poles, however, Lanskoi sent a steady stream of reports to St. Petersburg criticizing them. He especially objected to the decision to maintain the Polish army.

16. Ogiński, *Mémoires* 4:135.

17. Bojasiński, *Rządy tymczasowe,* pp. 13-17.

18. Harold Nicolson, *The Congress of Vienna: A Study in Allied Unity, 1812-1822,* (London, 1949), pp. 150, 175.

19. *Ibid.,* pp. 27-31, 169-170; Sir Charles Webster, *The Congress of Vienna,* (New York, 1966), pp. 118-120; Henry A. Kissinger, *A World*

Notes to Chapter One 151

Restored, (New York, 1964), pp. 152-154. Nicolson claims that Alexander's Kingdom of Poland ". . . would extend the boundaries of Russia to the very banks of the Oder."
20. Cited by A. Pogodin, "Pol'sha pered vosstaniem 1830 g",(Poland before the 1830 insurrection), *Russkoe Bogatstvo* 8 (1912:33).
21. Lanskoi to Alexander, May 15, 1815 (O.S.), reprinted in N.K. Shilder, *Imperator Aleksandr I, ego zhizn i tsarstvovanie* (Emperor Alexander I, his life and reign), 4 vols. (St. Petersburg, 1904), 3:551-552.
22. General A. I. Chernyshev to Alexander, April 16, 1815, quoted in N. Dubrovin, "Posle Otechestvennoi Voiny" (After the Fatherland War), *Russkaia Starina* 117 (1904): 482-483.
23. M.F. Orlov, "Primiechaniia M.F. Orlova, napisannyia v 1835" (M.F. Orlov's comments, written in 1835), *Russkaia Starina* 20 (1877): 661-662.
24. Czartoryski to Alexander, 1815, Adam Czartoryski, *Alexandre I et le prince Czartoryski; correspondance particulière et conversations, 1801-1823*, with an Introduction by Charles de Mazade, 2 vols. (Paris, 1865) 2:271.
25. A very useful discussion of this opposition is found in William L. Blackwell, "Alexander I and Poland: The Foundations of His Polish Policy" (Ph.D. dissertation, Princeton University, 1959) pp. 118-125.
26. Pozzo di Borgo's memorandum for the tsar on the Polish question at the Vienna Congress is found in Nicholas Turgenev, *La Russie et les Russes*, 3 vols. (Brussels, 1847) 1:310-322.
27. *Ibid.*
28. *Ibid.*
29. For a revealing study of Alexander's lifelong determination to act as his own Foreign Minister consult: Patricia Kennedy Grimsted, *The Foreign Ministers of Alexander I*, (Berkeley and Los Angeles, 1969).
30. Nicolson, *Congress of Vienna*, pp. 148-157, 164-181; Webster, *Congress of Vienna*, pp. 117-134; Kissinger, *World Restored*, pp. 152-172.
31. Leonard Chodźko (le comte d'Angeberg), *Receuil des traités, conventions et actes diplomatiques concernant la Pologne 1762-1862* (Paris, 1862), pp. 696-699.
32. Julian Niemcewicz, *Pamiętniki* (Memoirs), 2 vols. (Poznan, 1871), 2:253-255; Czartoryski to Alexander, June, 1815, Czartoryski, *Alexandre I et Czartoryski* 2:246-247; Marceli Handelsman, "The Polish Kingdom" in *The Cambridge History of Poland*, p. 275. Even Countess Potocka, a bitter critic of Alexander and Russia wrote that the announcement of the Congress Kingdom's birth elicited frenzied shouts and applause. Anna Potocka, *Pamiętniki* (Memoirs) (Warsaw, 1898), p. 150.

33. K. Lutostański, *Receuil des actes diplomatiques. I. Traités et documents concernant la Pologne* (Paris, 1918), p. 384.
34. Niemcewicz, *Pamiętniki* 2:219.
35. Potocka, *Pamiętniki,* p. 150.
36. Marceli Handelsman, *Konstytucje Polskie, 1791-1921* (Polish constitutions, 1791-1921), 3rd ed. (Warsaw, 1922), pp. 46-47, reprints the "Bases of the Polish Constitution," a joint effort by Czartoryski and Alexander enumerating the guiding principles for the Polish constitution.
37. *Ibid.*, "Introduction," p. xiv.
38. For the full details of this transitional period, Czartoryski's strenous efforts, and the difficulties encountered, consult Bojasiński, *Rządy tymczasowe, passim.*
39. Czartoryski to Alexander, July 29, 31, 1815, Czartoryski, *Memoirs of Czartoryski* 2:306-307; Czartoryski to Alexander, October 14, 1815, Czartoryski, *Alexandre I et Czartoryski* 2:261-264.

Notes to Chapter Two

1. Consult Leonard Chodźko (le comte d'Angeberg), *Receuil des traités, conventions et acts diplomatiques concernant la Pologne 1762-1862* (Paris, 1862), pp. 707-724, for the French (original) verson; *Dziennik Praw Królestwa Polskiego* (Bulletin of the Laws of the Kingdom of Poland), 49 vols. (Warsaw, 1815-1849), 1:1-103; S. Kieniewicz, ed., *Przemiany społeczne i gospodarcze w Królestwie Polskim* (Social and economic changes in the Polish Kingdom) (Warsaw, 1951), pp. 56-84; Z. Gołba, *Rozój władz Królestwa Polskiego w okresie powstania listopadowego* (The development of the government of the Polish Kingdom in the period of the November uprising) (Wroclaw, 1971), pp. 13-25; M. Handelsman *Konstytucje Polskie 1791-1921* (Polish constitutions, 1791-1921), 3rd ed. (Warsaw, 1922), pp. 47-66.
2. A Sejm is the Polish name for the national legislative gathering which has evolved into the present day Polish parliament. In pre-partition Poland, the Sejm, meeting irregularly, elected the Polish king and conducted the nation's business. Apparently, Alexander restored this traditional body as part of his program to conciliate the Poles. But events were to prove that the tsar never intended it to play a meaningful legislative role.
3. A.G.A.D., Protokoły Rady Administracyjnej, May 5, 1818.
4. *Ibid.*
5. *Dziennik Praw Królestwa Polskiego* 1:282-344, 361 ff., 395 ff.

Notes to Chapter Two 153

6. Helena Więckowska, *Opozycja Liberalna w Królestwie Kongresowem* (The Liberal Opposition in the Congress Kingdom) (Warsaw, 1925), p. 4.
7. Gołba *Rozwój władzp.* 22.
8. *Ibid.*
9. T. Mencel, "Udział społeczeństwa w życiu politycznym Królestwa Polskiego w latach 1815-1830" (The participation of the public in the political life of the Polish Kingdom in 1815-1830), *Przegląd Historyczny* 4 (1968): 646-647; 657-659. For the view that the 1815 constitution provided for no great modification of the Duchy's electoral system, see Jerzy Skowronek, "Skład społeczny i polityczny sejmów Księstwa Warszawskiego i Królestwa Kongresowego" (The social and political composition of the Sejms of the Duchy of Warsaw and the Congress Kingdom), *Przegląd Historyczny* 3 (1961): 474.
10. Mancel, "Udział społeczeństwa," p. 659.
11. Józef Bojasiński, *Rządy tymczasowe w Królestwie Polskim, Majgrudzień, 1815* (Provisional governments in the Polish Kingdom, May-December, 1815) (Warsaw, 1902), p. 137.
12. Czartoryski to Alexander, July 31, 1815, Adam Czartoryski, *Memoirs of Prince Adam Czartoryski,* trans. and ed. by Adam Gielgud, 2nd ed., 2 vols. (London, 1888), 2:307.
13. Czartoryski to Alexander, July 29, 1815, Adam Czartoryski, *Alexandre I et le prince Czartoryski, correspondence particulière et conaersations, 1801-1823,* with an Introduction by Charles de Mazade, 2 vols. (Paris, 1865), 2:252-256. In imperial Russia, the title tsesarevich was reserved for the eldest son as successor to the throne. By the special *ukaz* of October 28, 1799, Tsar Paul by-passed Alexander and bestowed the title on Constantine.
14. Czartoryski to Alexander, no date, *ibid.* 2:243-244.
15. *Ibid.*
16. A.G.A.D., P.R.A. January 12, 1816.
17. *Ibid.*
18. *Ibid.*
19. Cited in Szymon Askenazy, *Ministeryum Wielhorskiego* (Wielhorski's ministry) (Warsaw, 1898), p. 161.
20. Czartoryski to Alexander, January 28, 1816, Czartoryski, *Alexandre I et Czartoryski* 2:273-275.
21. Askenazy, *Ministeryum,* pp. 157-169, 522-525; Wacław Tokarz, *Armia Królestwa Polskiego, 1815-1830* (The Army of the Kingdom of Poland, 1815-1830) (Piotrków, 1917), pp. 49-50.
22. Marceli Handelsman, *Kryzys r. 1821 w Królestwie Polskim* (The

1821 crisis in the Kingdom of Poland) (Lwów, 1939), p. 3; Karol Hoffman, *Rzut oka na stan polityczny Królestwa Polskiego pod panowaniem Rossyjskiem* (A glance at the political state of the Kingdom of Poland under Russian rule) (Warsaw, 1831), pp. 114-115; Mieczysław Offmański, *Królestwo Polskie (1815-1830) (The Kingdom of Poland (1815-1830)) (*Warsaw, 1907), p. 27; Aleksander Kamiński, *Polskie związki młodzieży* (Polish youth societies) (Warsaw, 1963), p. 92; Bolesław Limanowski, *Historia demokracji Polskiej* (History of Polish democracy), 3rd ed. (Warsaw, 1946), p. 169; S.B. Gnorowski, *Insurrection of Poland in 1830-31; and the Russian Rule Preceding It since 1815* (London, 1839), p. 30; Piotr S. Wandycz, *The Lands of Partitioned Poland, 1795-1918* (Seattle and London, 1974), p. 77.

23. Handelsman, *Kryzys*, p. 3; Marceli Handelsman, "The Polish Kingdom" in *The Cambridge History of Poland*, W.F. Reddaway, et al., eds. (Cambridge, 1941; reprint ed., New York, 1971), p. 277.

24. Handelsman, "Polish Kingdom,:: p. 277; Kamiński, *Polskie związki*, p. 92; Allen McConnell, *Tsar Alexander I* (New York, 1970), p. 151; Stanisław Cieszkowski, *Aleksander I a konstytucya* (Alexander I and the constitution) (Warsaw-Lwów, 1909), p. 90.

25. Franklin A. Walker, "Constantine Pavlovich: An Appraisal," *Slavic Review* 26 (1967): 446-447; Władysław Bortnowski, *Wielki Książe Konstanty podczas powstania listopadowego* (Grand Duke Constantine during the November insurrection) (Warsaw, 1956), p. 197.

26. Marian Kukiel, *Czartoryski and European Unity 1700-1861* (Princeton, 1955), p. 133.

27. Constantine's devotion to Alexander seems to have known no bounds. Not only did the Grand Duke admire Alexander for his widely acclaimed charm and character, but he also loved him as a younger brother loves a heroic and idealized older brother. Moreover, as a military man Constantine felt duty bound to obey and execute all orders issuing from the commander-in-chief. A most revealing incident took place in autumn 1819, when Alexander told Constantine of his desire to abdicate. Constantine replied:

> Then I will beg of you a place as your second valet; I will serve you, and if necessary, clean your boots. If it were to do this now, it would be considered base, but when you leave the throne, I will demonstrate my devotion to you as my benefactor.

For a complete description of this scene see: N.K. Shilder, *Imperator Aleksandr I, ego zhizn i tsarstvovanie* (Emperor Alexander I, his life and reign), 4 vols. (St. Petersburg, 1904), 4:461-465.

28. Recently a full-length, scholarly biography of Zajączek appeared. However, JadwigaNadzieja, *General Józef Zajączek, 1752-1826* (Warsaw, 1975), consistently glamorizes Zajączek's radicalism and military exploits while quickly passing over his collaboration with Grand Duke Constantine and Novosil'tsov as the Congress Kingdom's Lord Lieutenant. More reliable if shorter descriptions of Zajączek, especially during his years as Viceroy, are found in: *Wielka Encyklopedia Powszechna* (The Great Universal Encyclopedia), 13 vols. (Warsaw, 1969), 12:610-611; Marcli Handelsman, *Francja-Polska, 1795-1845* (France-Poland, 1795-1845), 2 vols. (Warsaw, 1926), 2:61-62; Stanisław Smolka, *Polityka Lubeckiego przed powstaniem listopadowem* (Lubecki's policy before the November insurrection), 2 vols. (Cracow, 1907), 1:306-309. For a more sympathetic view of Zajączek and his activities see: Kajetan Koźmian, *Pamiętniki* (Memoirs), 3 vols. (Warsaw, 1972), 3:113-142.

29. A.G.A.D., P.R.A., January 12, 1816.

30. Cited in Julian Niemcewicz, *Pamiętniki* (Memoirs), 2 vols. (Poznan, 1871), 2:274.

31. Czartoryski to Alexander, January 28, February 6, May 13, 1816, Czartoryski, *Alexandre I et Czartoryski* 2:273-279; 280-281; 292-295.

32. A.G.A.D., Kancelaria Nowosilcowa no.173 "O vysoch. naznachenii tain. sov. senatora Novosil'tsova polnomochnii m. e. i. v. delegatom pri Gosudarstvennom Sovete ts.P." (On the imperial appointment of the secret counselor senator Novosil'tsov as plenipotentiary delegate to the Government Council of the Kingdom of Poland), Alexander's proclamation, December 1, 1815.

33. C.A. Przeclawski (Tsiprinus), "Kaleidoskop Vospominanii" (Kaleidoscope of Recollections), *Russkii Arkhiv* (1872): 1715-1716.

34. This interesting and complex man who played such an important role in both Russian and Polish affairs awaits his biographer. In the meantime, consult: "N.N. Novosil'tsov," *Entsiklopedicheskii Slovar* (Encyclopedic Dictionary), Brokgauz and Efron, eds., 82 vols. (St. Petersburg, 1897), 21:295; Grand Duke Nikolai Mikhailovich, *Graf Pavel Aleksandrovich Stroganov* (Count Paul Alexander Stroganov), 3 vols. (St. Petersburg, 1903), 1:*passim*; Przeclawski, "Kaleidoskop," pp. 1708-1760; Smolka, *Polityka Lubeckiego* 2:239-296, and *passim*. For a more sympathetic analysis: P. Kukol'nik, (Anti-Tsiprinus), "Vospominanie of Novosil'tsov" (Recollections of Novosil'tsov), *Russkii Arkhiv* 1 (1873): 203-0200; Modest I. Bogdanovich, *Istoriia tsarstvovaniia Imperatora Aleksandra I* (The history of the reign of Emperor Alexander I), 6 vols. (St. Petersburg, 1869-1871), 1:77ff.

35. Grand Duke Nikolai Mikhailovich, *Stroganov* 1:114. Count Andrault de Langeron, a French *émigré* who came to Russia after the French Revolution, became a general in the Russian army and took part in the numerous Russian campaigns against Napoleon.
36. Smolka, *Polityka Lubeckiego* 2:256-274, 574-581; Kukiel, *Czartoryski*, pp. 105-106; Szymon Askenazy, *Łukasiński*, 2 ed., 2 vols. (Warsaw, 1929), 1:59-68.
37. Count Charles Nesselrode, *Lettres et papiers du chancelier comte de Nesselrode*, 11 vols. (Paris, 1904-1905). 4:55.
38. Cited in I.A. Bychkov, "Aleksandr I i ego priblizhennye do epokhi Speranskago" (Alexander I and his retinue to the Speranskii era), *Russkaia Starina* 113 (February, 1903): 215.
39. Smolka, *Polityka Lubeckiego* 2:284-285; Bojasiński, *Rządy tymczasowe*, pp. 29-30; Szymon Askenazy, *Dwa stulecia XVIII-XIX* (Two centuries XVII-XIX), 2nd ed., 2 vols. (Warsaw, 1903), 1:304-341.
40. Koźmian, *Pamiętniki* 2:427.
41. Plater to Czartoryski, April 18, 1813, Biblioteka Czartoryskich, Folio no. 5511.
42. A.G.A.D., P.R.A., May 15, 1816.
43. *Ibid.*
44. A.G.A.D., K.N. no. 173, Novosil'tsov to Zajączek, May 16, 1816.
45. *Ibid.*, Minister-Secretary of State, I. Sobolewski to Novosil'tsov, June 29, 1816.
46. A.G.A.D., P.R.A., July 11, 1816.
47. Marc Raeff, *Michael Speransky* (The Hague, 1957), pp. 29-48; Grand Duke Nikolai Mikhailovich, *L'Empereur Alexandre Ier*, 2 vols. (St. Petersburg, 1912), *passim;* Kamiński, *Polskie związki*, p. 92.
48. Quoted in McConnel, *Tsar Alexander I*, p. 151.
49. Chodźko, *Receuil des traités*, pp. 733-734.
50. Hoffman, *Rzut oka na stan polityczny*, . 84.
51. M. Raeff, *Michael Speransky*, pp. 37-46.
52. S. Mel'gunov, "Sfinks na prestole (Cherty dlia kharakteristiki Aleksandra I)" (Sphinx on the throne (traits for the character of Alexander I), *Dela i liudi Aleksandrovskogo vremeni* (Affairs and people of Alexander's time) (Berlin, 1923), pp. 35-83; A.A. Kizevette, *"Imperator Aleksandr I i Arakcheev," Istoricheskie ocherki* (Historical essays) (Moscow, 1912), pp. 287-402; Raeff, *Speransky*, pp. 37-38. For a contemporary's evaluation see Baron von Nostitz' comments in F. Freksa and H. Hansen, eds., *A Peace Congress of Intrigue* (New York, 1919), p. 114. For different views on Alexander's character consult: E.M. Almedingen, *The Emperor Alexander I* (London, 1964); Constantine de Grunwald, *Alexandre Ier:*

le tsar mystique (Paris, 1955); Shilder, *Imperator Aleksandr I;* Maurice Paleologue, *The Enigmatic Tsar* (New York, 1937); Leonid I.Strakhovsky, *Alexander I of Russia* (New York, 1947); Alan Palmer, *Alexander I: Tsar of War and Peace* (London, 1974); Daria Olivier, *Alexandre Ier, Prince des Illusions* (Paris, 1973).

53. Quoted in Szymon Askenazy, *Szkice i portrety* (Sketches and portraits) (Warsaw, 1937), p. 139.

54. N.K. Shilder, "Imperator Nikolai I i Pol'sha v 1825-1831" (Emperor Nicholas I and Poland, 1825-1831), *Russkaia Starina,* 102 (1900): 66.

55. Schmidt to Bernsdorf, May 14, 1819, published in Askenazy, *Dwa stulecia,* 2:462, 560. Bernsdorf was Schmidt's superior at Berlin.

56. Wilhelm Feldman, *Dzieje Polskiej myśli politycznej* (History of Polish political thought) (Cracow, 1913), p. 72.

57. Quoted in Henryk Mościcki, *Pod znakiem orła i pogoni* (Under the banner of the eagle and the hunt) (Lwów, 1923), p. 17. Thè eagle and the hunt refer, respectively, to the Polish and Lithuanian coats of arms.

58. *Vosstanie dekabristov. Materialy* (The Decembrist uprising. Materials), M.N. Pokrovskii, M. Nechkina, eds., 13 vols. (Moscow, 1925-1975), 1:49-52, 139, 306; 3:6, 52-53, 73, 122.

Notes to Chapter Three

1. Stefan Kieniewicz and W. Kula, eds., Vol. 2 of *Historia Polski* (History of Poland) (Warsaw, 1958), p. 264.

2. Wacław Tokarz, *Armia Królestwa Polskiego, 1815-1830* (The Army of the Kingdom of Poland, 1815-1830) (Piotrków, 1917), pp. 116-119, 376.

3. Kieniewicz and Kula, eds., *Historia Polski,* 2:264-265.

4. Czartoryski to Alexander, 1815 (without date), January 1, February 6, April 5, April 17, May 13, 1816, Adam Czartoryski, *Mémoires du Prince Adam Czartoryski et correspondance avec l'empereur Alexandre Ier,* C. Mazade, ed., 2 vols. (Paris, 1887), 2:348-368; Natalia Kicka, *Pamiętniki* (Memoirs), Józef Dutkiewicz, ed., (Warsaw, 1972), pp. 152-154; P. Harro-Harring (pseud.), *Poland under the Dominion of Russia* (London, 1831), pp. 101-103 and *passim;* N.K. Shilder, Imperator Aleksandr I, ego zhizn i tsarstvovanie (Emperor Alexander I, his life and reign), 4 vols. (St. Petersburg, 1904), 4:17-21; A. Pogodin, 'Pol'sha pered vosstaniem 1830 g': (Poland before the 1830 revolution), *Russkoe Bogatstvo,* 8 (1912): 37-38; Allen McConnel, *Tsar Alexander I,* (New York, 1970), p. 151; Piotr S. Wandycz, *The Lands of Partitioned Poland, 1795-1918* (Seattle and London, 1974) p. 78.

5. Szymon Askenazy, *Łukasiński*, 2nd ed., 2 vols. (Warsaw, 1929), 1:13.
6. Ignacy A. Komorowski, *Wspomnienia podchorążego z czasów W. Ks. Konstantego* (Recollections of a Cadet officer from the times of Grand Duke Constantine) (Warsaw, 1900), p. 7.
7. Cited in Julian Niemcewicz, *Pamiętniki* (Memoirs), 2 vols. (Poznan, 1871), 2:278.
8. Minister-Secretary of State, Ignacy Sobolewski to Czartoryski, April 19, April 27, 1816, Biblioteka Czartoryskich, folio no. 5515; Niemcewicz, *Pamiętniki*, 2:331.
9. A.E. Koźmian, *Wspomnienia* (Recollections), 2 vols. (Posnan, 1867), 1:194.
10. The only full length biography of Constantine Pavolovich is the still valuable E. Karnovich, *Tsesarevich Konstantin Pavlovich* (St. Petersburg, 1899). A more recent interpretation is: Franklin A. Walker, "Constantine Pavolovich: An Appraisal," *Slavic Review* 26 (1967): 445-452. See also: Shilder, *Imperator Aleksandr I;* Czartoryski, *Mémoires du Prince Czartoryski;* Tokarz, *Armia;* Alexander Moriolles, *Mémoires du Comte de Moriolles sur l'émigration, la Pologne et la cour du Grand-Duc Constantin (1789-1833)*, 2nd. ed. (Paris, 1902).
11. Stanisław Smolka, *Polityka Lubeckiego przed powstaniem listopadowem* (Lubecki's policy before the November insurrection), 2 vols. (Cracow, 1907), 1:106; J. Bojasiński, *Rządy tymczasowe w Królestwie Polskim, Maj-grudzień 1815* (Provisional governments in the Polish Kingdom, May-December 1815) (Warsaw, 1902), pp. 98-99. Bojasiński indicates the convertible value of the Polish zloty at that time: 20 zlotys equaled 50 groszy or one Russian assignat ruble. Bojasiński notes that officially fixed prices in April and May, 1815 were as follows: one bushel of wheat, 29 to 39 zlotys; one bushel of rye, 25 to 29 zlotys; one bushel of oats, 11 to 13 zlotys; one pound of best beef, 11 groszy.
12. G. Pisarevskii, *Iz istorii kongressovogo Tsarstva Pol'skogo* (From the history of the Polish Congress Kingdom), (Smolensk, 1926), p. 1.
13. *Ibid.*
14. S. Siegel, *Ceny w Warsawie w latach 1816-1914* (Prices in Warsaw, 1816-1914), (Poznan, 1949), pp. 174, 259-269.
15. Smolka, *Polityka,* 1:71-131; Kieniewicz and Kula, eds., *Historia Polski,* 2:202-254.
16. A.G.A.D., Protokoły Rady Administracyjnej, December 28, 1815.
17. No full length biography of Potocki exists. Consult: Kieniewicz and Kula, eds., *Historia Polski,* 2:267-277; E.Kipa, "Stanisław K. Potocki jako

Minister Wyznań Religijnych" (Stanislaw K. Potocki as Minister of Religions), *Rocznik Historii Sztuki* (Annual of the History Craft), 1 (1956): 442-449; Marceli Handelsman, *Kryzys r. 1821 w Królestwie Polskim* (The 1821 crisis in the Kingdom of Poland), (Lwów, 1939), pp. 7-9.

18. Kieniewicz and Kula, eds., *Historia Polski*, 2:271.
19. Handelsman, *Kryzys*, p. 8.
20. A.G.A.D., Rada Stanu Królestwa Polskiego no. 140, "Raport Rady Stanu z czynności rządu z r. 1822" (Report of the State Council on the government's activities for 1822).
21. *Dziennik Praw Królestwa Polskiego* (Bulletin of the Laws of the Kingdom of Poland), 49 vols. (Warsaw, 1815-1849), 13:91.
22. A.G.A.D., R.S. no. 140.
23. A.G.A.D., R.S. no. 103, "Sprawozdanie z działalności Komisji Rządowej Wojny i Komisji Rządowej Wyznań Religijnych i Oświecenia Publicznego" (Report of the Activity of the War Ministry and the Education Ministry).
24. Kieniewicz and Kula, eds., *Historia Polski*, 2:270; For additional information on higher education see: R. Gerber, ed., *Księga protokołów Rady Ogólnej Uniwersytetu Warszawskiego (1817-1819)* (The minutes of Warsaw University's General Council), (Warsaw, 1958); Józef Bieliński, *Królewski Uniwersytet Warszawski* (The Royal Warsaw University), 3 vols. (Warsaw, 1907-1912); Józef Bieliński, *Uniwersytet Wileński* (Wilno University), 3 vols. (Cracow, 1899-1900); Tadeusz Manteuffel, *Centralne władze oświatowe na terenie b. Królestwa Kongresowego, 1807-1915* (Central education authorities on the land of the former Congress Kingdom, 1807-1915), (Warsaw, 1929).
25. A.G.A.D., R.S. no. 127, "Raport Rady Stanu z odbytych czynności z roku 1818 i 1819" (Report of the State Council on activities performed in 1818 and 1819); R.S. no. 133, "Sprawozdanie z działalności rządu w latach 1818-1819 i z petycji wniesionych przez Izbę Poselską na Sejm" (Report of the activities of the government in 1818-1819 and on petitions entered by the House of Representatives at the Sejm).
26. Kieniewicz and Kula, eds., *Historia Polski*, 2:269-270.
27. Shilder, *Imperator Aleksandr I*, 3:352-354; Michał Ogiński, *Mémoires de Michel Ogiński sur la Pologne et les Polonais depuis 1788 jusqu'a la fin de 1815*, 4 vols. (Paris, 1826-1827), 4:231-242.
28. Shilder, *Imperator Aleksandr I*, 3:354-355; Ogiński, *Mémoires*, 4:231-242; Leonard Chodźko (le comte d'Angeberg), *Receuil des traités' conventions et actes diplomatiques concernant la Pologne 1762-1862* (Paris, 1862), pp. 705-706.

29. Bolesław Limanowski, *Historia demokracji Polskiej* (History of Polish democracy), 3rd ed., (Warsaw, 1946), p. 158.
30. K. Lutostański, *Receuil des actes diplomatiques*. I. *Traités et documents concernant la Pologne* (Paris, 1918), p. 388.
31. Szymon Askenazy, *Rosya-Polska, 1815-1830* (Russia-Poland, 1815-1830), (Lwów, 1907), pp. 17-18, 119-120; Handelsman, *Kryzys*, p. 19.
32. Alexander's opening and closing addresses to the 1818 Sejm: in the original French, Chodźko, *Receuil des traités*, pp. 734-737, 737-739; in Polish, *Dyariusz Seymu Królestwa Polskiego 1818* (Diary of the 1818 Sejm of the Kingdom of Poland), 3 vols. (Warsaw, 1818), 1:10-11; 3:74-75; in Russian, P. M. Maikov, "Tsarstvo Pol'skoe posle vienskago kongressa" (The Kingdom of Poland after the Vienna Congress), *Russkaia Starina*, 113, (1903): 422-425; 430-432.
33. *Ibid.*
34. Shilder, *Imperator Aleksandr I*, 4:82-84. Shilder relates the story of the preparations for the Sejm speeches from Capo d'Istria's unpublished notes.
35. "Iz Vospominanii Mikhailovskago-Danilevskago" (From the Memoirs of Mikhailovskii-Danilevskii), *Russkaia Starina*, 91 (1897): 72.
36. See footnote 32.
37. S. Cieszkowski, *Alexander I a Konstytucya* (Alexander I and the Constitution), (Warsaw, 1909), p. 85.
38. "Iz Vospominanii Mikhailovskago-Danilevskago" *Russkaia Starina*, 91 (1897): 71-72.
39. Prince Shcherbatov, *General-fel'dmarshal Kniaz Paskevich*, 7 vols. (St. Petersburg, 1888), 1:330.
40. Praga is the right bank, or eastern shore, district of Warsaw, Praga was the scene of a bloody battle in November, 1794, when the Russian armies under Suvorov stormed the suburb and annihilated its defenders. This action ended the uncessful Kościuszko revolt which had been provoked by the second partition.
41. Shcherbatov, *Paskevich*, 1:330.
42. "Pis'ma A.P. Ermolov k A.A. (vposledstvii grafa) Zakrevskomu" (Letters of A.P. Ermolov to A.A. (later count) Zakrevskii), *Sbornik Imperatorskago Russkago Istoricheskago Obshchestva* (Collection of the Imperial Russian Historical Society), (St. Petersburg, 1867-1916), 73: 280-281.
43. "Pis'ma A.A. Zakrevskii k P.D. Kiselevy" (Letters of A.A. Zakrevskii to P.D. Kiselev), *ibid.*, 78: 2.

44. "Pis'ma P.D. Kiseleva k A.A. Zakrevskomu" (Letters of P.D. Kiselev to A.A. Zakrevskii), *ibid.*, 78: 192.

45. F.V. Rostopchin to S.R. Vorontsov, January 26, 1819, as excerpted in Shilder, *Imperator Aleksandr I*, 4: 459.

46. N.M. Karamzin to I.I. Dmitriev, April 1818, quoted in *ibid.*, 4: 92.

47. Nicholas Turgenev, *La Russie et les Russes*, 3 vols. (Brussels, 1847), 1:67.

48. A. Pogodin, "Pol'sha pered vosstaniem 1830 g." (Poland before the 1830 insurrection), *Russkoe Bogatstvo*, 8 (1912): 39.

49. "Pis'ma Speranskago k A.A. Stolypinu" (Letters of Speranskii to A.A. Stolypin), dated May 5, 1818 (O.S.), *Russkii Arkhiv* (1869): 1697-1698.

50. *Ibid.*, pp. 1698-1699.

51. *Ibid.*, p. 1703.

52. L.Dembowski, *Moje wspomnienia* (My recollections), 2 vols. (St. Petersburg, 1898), 1: 30.

53. At least one contemporary observer felt that Constantine's election to the Sejm was a government plan to intimidate the more outspoken deputies, and to maintain a high level of order and decorum. See: Karol Hoffman, *Rzut oka na stan polityczny Królestwa Polskiego pod panowaniem Rossyjskiem* (A glance at the political state of the Kingdom of Poland under Russian rule), (Warsaw, 1831), pp. 126-127.

54. Constantine to Sipiagin, published in Shilder, *Imperator Aleksandr I*, 4: 89-90.

55. For the project's text consult: *Dyariusz Sejmu*, 2: 85-115.

56. Helena Więckowska, *Opozycja Liberalna w Królestwie Kongresowem, 1815-1830* (The Liberal Opposition in the Congress Kingdom, 1815-1830), (Warsaw, 1925), pp. 32-33.

57. *Dyariusz Sejmu*, 2: 85-115.

58. Więckowska, *Opozycja Liberalna*, p. 35.

59. *Dyariusz Sejm*, 3: 51.

60. *Ibid.*, 3: 45-51.

61. Cited in Alexander Rembowski, *Pisma Aleksandra Rembowskiego* (The writings of Alexander Rembowski), vol. 1: *Nasze poglądy polityczne w 1818 r.* (Our political views in 1818), (Warsaw, 1901), pp. 113, 141-143.

62. A.G.A.D., R.S. no. 127.

63. Quoted in W.M. Kozłowski, *Autonomia Królestwa Polskiego (1815-1830)* (The Autonomy of the Polish Kingdom, 1815-1830), (Warsaw, 1907), pp. 148-149.

Notes to Chapter Four

1. Szymon Askenazy, *Szkice i portrety* (Sketches and portraits), (Warsaw, 1937), pp. 138-139.
2. Richard Pipes, editor and translator, *Karamzin's Memoir on Ancient and Modern Russia* (New York, 1969), pp. 68-75, 132.
3. *Ibid.*, p. 132.
4. *Ibid.*, pp. 145, 189-190.
5. A.N. Pypin, *Obshchestvennoe dvizhenie v Rossii pri Aleksandr I* (The social movement in Russia under Alexander I), 3rd ed., (St. Petersburg, 1900), p. 215.
6. N.K. Shilder, *Imperator Aleksandr I, ego zhizn i tsarstvovanie* (Emperor Alexander I, his life and reign), 4 vols. (St. Petersburg, 1904), 4: 173-174, 468.
7. Jan Kucharzewski, *The Origins of Modern Russia* (New York, 1948), p. 220 ff. Kucharzewski's work, an abridged version of his famous *Od białego caratu do czerwonego* (From white tsardom to red), reprints significant sections of Karamzin's *Opinion of a Russian Citizen*. The entire essay is found in *Neizdannye sochineniia i perepiska Karamzina* (The Unpublished Works and Correspondence of Karamzin), (St. Petersburg, 1868), pp. 3-8. J.L. Black, *"Interpretations of Poland in Nineteenth Century Russian Nationalist-Conservative Historiography," Polish Review*, 17 (1972): 20-41, discusses the evolution of anti-Polish views by three major Russian historians (Karamzin, M.P. Pogodin, and S.M. Solov'ev) during the nineteenth century.
8. Kucharzewski, *Origins*, p. 220.
9. *Ibid.*
10. *Ibid.*, p. 221.
11. *Ibid.*
12. Pipes, ed., *Karamzin's Memoir*, pp. 89-92; Anatole G. Mazour, *The First Russian Revolution* (Stanford, 1937), pp. 29-30. A recent excellent study of Karamzin's impact upon Russian society is J.L. Black, *Nicholas Karamzin and Russian Society in the Nineteenth Century* (Toronto and Buffalo, 1975).
13. Cited in Kucharzewski, *Origins*, p. 221.
14. *Ibid.*
15. P.A. Viazemskii, *Polnoe sobranie sochinenii Kniazia P.A. Viazemskago* (The complete collected works of Prince P.A. Viazemskii), S.D. Sheremetev, ed., Vol. 1: "Avtobiograficheskoe vvedenie" (Autobiographical preface), (St. Petersburg, 1878-1896), pp. xxxv-xxxvii.

Notes to Chapter Four 163

16. For a full discussion of the 1819-1820 Russian constitution as prepared by Novosil'tsov, consult: George Vernadsky, *La charte constitutionnelle de l'empire Russe de l.an 1820* (Paris, 1933). See also: Shilder, *Imperator Aleksandr I*, 4: 150-152, 465-466.
17. Viazemskii, *Sobranie sochinenii Viazemskago*, I: xxxv-xxxvi.
18. This revealing incident, based on documents from Gosudarstvennyi Arkhiv (The State Archive), is related in Shilder, *Imperator AleksandrI*, 4:465-466.
19. "Vsepoddannieishaia zapiska N.N. Novosil'tsova Aleksandru I" (A most devoted memorandum of N.N. Novosil'tsov to Alexander I), *Russkaia Starina*, 35 (1882): 142-144.
20. Szymon Askenazy, *Rosya-Polska 1815-1830* (Russia-Poland, 1815-1830), (Lwów, 1907), pp. 17-18, 119-120.
21. S.Smolka, *Polityka Lubeckiego przed powstaniem listopadowem* (Lubecki's policy before the November revolution), 2 vols. (Cracow, 1907), 1: 324-326.
22. Natalia Gąsiorowska, *Wolność druku w Królestwie Kongresowem, 1815-1830* (Freedom of the press in the Congress Kingdom, 1815-1830), (Warsaw, 1916), pp. 9-11.
23. *Ibid.*, pp. 11-13.
24. P.M. Maikov, "Melkiia zamietki ob otnosheniiakh imperatora Aleksandra k Poliakam" (Small Notes about the Relations of Emperor Alexander to the Poles), *Russkaia Starina*, 116 (1903): 443-444; Gąsiorowska, *Wolność druku*, pp. 16-20.
25. Gęsiorowska, *Wolność druku*, pp. 14-23.
26. *Ibid.*, p. 21; *Dziennik Praw Królestwa Polskiego* (Bulletin of the Laws of the Kingdom of Poland), 49 vols. (Warsaw, 1815-1849), 1: 10, 2: 32.
27. A.G.A.D., Protokoły Rada Administracyjnej, February 17, 1816. A.G.A.D., Rada Stanu Królestwa Polskiego no. 182, "Cenzura i wolność druku" (Censorship and freedom of the press).
28. A.G.A.D., R.S. no. 182.
29. *Ibid.*
30. A.G.A.D., P.R.A., March 16, 1816.
31. A.G.A.D., R.S. no. 99, "Raporta roczne Komisji Obrządków Religijnych i Oświecenia Publicznego" (Yearly reports of the Education Ministry), Report for 1817.
32. *Ibid.*, 1816-total value of imported books—188, 383 zlotys; 1817-total value of imported books—236,349 zlotys.
33. Maikov, "Melkiia zamietki," p. 444.

34. Kajetan Koźmian, *Pamiętniki* (Memoirs), 3 vols. (Wrocław, 1972), 2: 238.
35. Gąsiorowska, *Wolność druku*, pp. 52-58.
36. A.G.A.D., P.R.A., May 22, 1819; *Dziennik Praw*, 6: 327-329.
37. A.G.A.D., P.R.A., June 12, 1819.
38. Gąsiorowska, *Wolność druku*, p. 68.
39. A.G.A.D., P.R.A., July 13, 1819.
40. A.G.A.D., P.R.A., July 16, 1819; *Dziennik Praw*, 6: 362; Leonard Chodźko, (le comte d'Abgeberg), *Receuil des traités, conventions et actes diplomatiques concernant la Pologne 1762-1862* (Paris, 1862), p. 741.
41. A.G.A.D., P.R.A., June 19, 1819.
42. A.G.A.D., R.S. no. 182.
43. A.G.A.D., P.R.A., December 28, 1819.
44. Chodźko, *Receuil des traités*, p. 741.
45. The role of secret societies in the Polish military is an important one. However, their activities, which have been the subject of numerous investigations, are beyond the immediate scope of this work. The most recent examination of secret, military societies is Hanna Dylągowa's excellent study, *Towarzystwo Patriotyczne i sąd sejmowy, 1821-1829 (The Patriotic Society and the Sejm court, 1821-1829), (Warsaw, 1970)*. Older although still valuable are: Szymon Askenazy, *Łukasiński*, 2nd ed., 2 vols. (Warsaw, 1929); Bolesław Limanowski, *Łukasiński*, (Warsaw, no date); and B. Gembarzewski, *Wojsko Polskie. Królestwo Polskie 1815-1830* (The Polish Army. The Kingdom of Poland, 1815-1830), (Warsaw, 1903). For the Decembrists' contacts with Polish secret, military societies, consult: Dyągowa, *Towarzystwo Patriotyczne*, M. Nechkina, *Dvizhenie dekabristov* (The Decembrist Movement), 2 vols. (Moscow, 1955); *Vosstanie dekabristov. Materialy* (The Decembrist uprising: Materials), M.N. Pokrovskii, M. Nechkina, eds. 1-13 vols. (Moscow, 1925-1975); Leon Baumgarten, *Dekabryści a Polska* (The Decembrists and Poland), (Warsaw, 1952); P.N. Ol'shanskii, *Dekabristy i pol'skoe natsional'no-osvoboditel'noe dvizhenie* (The Decembrists and the Polish national liberation movement), (Moscow, 1959). For Lieutenant Peter Wysocki's conspiratorial organization whose attack on Belvedere palace touched off the November insurrection, see: Wacław Tokarz, *Sprzysiężenie Wysockiego i noc listopadowa* (Wysocki's conspiracy and the November night), (Cracow, 1925); and Julius S. Harbut, *Noc listopadowa* (The November night), (Warsaw, 1926).
46. For the *Burschenschaft* movement: Paul Wentzcke, *Geschichte der deutschen Burschenschaft*, 4 vols. (Heidelberg, 1919-1939); H. Haupt, ed., *Quellen und Darstellung zur Geschichte der Burschenschaft und deutschen*

Einheitsbewegung (Heidelberg, 1910); Maria Wawrykowa, *Ruch studencki w Niemczech 1815-1825* (The student movement in Germany 1815-1825), (Warsaw, 1969); G.W. Spindler, *Karl Follen* (Chicago, 1917).

47. Alexander Kamiński, *Polskie związki młodzieży* (Polish youth societies), (Warsaw, 1963), pp. 227-242. Kamiński is the leading contemporary expert on Polish student secret societies in the first half of the nineteenth century.

48. *Ibid.*, pp. 71-72, 95-96, 147-149, 167, 377-383, and *passim*; Askenazy, *Łukasiński,* 1: 249-268; 2: 102-109, 381-384; Stanisław Małachowski-Łempicki, *Raporty szpiega Mackrotta o Wolnomularstwie Polskim 1819-1822* (The reports of the spy Mackrott about Polish Freemasonry 1819-1822), (Warsaw, 1931). See also: Stanisław Małachowski-Łempicki, *Wykaz Polskich lóż Wolnomularskich w latach 1738-1821* (The Register of Polish Freemason lodges in the years 1738-1821), (Cracow, 1929); W. Łukaszewicz, *Wpływ Masonerii, karbonaryzmu i J. Mazziniego na polska myśl rewolucyjną w latach poprzedzających Wiosnę Ludów* (The influence of the Masons, *Carbonari,* and J. Mazzini on Polish revolutionary thought in the years preceding the revolutions of 1848), (Warsaw, 1948).

49. Marceli Handelsman, *Francja-Polska, 1795-1845* (France-Poland, 1795-1845), 2 vols. (Warsaw, 1926), 2: 90, 94, 103.

50. *Ibid.*, 2: 92-94.

51. *Ibid.*, 2: 94-95; Kamiński, *Polskie związki,* p. 133; Marceli Handelsman, *Les idées françaises et la mentalité politique en Pologne au XIXe siècle* (Paris, 1927), 67-68.

52. Kamiński, *Polskie związki,* pp. 124-129.

53. *Ibid.*, pp. 110-113.

54. Mackrott, following the example of his father who had engaged in spying for many years, supplied Constantine with voluminous reports in neat, precise, French. Captured intact during the 1830-1831 rebellion, they not only sealed Mackrott's fate but also revealed to the patriots the names of many other spies. Running into the thousands of pages, Mackrott's reports comprise the bulk of *Kancelaria Tajna Wielkiego Księcia Konstantina* (Grand Duke Constantine's Secret Chancellery). Serving chiefly to satiate Constantine's abnormal desire for gossip, the reports also contain valuable information about student activities and the events surrounding the 1820 Sejm. See A.G.A.D., K.T.K no. 40a-100. See below: footnote no. 69.

55. A.G.A.D., K.T.K no. 40a, March 22, May 2, 3, 4, 1820.

56. *Ibid.*, no. 102, "Personels (sic) de Makrot."

57. Quoted in Alexander Kraushar, *Miscellanea historyczne* (Historical miscellanea), Vol. 15: *Panta Koina* (Warsaw, 1907), p. 40.

58. Kamiński, *Polskie związki*, p. 138.
59. Quoted in *ibid.*
60. Consult the lengthy reproduction in Kraushar, *Panta Koina*, pp. 22-24.
61. Kamiński, *Polskie związki*, p. 137.
62. *Ibid.*, pp. 140-141; Kraushar, *Panta Koina*, pp. 10-47.
63. Handelsman, *Francja-Polska*, 2: 89, 103-106; Kamiński, *Polskie związki*, pp. 132-134. For the decree forbidding Warsaw university students to associate, see: R. Gerber, ed., *Księga protokołów Ray Ogólnej Uniwersytetu Warszawskiego (1817-1819)* (The minutes of Warsaw University's General Council (1817-1819)), (Warsaw, 1958); for the 1821 decree outlawing all secret societies, A.G.A.D., P.R.A., November 6, 1821.
64. Handelsman, *Francja-Polska*, 2: 78-90. What follows is an analysis of the Liberal Opposition's basic philosophy as distilled from Wincenty Niemojowski's *O monarchij konstytucyjnej i rękojmach władz publicznych* (On constitutional monarchy and the guarantees of public authorities), a translation of Benjamin Constant's *Réflexions sur les constitutions*, embellished with a preface and footnotes. This work, together with W. Niemojowski's own pamphlet, *O władzach publicznych w monarchij konstytucyjnej* (On public authorities in a constitutional monarchy), a further restatement of Constant's ideas, served as the Liberal Opposition's "Bible." The question of Polish liberal movements during the Congress Kingdom has not received a great deal of attention. The best available work is Helena Więckowska's admirable monograph, *Opozycja Liberalna w Królestwie Kongresowym, 1815-1830* (The Liberal Opposition in the Congress Kingdom, 1815-1830), (Warsaw, 1925). See also: Helena Więckowska Braunsteinowna, "Charakterystyka braci Niemojowskich" (Characterization of the Niemojowski brothers), *Przegląd Historyczny* (1922): 61-85; Handelsman, *Francja-Polska*, 2: 70-85; Piotr Chmielowski, *Liberalizm i obskurantyzm na Litwie i Rusi, 1815-1823* (Liberalism and obscurantism in Lithuania and Ruthenia, 1815-1823), (Warsaw, 1898). A good English language treatment of the subject is found in George T. Bujarski, *"Polish Liberalism, 1815-1823," Polish Review*, 17 (1972): 3-37. Bujarski's article is especially valuable in conjunction with the flawed and biased work by the contemporary Polish historian, Jerzy Szacki, *Z historii rozwoju ideologii szlachecko-rewolucynej w Polsce drugiego i trzeciego dziesieciolecia XIX wieku* (From the history of the evolution of gentry-revolutionary ideology in Poland during the second and third decades of the 19th century), (Warsaw, 1955).
65. Koźmian, *Pamiętniki*, 3: 41.
66. Braunsteinowna, *"Charakterystyka," pp. 61-85.*

67. Wincenty Niemojowski, *Głos posła Kaliskiego na Sejmie Królestwa Polskeigo* (The Voice of a Kalisz deputy at the Sejm of the Polish Kingdom), (Poznan, 1818).
68. Więckowska, *Opozycja Liberalna* (The Liberal Opposition), p. 82.
69. Mackrott composed detailed, daily reports about events surrounding the 1820 Sejm which shed much light on day to day happenings, personalities, issues, and public sentiment. His superiors wrote of him, "In 1820 he watched over the Polish Sejm—he sent reports to his superiors on the numerous secret enterprises of several deputies who distinguished themselves during this Sejm by a manner of liberal thought." A.G.A.D., K.T.D., no. 40b, September 1, 4, 5, 11, 1820; no. 102.
70. Stefan Kieniewicz and W. Kula, eds., Vol. 2 of *Historia Polski* (History of Poland), (Warsaw, 1958), pp. 278-279.
71. For Niemojowski's speech, *Dziennik posiedzeń Izby Poselskiey w czasie Seymu Królestwa Polskiego w dniu 1820 odbytego* (Bulletin of the sessions of the House of Representatives at the time of the Sejm of the Kingdom of Poland held in 1820), 2 vols. (Warsaw, 1820), 1: 96-101. For numerous comments against the government bill, 1: 55-74.
72. A.G.A.D., K.T.K., no. 40b, September 14, 1820.
73. *Dziennik posiedzeń*, 1: 172.
74. *Ibid.*, 1: 296-302.
75. *Ibid.*, 1: 339.
76. *Ibid.*, 1: 316-320.
77. Więckowska, *Opozycja Liberalna*, p. 90.
78. *Dziennik posiedzeń*, 1: 335-342.
79. *Ibid.* 1: 345-355.
80. *Ibid.* 1:391; A.G.A.D., K.T.K., no 40b, September 27, 1820.
81. Shilder, *Imperator Aleksandr I*, 4: 179.
82. *Sziennik posiedzeń*, 1: 393, 400-404, 440-478, 487-488; 2: 64, 66-67. A.G.A.D., K.T.K., no. 40b, October 10, 13, 1820.
83. This incident is described in Alexander Kraushar, *"Z tajnego archiwum Senatora Nowosilcowa: Uwagi nad konstytucya Królestwa z roku 1815"* (From the secret archive of Senator Novosil'tsov: Observations on the Kingdom's constitution from 1815," *Przegląd Historyczny*, 1 (1906): 114.
84. I. Sobolewski's September 10, 1820 order to the Lord Lieutenant is published in a Polish translation in Gąsiorowska, *Wolność druku*, pp. 340-341.
85. Chodźko, *Receuil des traités*, pp. 745-746.
86. *Ibid.*

87. P.M. Maikov, "Tsarstvo Pol'skoe posle vienskago kongressa" (The Kingdom of Poland after the Vienna Congress), *Russkaia Starina*, 115 (1903): 14-15.
88. A.G.A.D., R.S., no. 127, "Raporta Rady Stanu z obdytych czynności z roku 1818 i 1819" (Report of the State Council on activities performed in 1818 and 1819).
89. A.G.A.D., R.S., no. 128, "Niekompletne uwagi komisjów izb sejmowych nad raportem Rady Stanu zdanym w roku 1818 i 1819" (Incomplete observations of the Sejm house commissions on the report of the State Council from 1818 to 1819).
90. A.G.A.D., R.S., no. 130, "Observations de la Chambre de Senat sur le rapport du Conseil d'Etat presenté en 1820...
91. A.G.A.D., R.S., no. 132, "Observations de la Chambre des Nonces sur les rapport (sic) du Conseil d'Etat presenté en 1820."
92. A.G.A.D., R.S., no. 137, "Odpowiedzi Rady Stanu na uwagi izb sejmowych poczynione nad raportem tejże Rady, zdanym z czynności w r. 1820." (Replies of the State Council to the observations of the Sejm houses made on the report of this Council, on the activities for 1820).

Notes to Chapter Five

1. Alexander Moriolles, *Mémoires du Comte de Moriolles sur l'émigration, la Pologne et la cour de Grand-Duc Constantin (1789-1833)*, 2nd ed. (Paris, 1902), pp. 79-80, 134-135.
2. A. Pogodin, "Pol'sha pered vosstaniem 1830 g." (Poland before the 1830 insurrection), *Russkoe Bogatstvo*, 8 (1912): 47.
3. Novosil'tsov's proposed *ukaz* is published in Szymon Askenazy, *Rosya-Polska, 1815-1830* (Russia-Poland, 1815-1830), (Lwów, 1907), pp. 188-189.
4. Novosil'tsov's memorial on constitutions is published in: D. Tsvietaev, "Novosil'tsov o konstitutsii Tsarstva Pol'skago" (Novosil'tsov about the constitution of the Kingdom of Poland), *Russkaia Starina*, 121 (1905): 601-604. It is excerpted in G. Pisarevskii, *Iz istorii kongressovago Tsarstva Pol'skogo* (From the history of the Polish Congress Kingdom), (Smolensk, 1926), pp. 7-8; and A. Kraushar, *"Z tajnego archiwum Senatora Nowosilcowa: Uwagi nad konstytucya Krolestwa z roku 1815"* (From the secret archive of Senator Novosil'tsov: Observations on the Kingdom's constitution from 1815), *Przegląd Historyczny*, 1 (1906): 111-112 (erroneously claims to publish the entire document). Tsvietaev's dating this memorandum as 1815 appears unwarranted in light of Novosil'tsov's complete dependence on Alexander and the Emperor's role in preparing

Notes to Chapter Five   169

the Polish constitution. References in the memorial to European conflagrations and unruly Sejm representatives basing their demands for unfettered freedom of speech on constitutional provisions set its date as sometime shortly after the second Sejm. Its elegance and verbosity indicate that Novosil'tsov did not hurry the project. Perhaps he prepared it during winter, 1820/1821 for presentation to Alexander when the emperor stopped at Warsaw on his return from Laibach in May, 1821.

    5. Szymon Askenazy, "Dwie rozmowy w Belwederze" (Two conversations at Belvedere), *Wczasy Historyczne* (Historical Holidays), (Warsaw, 1910), pp. 246, 454.

    6. Pisarevskii, *Iz istorii*, pp. 6-7; Pogodin, "Pol'sha pered vosstaniem 1830 g.," p. 47; Marceli Handelsman, *Kryzys r. 1821 w Krolestwie Polskim* (The 1821 crisis in the Kingdom of Poland), (Lwów, 1939), p. 20; Stefan Kieniewicz, *Historia Polski, 1795-1918* (Warsaw, 1969), p. 72. Askenazy reconstructed Alexander's *"carte blanche"* promise from Czartoryski's notes made when the Polish statesman conferred with Grand Duke Constantine in 1827. At this time Czartoryski played a key role in the Sejm Court, Poland's highest judicial body, which had been convened to judge the culpability of several Poles remotely linked to the Decembrists. Constantine, attempting to win Czartoryski's support, invited Prince Adam to Belvedere Palace for consultations on two occasions. During their second meeting, Constantine related Alexander's offer of *"carte blanche"* in the Congress Kingdom. Czartoryski's notes on the conversations, in French, are published in "Dwie rozmowy," pp. 448-454.

    7. Constantine to Alexander, April 30, 1822, Pisarevskii, *Iz istorii*, p. 46.

    8. Novosil'tsov's report to Alexander, May 24, 1821, partially reprinted in Szymon Askenazy, *Łukasiński*, 2nd. ed., 2 vols. (Warsaw, 1929), 1: 408-410.

    9. Proclamation of the Minister-Secretary of State for Poland, May 25, 1821. Quoted in S. Gnorowski, *Insurrection of Poland in 1830-1831 and the Russian Rule Preceding It Since 1815* (London, 1839), p. 25.

    10. Czartoryski to Alexander, August 21, 1821, Adam Czartoryski, *Memoirs of Prince Adam Czartoryski*, trans. and ed. Adam Gielgud, 2nd ed., 2 vols. (London, 1888), 2: 311.

    11. *Ibid.*, p. 313.

    12. The succession crisis has received very little scholarly attention. Pisarevskii, *Iz istorii*, pp. 21-31, 35-48, publishes several valuable documents. See also: N.K. Shilder, *Imperator Aleksandr I, ego zhizn i tsarstvovanie* (Emperor Alexander I, his life and reign), 4 vols. (St. Petersburg, 1904), 4: 146, 175-176, 278-282, 465, 468, 478; N. Chechulin,

"Konstantin Pavlovich" in *Russkii Biograficheskii Slovar*, 25 vols. (St. Petersburg, 1903), 9: 193-201; Karol Hoffman, *Rzuc oka na stan polityczny Królestwa Polskiego pod panowaniem Rossyjskiem* (A glance at the political state of the Kingdom of Poland under Russian rule), (Warsaw, 1831), pp. 114-116; Gnorowski, *Insurrection of Poland*, pp. 30-31.

13. Mieczysław Offmański, *Królestwo Polskie, 1815-1830* (The Kingdom of Poland), (Warsaw, 1907), p. 27; Chechulin, "Konstantin Pavlovich," p. 193.

14. Shilder, *Imperator Aleksandr I*, 4: 175.

15. Askenazy, *Łukasiński*, 1: 163.

16. Marceli Handelsman, "The Polish Kingdom, 1815-1830," *The Cambridge History of Poland*, W.F. Reddaway et al., eds., 2 vols. (Cambridge, 1951), 2: 20.

17. Warren B. Walsh, ed., *Readings in Russian History*, 4th ed., 3 vols. (Syracuse, 1963), 2: 303.

18. *Ibid.*

19. The project of this rescript, without date, is published in Pisarevskii, *Iz istorii*, pp. 37-38.

20. *Ibid.*

21. *Ibid.*

22. "Au Lieutenant en Conseil," without date, published in *ibid.*, p. 38.

23. For the Lord Lieutenant's and Novosil'tsoa's comments, see respectively: "Observations sur le project connumiqué" without date, and "Observations sur les deux projects de rescrits que Votre Altesse Impériale m'a fait l'honneur de me communiquer," April 24, 1822, published in *ibid.*, pp. 38-39; 40-42.

24. *Ibid.*, pp. 40-41.

25. Constantine to Alexander, April 30, 1822, published in *ibid.*, pp. 42-48.

26. Novosil'stov to Constantine, April 24, 1822, published in *ibid.*, p. 40.

27. Askenazy, *Łukasiński*, 1: 166-167.

28. A.G.A.D., K.N., no. 592, "O diplomaticheskikh snosheniiakh Tsarstva s inostrannymi derzhavymi" (On the diplomatic relations of the Kingdom with foreign powers), Nesselrode to Constantine, September 16, 1822; Constantine to Novosil'tsov, September 23, 1822.

29. *Ibid.*, Nesselrode to Constantine, September 16, 1822.

30. A.G.A.D., K.N., no. 579, "Ob otkrytom soiuze vol'nykh poliakov i tainom politicheskom soiuze v gorode Krakove" (About the discovery of a society of free Poles and a secret political society in Cracow),

Novosil'tsov to Alexander, April 13, 1822; Novosil'tsov to Alexander, published in Askenazy, *Łukasiński*, 2: 412.

31. Marc Raeff, *The Decembrist Movement* (Englewood Cliffs, N.J., 1966), p. 4.

Notes to Chapter Six

1. Prince Klemens Metternich, *Memoirs of Prince Metternich*, Richard Metternich, ed., A. Napier trans., 5 vols. (New York, 1881), 3: 399.
2. M.V. Nechkina, *Russia in the Nineteenth Century*, Sir Bernard Pares and Oliver J. Frederiksen, trans. (Ann Arbor, 1953), pp. 127-133; Allen McConnell, *Tsar Alexander I* (New York, 1970), pp. 161, 175-176; F.B. Artz, *Reaction and Revolution, 1814-1832* (New York, 1934), pp. 164-165, 167-168.
3. Metternich, *Memoirs*, 3: 402.
4. A.G.A.D., Kancelaria Nowosilcowa, no. 481, "O tsenzure Tsarstva" (About the Kingdom's censorship), Novosil'tsov to Constantine, February 7, 1820.
5. A.G.A.D., Protokoły Rady Administracyjnej, February 8, 1820.
6. *Ibid.*
7. A.G.A.D., K.N., no. 481, Novosil'tsov to Alexander, February 13, 1820.
8. *Ibid.*
9. A.G.A.D., P.R.A., February 29, 1820.
10. *Ibid.*, March 4, 1820.
11. Zajączek to the Minister of the Interior, March 28, 1820, as quoted in Natalia Gąsiorowska, *Wolność druku w Królestwie Kongresowem* (Freedom of the press in the Congress Kingdom), (Warsaw, 1916), p. 313.
12. A.G.A.D., P.R.A., April 4, 1820.
13. A.G.A.D., P.R.A., June 13, 1820.
14. "Mnenie Kapodistrii o tsensure v Tsarstve Pol'skom" (The opinion of Capo d'Istria about censorship in the Kingdom of Poland), *Russkaia Starina*, 116 (1903): 446-455. See also, Gąsiorowska, *Wolność druku*, pp. 100-110.
15. Novosil'tsov to Alexander, May 24, 1821; partially reprinted in Gąsiorowska, *Wolność druku*, pp. 341-344.
16. *Ibid.*, pp. 130-132.
17. *Ibid.*, pp. 133-139.
18. A.G.A.D., K.N., no. 481, Constantine to Zarzecki, February 19, 1822.

19. *Ibid.*, Zarzecki to ?, February 24, 1822; Wodzicki (President of the Cracow Senate) to Novosil'tsov, February 24, 1822.
20. Aleksander Kraushar, *Miscellanea historyczne* (Historical Miscellanea), vol. 54: *Senator Nowosilcow i cenzura za Królestwa Kongresowego (1819-1829)* (Senator Novosil'tsov and censorship for the Congress Kingdom (1819-1829)), (Cracow, 1911), p. 40.
21. A.G.A.D., K.N., no. 481, Novosil'tsov to Alexander, May 3, 1822.
22. *Ibid.*, The Lord Lieutenant's decree, May 7, 1822. See also: A.G. A.D., P.R.A., May 7, 1822; *Dziennik Praw Królestwo Polskiego* (Bulletin of the Laws of the Kingdom of Poland), 49 vols. (Warsaw, 1815-1849), 7: 369 ff.
23. Gąsiorowska, *Wolność druku*, pp. 161-167.
24. A.G.A.D., K.N., no. 481, Constantine to Novosil'tsov, November 21, 1822.
25. *Ibid.*, Novosil'tsov to Zajączek, November 25, 1822.
26. Gąsiorowska, *Wolność druku*, p. 184.
27. A.G.A.D., K.N., no. 481, Novosil'tsov to Nesselrode, January 31, 1823.
28. *Ibid.*, Szaniawski to Novosil'tsov, February 17, 1823.
29. *Ibid.*, Novosil'tsov to Alexander, February 4/20 (sic), 1823.
30. A.G.A.D., K.N., no. 548, "Delo o preobrazovanii uchilishch v Tsarstve i naznachenii general'nago kuratora nad onimi" (The matter of reform of schools in the Kingdom and appointment of a general curator over them), Novosil'tsov to Golovkin, June 6, 1821.
31. Tadeusz Manteuffel, *Centralne władze oświatowe na terenie b. Królestwa Kongresowego* (Central educational authorities on the land of the former Congress Kingdom), (Warsaw, 1929), p. 19.
32. E.Kipa, "Stanisław K. Potocki jako Minister Wyznań Religijnych" (Stanisław K. Potocki as Minister of Religions), *Rocznik Historii Sztuki* (Annual of the History Craft), 1 (1956): 447-449.
33. A.G.A.D., Rada Stanu Królestwa Polskiego, 1815-1831, no. 162, "Organizacja Komisji Wyzań Religijnych i Oświecenia Publicznego" (Organization of the Religions and Public Education Ministry); *Dziennik Praw Królestwo Polskiego*, 7: 174-229; Manteuffel, *Centralne władze*, pp. 19-21.
34. Marceli Handelsman, *Kryzys r. 1821 w Królestwie Polskim* (The 1821 crisis in the Kingdom of Poland), (Lwów, 1939), p. 11.
35. Marja Manteufflowa, *J.K. Szaniawski: ideologia i dziatalność* (J.K. Szaniawski: ideology and activity), (Warsaw, 1936), p. 106.
36. Niemcewicz's characteristic bon mot is related in Natalia Kicka, *Pamiętniki* (Memoirs), Józef Dutkiewicz, ed., (Warsaw, 1972), p. 101.

37. Quoted in Manteufflowa, *Szaniawski*, p. 75.
38. *Ibid.*
39. Szaniawski's inaugural speech to the Society for Elementary Textbooks, quoted in Stefanja Koelichenówna, *Przejawy reakcji w działalności Towarzystwa do Ksiąg Elementarnych (1821-1830)* (Indications of reaction in the activity of the Society for Elementary Textbooks), (Warsaw, 1929), p. 4.
40. Szaniawski's Education Commission Report of January 25, 1822, as reprinted in Gąsiorowska, *Wolność druku*, pp. 350-356.
41. B.P.P., Archiwum Wielkiego Księcia Konstantego, no. 340, Novosil'tsov to Alexander, January 9, 1822.
42. Manteufflowa, *Szaniawski*, pp. 56, 85, 92-93.
43. A.G.A.D., K.N., no. 549, "Delo o novom plane obrazovaniia uchilishch v Tsarstve" (The matter of a new plan of education for schools in the Kingdom), Prażmowski at the Education Reform Committee's meeting, March 12, 1827.
44. For Russian and European educational policies see: M.I. Demkov, *Istoriaa russkoi pedagogii* (A history of Russian pedagogy), (Moscow, 1909); S.V. Rozhdestvenskii, *Istoricheskii obzor deiatel' nosti Ministerstva Narodnago Prosveshcheniia 1802-1902* (A historical review of the activity of the Ministry of Public Education, 1802-1902), (St. Petersburg, 1902); Nicholas A. Hans, *History of Russian Educational Policy (1701-1917)*, (London, 1931); William H.E. Johnson, *Russia's Educational Heritage* (Pittsburgh, 1950); J. Flynn, "The Universities in the Russia of Alexander I" (Ph.D. dissertation, Clark University, 1964); J.W. Adamson, *English Education, 1789-1902* (Cambridge, 1930); E.H. Reisner, *Nationalism and Education since 1789* (New York, 1922); Daniel Beauvois, *Lumière et Société en Europe de l'est*, 2 vols.(Lille, 1977).
45. A.G.A.D., K.N., no. 564, "O tainom obshchestve otkryvshemsia mezhdu uchenikami varshavskago i krakovskago universitetov, pod nazvaniem Bratstva Burshov" (On the secret society uncovered between the students of Warsaw and Cracow universities under the name: *Burschenschaft*), Novosil'tsov to Secretary of State for Poland, I. Sobolewski, November 2, 9, 10, 1821.
46. A.G.A.D., K.N., no. 548, Sobolewski to Novosil'tsov, November 20, 1821.
47. *Ibid.*, Sobolewski to Novosil'tsov, December 16, 1821.
48. A.G.A.D., K.N., no. 564, Novosil'tsov to Alexander, September 14, 1821.
49. *Ibid.*
50. *Ibid.*

51. *Ibid.*
52. Manteufflowa, *Szaniawski*, pp. 65-66.
53. A.G.A.D., P.R.A., December 18, 1821.
54. B.P.P., A.W.K.K., Novosil'tsov to Alexander, January 9, 1822.
55. A.G.A.D., K.N., no. 564, Novosil'tsov to Alexander, January 19, 1822.
56. *Ibid.*, Novosil'tsov to Alexander, March 24, 1822.
57. Manteufflowa, *Szaniawski*, pp. 70-72.
58. A.G.A.D., R.S., no. 142, "Względem zdania raportu z czynności rządu z lat 1820, 1821, 1822, i 1823 na Sejm w. r. 1825" (About the opinion of the report on the government's activities from 1820, 1821, 1822, and 1823 at the 1825 Sejm).
59. Manteufflowa, *Szaniawski*, pp. 70-72.
60. A.G.A.D., K.N., no. 548, Minister-Secretary of State, Stefan Grabowski to Novosil'tsov, June 10, 1823.
61. *Ibid.*, Novosil'tsov to Alexander, February 7, 1823; Stefan Grabowski to Novosil'tsov, March 25, 1823.
62. *Ibid.*, Stefan Grabowski to Novosil'tsov, March 25, 1823.
63. *Ibid.*, Stefan Grabowski to Novosil'tsov, June 10, 1823.
64. A.G.A.D., R.S., no. 109, "Raporta z czynności Komisji Rządowej Spraw Wewnętrznych i Policji z lat 1821-1824" (Report on the activities of the Interior Ministry from 1821-1824); R.S., no. 141, "Raport roczny z czynności rządu w r. 1824 obdytych" (Yearly report for the government's activities, 1824).
65. Manteufflowa, *Szaniawski*, p. 72.
66. A.G.A.D., K.N., no. 549, Novosil'tsov to Constantine, without date (probably mid-1826).
67. *Ibid.*
68. Manteufflowa, *Szaniawski*, pp. 76-77, 85.
69. A.G.A.D., K.N., no. 548, Minutes of the Educational Reform Committee, February 27, 1822.
70. Manteufflowa, *Szaniawski*, p. 98.
71. Koelichenówna, *Przejawy reakcji*, pp. 5-6.
72. Manteufflowa, *Szaniawski*, p. 105.
73. A.G.A.D., K.N., no. 564, Novosil'tsov to Alexander, November 14, 1821; K.N., no. 548, Minutes of the Educational Reform Committee, February 10, 1822.
74. A.G.A.D., K.N., no. 564, Novosil'tsov to Alexander, November 14, 1821.
75. Koelichenówna, *Przejawy reakcji*, pp. 1-3.
76. *Ibid.*, p. 11.

Notes to Chapter Six

77. *Ibid.*, pp. 12-14.
78. *Ibid.*, pp. 1-3.
79. P.M. Maikov, "Tsarstvo Pol'skoe posle vienskago kongressa" (The Kingdom of Poland after the Vienna Congress), *Russkaia Starina*, 120 (1904): 619-620.
80. A.G.A.D., R.S., no. 142.
81. A.G.A.D., Kancelaria Tajna Wielkiego Księcia Konstantina, no. 47, 63.
82. For the genesis and detailed development of this proposal consult A.G.A.D., K.N., no. 564, Novosil'tsov to Stefan Grabowski, November 2, 9, 1821. See also: A.G.A.D. Komisja Rządowa Spraw Wewnętrznych i Policji no. 7471 for the Lord Lieutenant's projected decree. Also: A.G. A.D., P.R.A., December 30, 1820; January 15, February 5, March 26, April 23, 1822. For the actual decree: *Dziennik Praw*, 8: 3.
83. *Zbiór przepisów administracyjnych Królestwa Polskiego* (Collection of administrative regulations of the Kingdom of Poland); "Wydział Oświecenia" (Education Ministry), 6 vols. (Warsaw, 1866), 1: 121-123, for the decrees of July 16 and August 13, 1821.
84. Manteufflowa, *Szaniawski*, p. 163. The author supplies statistical tables based on the Education Ministry's yearly reports.
85. Quoted in Hanna Dylagowa, *Towarzystwo Patriotyczne i sąd sejmowy, 1821-1829* (The Patriotic Society and the Sejm court, 1821-1829), (Warsaw, 1970), p. 20.
86. A.G.A.D., P.R.A., December 7, 1816.
87. Szymon Askenazy, *Łukasiński*, 2nd ed., 2 vols. (Warsaw, 1929), 1: 339-341. For the development of the Russian gendarmerie consult: Sidney Monas, *The Third Section* (Cambridge, Mass., 1961) and P.S. Squire, *The Third Department* (Cambridge, England, 1968).
88. A.G.A.D., R.S., no. 282, "Żandarmeria" (Gendarmerie).
89. *Ibid.*
90. Askenazy, *Łukasiński*, 1: 354; Dylągowa, *Towarzystwo Patriotyczne*, p. 21; Szymon Askenazy, *Dwa stulecia XVIII-XIX* (Two centuries XVIII-XIX), 2nd ed., 2 vols. (Warsaw, 1903), 1: 455-456, 558.
91. For details of Mackrott's career as spy see: Chapter 4; for Schley see: Askenazy, *Łukaniński*, 1: 344-347; Stanisław Małachowski-Łempicki, *Raporty szpiega Mackrotta o Wolnomularstwie Polskim 1819-1822* (The reports of the spy Mackrott about Polish Freemasonry 1819-1822), (Warsaw, 1931), p. 15.
92. Askenazy, *Łukasiński*, 1: 347; Dylągowa, *Towarzystwo Patriotyczne*, p. 20; Małachowski-Łempicki, *Raporty Mackrotta*, p. 15.
93. Askenazy, *Łukasiński*, 1:322-377, 429-437. For more details

about the police and spy networks honeycombing Poland at this time: Małachowski-Łempicki, *Raporty Mackrotta*, pp. 5-23; Dylągowa, *Towarzystwo Patriotyczne*, pp. 20-22.

94. Askenazy, *Łukasiński*, 1: 350-355; Dylągowa, *Towarzystwo Patriotyczne*, p. 21.
95. Askenazy, *Łukasiński*, 1: 375-377.
96. Małachowski-Łempicki, *Raporty Mackrotta*, pp. 16-22.
97. A.G.A.D., K.N., no. 486, "O sushchestvovanii tainago obshchestva v Germanii, imeiushchago tselei revoliutsionnykh" (On the existence of a secret society in Germany having revolutionary aims), Novosil'tsov to Alexander, August 10, 1821; K.N., no. 562, "Delo ob uchrezhdenii varshave komiteta tsentral'noi politsii" (The matter about establishment in Warsaw of a central police committee) for Novosil'tsov's project of Central Police Bureau.
98. *Ibid.*

Notes to Chapter Seven

1. Minister-Secretary of State for Poland, I. Sobolewski to Zajączek, October 18, 1820, reprinted in Helena Więckowska, *Opozycja Liberalna w Królestwie Kongresowem* (The Liberal Opposition in the Congress Kingdom), (Warsaw, 1925), pp. 176-179.
2. Sobolewski to Zajączek, *ibid.*, pp. 179-180.
3. Zajączek to Sobolewski (?), December 22, 1820, excerpted in P.M. Mailov, "Tsarstvo Pol'skoe posle vienskago kongressa" (The Kingdom of Poland after the Vienna Congress), *Russkaia Starina*, 115 (1903): 16.
4. Alexander's proclamation, August 12, 1821; published in Więckowska, *Opozycja Liberalna*, pp. 180-181.
5. A.G.A.D., Kancelaria Tajna Wielkiego Księcia Konstantina, no. 40a, 40b, 63.
6. G. Pisarevskii, *Iz istorii kongressovogo Tsarstva Pol'skogo* (From the history of the Polish Congress Kingdom), (Smolensk, 1926), p. 13.
7. A.G.A.D., Kanceleria Nowosilcowa, no. 564, "O tainom obshchestve otkryvshemsia mezhdu uchenikami varshavskago i krakovskago universitetov pod nazvaniem Bratstva Burschov" (On the secret society uncovered between the students of Warsaw and Cracow universities under the name: *Burschenschaft*), Novosil'tsov to Alexander, September 21, 1821.
8. Więckowska, *Opozycja Liberalna*, p. 108.
9. A.G.A.D., K.N., no. 564, Novosil'tsov to Alexander, November 25, 1821.

10. *Ibid.*
11. Więckowska, *Opozycja Liberalna*, pp. 108-109.
12. B.P.P., Archiwum Wielkiego Księcia Konstantego, no. 340, Novosil'tsov to Alexander, December 29, 1821.
13. B.P.P., A.W.K.K., no. 340, Novosil'tsov to Alexander, December 29, 1821; Novosil'tsov to Alexander, January 9, 1822.
14. A.G.A.D., K.N., no. 564, Novosil'tsov to Alexander, January 19, 1822; B.P.P., A.W.W.K., no. 340, Novosil'tsov to Alexander, January 9, 1822.
15. Pisarevskii, *Iz istorii*, pp. 14-15.
16. B.P.P., A.W.K.K., no. 340, The proclamation dissolving the Kalisz Council, countersigned by the Treasury Minister, Lubecki, July 23, 1822.
17. A.G.A.D., Protokoły Rady Administracyjnej, January 13, 1824.
18. Więckowska, *Opozycja Liberalna*, p. 112; Ryszard Przelaskowski, *Sejm Warszawski r. 1825* (The 1825 Warsaw Sejm), (Warsaw, 1929), p. 56.
19. T. Mencel, "Udział społeczeństwa w życiu politycznym Królestwa Polskiego w latach 1815-1830" (The participation of the public in the political life of the Polish Kingdom in 1815-1830), *Przegląd Historyczny*, 4 (1968): 653.
20. Quoted in *ibid.*
21. *Ibid.*, pp. 653-654.
22. *Ibid.*, p. 654.
23. Przelakowski, *Sejm 1825*, pp. 63-64.
24. *Ibid.*, pp. 58-65; Więckowska, *Opozycja Liberalna*, pp. 102-103; Mencel, "Udział społeczeństwa," pp. 654-656.
25. Quoted in Więckowska, *Opozycja Liberalna*, p. 102.
26. Quoted in Pisarevskii, *Is istorii*, p. 18.
27. *Ibid.*
28. Constantine to Alexander, March 31, 1822, reproduced in *ibid.*, pp. 35-37.
29. Przelaskowski, *Sejm 1825*, pp. 24-25.
30. A.G.A.D., P.R.A., September 10, 1822.
31. Constantine to Alexander, March 31, 1822, reproduced in Pisarevskii, *Iz istorii*, pp. 35-37.
32. Przelaskowski, *Sejm 1825*, pp. 82-84.
33. *Ibid.*, pp. 84-85; Szymon Askenazy, *Łukasiński*, 2nd ed., 2 vols. (Warsaw, 1929), 1: 189-190. For Alexander's proposed project consult "Proekt adresa predstavitelei Tsarstva Pol'skago, sobstvennoruchno pisannyi Imperatorom Aleksandrom I" (Project of an address of the Polish Kingdom's representatives, hand written by Emperor Alexander I), *Russkaia Starina*, 34 (1882): 256-257.

34. *Dziennik Praw Królestwa Polskiego* (Bulletin of the Laws of the Kingdom of Poland), 49 vols. (Warsaw, 1815-1849), 9: 90 ff. Marceli Handelsman, *Konsytyucje Polskie 1791-1921* (Polish constitutions, 1791-1921), (Warsaw, 1922), pp. 66-67; N.K. Shilder, *Imperator Aleksandr I, ego zhizn i tsarstvovanie* (Emperor Alexander I, his life and reign), 4 vols. (St. Petersburg, 1904), 4: 481.

35. Jan Zdzitowiecki, *Ziążę-Minister Franciszek Zawery Drucki-Lubecki, 1778-1846* (Prince-Minister Franciszek Zawery Drucki-Lubecke), (Warsaw, 1948), p. 507.

36. A. Pogodin, "Pol'sha pered vosstaniem 1830 g." (Poland before the 1830 insurrection), *Russkoe Bogatstvo*, 9 (1912): 48-49.

37. Więckowskia, *Opozycja Liberalna*, pp. 111-112.

38. The constitution granted the Senate the right to expel any House members "finding themselves in an accused state" at the time the Sejm gathered.

39. Więckowska, *Opozycja Liberalna*, pp. 125-128.

40. Przelaskowski, *Sejm 1825*, pp. 88-91.

41. *Ibid.*, pp. 93-94, 97; Więckowska, *Opozycja Liberalna*, pp. 118-120; Pogodin, "Pol'sha pered vosstaniem," p. 49.

42. Schmidt (Prussian consul at Warsaw) to Bernstorff, October 4, 7, 17, 18, 1819, published in Szymon Askenazy, *Dwa stulecia, XVIII-XIX* (Two centuries, XVIII-XIX), 2nd ed., 2 vols. (Warsaw, 1903), 1: 463, 561; M. Kukiel, *Dzieje Polski porozbiorowe* (History of Poland after the partitions), 2nd ed. (London, 1963), p. 195.

43. Alexander to Arakcheev, May 23, 1825, published in Shilder, *Imperator Aleksandr I*, 4: 334.

44. Alexander's closing speech to the 1825 Sejm, June 13, 1825, *ibid.*, 4: 332; N. Gąsiorowska, *Wolność druku w Królestwie Kongresowem* (Freedom of the press in the Congress Kingdom), (Warsaw, 1916), p. 204; Leonard Chodźko (le comte d'Angeberg), *Receuil des traités conventions et actes diplomatiques concernant la Pologne 1762-1862* (Paris, 1862), pp. 750-751.

45. Hanna Dylągowa, *Towarzystwo Patriotyczne i sąd sejmowy, 1821-1829* (The Patriotic Society and the Sejm court, 1821-1829), (Warsaw, 1970), pp. 33, 173-174.

46. Novosil'tsov to Alexander, May 24, 1821, published in Askenazy, *Łukasiński*, 1: 409.

47. A.G.A.D., K.N., no. 565, "O masonskikh lozhakh, arkhivakh, i bibliotekakh v Tsarstve Pol'slom i o masonskom tainom obshchestve pod nazvaniem: Natsional'noe Masonstvo" (About masonic lodges, archives

and libraries in the Polish Kingdom and about the secret masonic society named: National Masons), Novosil'tsov to Alexander, September 29, 1821.
48. A.G.A.D., K.N., no. 486, "O sushchestvovanii tainago obshchestva v Germanii, imeiushchago tselei revoliutsionnykh" (On the existence of a secret society in Germany having revolutionary aims), Constantine to Novosil'tsov, June 24, 1821.
49. A.G.A.D., K.N., no. 486, Novosil'tsov to Alexander, June 29, 1821.
50. *Ibid.*, Novosil'tsov to Alexander, July 6, July 29, August 17, November 10, 1821.
51. A.G.A.D., K.N., no. 564, Novosil'tsoa to Alexander, August 17, 24, September 3, 21, November 2, 10, 1821; January 7, 19, March 24, 1822. Aleksander Kamiński, *Polskie zwiąska młodzieży* (Polish youth societies), (Warsaw, 1963), pp. 151-152, 211-218.
52. A.G.A.D., K.N., no. 564, Novosil'tsov to Alexander, September 9, 1821.
53. *Ibid.*, Novosil'tsov to Alexander, September 3, 21, 1821; A.G.A.D., K.N., no. 583, "O sushchestvovanii tainago obshchestva pod nazvaniem' Pantakoina" (About the existence of a secret society named: Pantakoina), Novosil'tsov to Alexander, February 3, 1823; B.P.P., A.W.K.K., no. 340, Novosil'tsov to Alexander, January 9, 1822.
54. Novosil'tsov to Alexander, May 3, 1822, published in Przelaskowski, *Sejm 1825*, p. 69.
55. A.G.A.D., P.R.A., November 6, 1821.
56. A.G.A.D., K.N., no. 579, "Ob otkrytom soiuze vol'nykh poliakov i tainom politicheskom soiuze v gorode Krakove" (About the discovery of a union of free Poles and a secret political society in Cracow), Novosil'tsov to Alexander, July 26, 1822.
57. Askenazy, *Łukasiński*, 2: 109-112, 384-386. For the fate of Polish Freemasonry see: Ludwik Hass, *"'Diaspora' polskiego wolnomularstwa, 1821-1908"* (The "Diaspora" of Polish Freemasonry), *Przegląd Historyczny*, 2 (1971), 197-224.
58. A.G.A.D., P.R.A., July 9, 1822.
59. A.G.A.D., Komisja Rządowa Spraw Wewnętrznych i Policji no. 7282; the "loyalty oath" matter, May 13, 1822.
60. B.P.P., A.W.K.K., Novosil'tsov to Alexander, January 9, 1822; A.G.A.D., K.N., no. 564, Novosil'tsov to Alexander, September 3, 1821, January 19, 1822; K.N., no. 583, Novosil'tsov to Alexander, August 2, 1822.
61. A.G.A.D., K.N., no. 823, "Delo o sushchestvovanii v Varshave

mezhdu studentami i drugimi molodymi liudami tainom obshchestve vol'nykh poliakov" (The matter about the existence in Warsaw among students and other young people of a secret society of free Poles), Heltman's confession.

62. Kamiński, *Polskie związki*, pp. 146-149.
63. A.G.A.D., K.N., no. 823, Heltman's confession.
64. Kamiński, *Polskie związki*, pp. 152-154.
65. *Ibid.*, pp. 154-155.
66. *Ibid.*, pp. 155-160.
67. Since the late 19th century, detailed materials on the Wilno Filomats have been published. Undoubtedly, the most useful source is the *Archiwum Filomatów*, a ten volume collection of primary sources still in publication. Recent Polish historiography, reflecting the current regime's ideological precepts, has imparted to the Filomats a "progressive-revolutionary" character not at all justified by the evidence. Even the strongest propagators of his position frequently stumble over the historical evidence. See: Jerzy Szacki, *Z historii rozwoju ideologii szlachecko-rewolucynej w Polsce drugiego i trzeciego dziesięciolecia XIX wieku* (From the history of the evolution of gentry-revolutionary ideology in Poland during the second and third decades of the 19th century), (Warsaw, 1955). For the Filomats' adverse comments about Warsaw life in general, and student activity there in particular, consult: *Archiwum Filomatów*, Part I: *Korespondencja, 1815-1823* (Correspondence, 1815-1823), Jan Czubek, ed., 5 vols. (Cracow, 1913), 1: 89, 2: 104, 3: 167-168; 4: 56-59, 90-91, 102, 136-137, 151, 170.
68. A.G.A.D., K.T.K., no. 1. This folio contains the November, 1822, and February 20, 1823, reports of the Russian spy stationed in Western Europe, who used the pseudonym "Chevegrois-Schweizer."
69. B.P.P., A.W.K.K., Novosil'tsov to Alexander, July 12, 1823.
70. Kamiński, *Polskie związki*, p. 370.
71. Czartoryski to Constantine, May 30, 1823, Adam Czartoryski, *Alexandre I et le prince Czartoryski; correspondance particulière et conversations' 1801-1823*, with an Introduction by Charles de Mazade, 2 vols. (Paris, 1865), 2: 351-353.
72. Czartoryski to Constantine, without date, *ibid.*, 2: 354-368.
73. Czartoryski to Alexander, 1823, *ibid.*, 2: 330-331.
74. For Czartoryski's career as Curator of the Wilno Education District and his considerable success in promoting Polish cultural activities in the western *gubernii* see: Daniel Beauvois, "Adam Jerzy Czartoryski jako kurator wileńskiego okręgu naukowego" (Adam George Czartoryski

as Curator of the Wilno Education District), *Przegląd Historyczny*, 1 (1974): 61-85.

75. Joachim Lelewel, *Nowosilcow w Wilnie w roku szkolnym 1823/4* (Novosil'tsov at Wilno in the school year 1823/4), reprinted in M.H. Serejski, et al., eds., *Joachim Lelewel, Dzieła* (Lelewel's Works), 10 vols. (Warsaw, 1957-1972), 8: 545-606. Lelewel's description of the Wilno purge, although decidedly anti-tsarist and anti-Novosil'tsov, nevertheless manages to marshal the facts and to present first-hand observations. The author, a leading Polish historian and liberal activist who later played a key role during the 1830-31 insurrection, was one of the four professors expelled from Wilno University on the strength of the tsar's August, 1824, *ukaz*.

76. Serejski, et al., eds., *Lelewel, Dzieła*, 8: 557-560, 573-577.

77. *Ibid.*, 8: 564. Alexander Kraushar in his *Bajkow*, 2nd ed., (Cracow, 1913), publishes excerpts from Bajkow's diary. Leon S. Bajkow, Novosil'- tsoa's secretary and cohort in carousing, describes Novosil'tsov as tipsily conducting an academic examination, drunkenly accosting prostitutes and maliciously inciting Wilno students at a picnic honoring the emperor's name's day to beat up and rob Jews who arrived on the scene to sell pastries. Another contemporary, Natalia Kicka, *Pamiętniki* (Memoirs), Józef Dutkiewicz, ed., (Warsaw, 1972), pp. 35-36, describes Novosil'tsov's visit to her father's manor during which the new curator drunkenly boasted that henceforth Polish students would only learn crafts since this training would then enable them to work at factories he planned to establish at his Słonim estate.

78. Serejski, et al., eds., *Lelewel, Dzieła*, 8: 577-581.

79. Kamiński, *Polskie związki*, pp. 278-279, 287-288, 373. Józef Bieliński, *Uniwersytet Wileński, 1579-1831* (The University of Wilno, 1579-1831), 3 vols. (Cracow, 1899-1900), 3: 8-12, first formulated the hypothesis that Novosil'tsov did not pursue a policy of Russification, but only desired to purge the Lithuanian Educational District of liberals and "revolutionaries."

80. Kamiński, *Polskie związki*, pp. 128-129, 132-134, 160-161, *passim*; Dylągowa, *Towarzystwo Patriotyczne*, pp. 25-29; Marceli Handelsman, *Francja-Polska, 1795-1845* (France-Poland, 1795-1845), 2 vols. (Warsaw, 1926), 2: 98-100, 108.

81. Kamiński, *Polskie związki*, pp. 183-191; 533-536. Note that Professor Kamiński devotes less than a dozen pages of his very extensive work to student secret societies at the time of the November insurrection.

SELECTED BIBLIOGRAPHY

I. MANUSCRIPT SOURCES

Archiwum Główne Akt Dawnych w Warszawie (The Central Archive of Old Records in Warsaw), *A.G.A.D.*

K.N. Kancelaria Nowosilcowa (Novosil'tsov's Chancellery).
K.T.K. Kancelaria Tajna Wielkiego Księcia Konstantina (Grand Duke Constantine's Secret Chancellery).
P.R.A. Protokoły Rady Administracyjnej Królestwa Polskiego (Minutes of the Polish Kingdom's Administrative Council).
R.S. Rąda Stanu Królestwo Polskiego (State Council of the Kingdom of Poland).
K.R.S.W. i P. Komisja Rządowa Spraw Wewnętrznych i Policji (The Interior Ministry).

Biblioteka Polska w Paryżu (The Polish Library in Paris), *B.P.P.*
A.W.K.K. Archiwum Wielkiego Księcia Konstantego (Grand Duke Constantine's Archive), folio no. 340.
R.P.A.C. Różne Pisma Adama Czartoryskiego (Various Letters of Adam Czartoryski), folio no. 54.

Biblioteka Czartoryskich w Krakowie, Dział Rękopisów (The Library of the Czartoryskis in Cracow, Manuscript Division).

II. PUBLISHED SOURCES

Archiwum Filomatów (The Filomats Archive). Part 1, *Korespondencja, 1815-1823* (Correspondence, 1815-1823), ed. Jan Czubek. 5 vols. Cracow: 1913.
Bobkowska, Wanda (ed.) *Korespondencja Metternicha w sprawie Uniwersytetu Krakowskiego, 1820-1829* (Metternich's Correspondence on the Matter of the University of Cracow, 1820-1829). Cracow: 1935.
Chodźko, Leonard (le comte d'Angeberg). *Receuil des traités, conventions et actes diplomatiques concernant la Pologne 1762-1862*. Paris: 1862.
Czartoryski, Prince Adam. *Alexandre I et le prince Czartoryski. correspondence particuliére et conversations, 1801-1823*. With an introduction by Charles Mazade. 2 vols. Paris: 1865.

Czartoryski, Prince Adam. *Mémoires du Prince Adam Czartoryski et correspondence avec l'empereur Alexandre Ier,* ed. Charles Mazade. 2 vols. Paris: 1887.

Czartoryski, Prince Adam. *Memoirs of Prince Adam Czartoryski,* trans. and ed. Adam Gielgud. 2 vols. 2nd ed. London: 1888.

Dziennik posiedzeń Izby Poselskiey w czasie Seymu Królestwa Polskiego w dniu 1820 odbytego (Bulletin of the Sessions of the House of Representatives at the Time of the Sejm of the Kingdom of Poland Held in 1820). 2 vols. Warsaw: 1820.

Dyarjusz Seymu Krolestwa Polskiego 1818 (Diary of the 1818 Sejm of the Kingdom of Poland). 3 vols. Warsaw: 1818.

Dziennik Praw Królestwa Polskiego (Bulletin of the Laws of the Kingdom of Poland). 49 vols. Warsaw: 1815-1849.

Gerber, R. (ed.). *Księga protokłow Rady Ogólnej Uniwersytetu Warszawskiego (1817-1819)* (The Minutes of Warsaw University's General Council (1817-1819)). Warsaw: 1958.

Handelsman, Marceli. (ed.) *Konstytucje Polskie 1791-1921* (Polish Constitutions 1791-1921). Warsaw: 1922.

Kieniewicz, Stefan (ed.). *Przemiany społeczne i gospodarcze w Królestwie Polskim (1815-1830)* (Social and Economic Transformations in the Polish Kingdom (1815-1830)). Warsaw: 1951.

Lutostański, K. *Recueil des actes diplomatiques* Vol. 1. *Traités, et documents concernant la Pologne.* Paris: 1918.

"Mnenie Kapodistrii o tsenzure v Tsarstve Pol'skom" (The Opinion of Capo d'Istria about Censorship in the Kingdom of Poland). *Russkaia Starina,* 116 (October-December 1903): 446-455.

Nesselrode, Count Charles. *Lettres et papiers du chancelier comte de Nesselrode.* 11 vols. Paris: 1904-1912.

Niemojowski, Wincenty. *Głos posła Kaliskiego na Sejmie Królestwa Polskiego (The Voice of a Kalisz Deputy at the Sejm of the Polish Kingdom).* Poznan: 1818.

"Obrazovanie Verkhovnago Vremennago Sovieta, uchrezhdennago dlia uprav leniia Varshavskim Gertsogstvom" (Formation of the Supreme Provisional Council, Established for Governing the Duchy of Warsaw). *Russkii Arkhiv,* 9 (1871): 1570-1578.

"Pis'ma A.A. Zakrevskii k P.D. Kiselevy" (Letters of A.A. Zakrevskii to P.D. Kiselev). *Sbornik Imperatorskago Russkago Istoricheskago Obshchestva,* 78: 191-192.

"Pis'ma A. P. Ermolov k A.A. Zakrevskomu" (Letters of A.P. Ermolov to A.A. Zakrevskii). *Sbornik Imperatorskago Russkago Istoricheskago Obshchestva,* 73:279-282.

"Pis'ma P.D. Kiselev k A.A. Zakrevskom" (Letters of P.D. Kiselev to A.A. Zakrevskii). *Sbornik Imperatorskago Russkago Istoricheskago Obshchestva,* 78: 1-2.

"Pis'ma Speranskago k A.A. Stolypinu" (Letters of Speranskii to A.A. Stolypin), *Russkii Arkhiv* (1869):1682-1708.

"Proekt adresa predstavitelei Tsarstva Pol'skago, sobstvennoruchno pisannyi Imperatorom Aleksandrom I" (Project of an Address of the Polish Kingdom's Representatives, Handwritten by the Emperor Alexander I). *Russkaia Starina,* 34 (1882):256-257.

Raeff, Marc (ed.). *The Decembrist Movement.* Englewood Cliffs, New Jersey: 1966.

Smolka, S. (ed.). *Korespondencya Lubeckiego z Ministrami Sekretarzami Stanu Ignacym Sobolewskim i Stefanem Grabowskim* (Lubecki's Correspondence with the Ministers-Secretaries of State, Ignacy Sobolewski and Stefan Grabowski). 4 vols. Cracow: 1909.

Tsvietaev, D. "Novosil'tsov o konstitutsii Tsarstva Pol'skago" (Novosil'tsov about the Constitution of the Kingdom of Poland). *Russkaia Starina,* 121 (January-March, 1905):599-605.

Vosstanie dekabristov. Materialy (The Decembrist Uprising. Materials), eds. M.N. Pokrovskii, M. Nechkina. 1-13 vols. Moscow: 1925-1979.

"Vsepoddannieishaia zapiska N.N. Novosil'tsova Aleksandru I" (A Most Devoted Memorandum of N.N. Novosil'tsov to Alexander I). *Russkaia Starina,* 35 (1882):142-144.

Walsh, Warren B. (ed.). *Readings in Russian History.* 3 vols. 4 ed. Syracuse: 1963.

Zbiór przepisów administracyjnych Królestwa Polskiego (Collection of Administrative Regulations of the Kingdom of Poland). "Wydział Oświecenia" (Education Ministry). 6 vols. Warsaw: 1866.

III. Memoirs

Dembowski, L. *Moje wspomnienia* (My Recollections). 2 vols. St. Petersburg: 1898.

Fiszerowa, Wirydianna. *Dzieje Moje Własne* (My Own History). trans. Edward Raczyński. London: 1975.

Harro-Harring, P. (pseud.). *Poland Under the Domination of Russia.* London: 1831.

"Iz Vospominanii Mikhailovskago-Danilevskago" (From the Memoirs of Mikhailovskii-Danilevskii). *Russkaia Starina, 91 (1897):69-102.*

Kicka, Natalia. *Pamiętniki* (Memoirs), ed. Józef Dutkiewicz. Warsaw: 1972.

Komorowski, Ignacy A. *Wspomnienia podchorążego z czasów W. Ks. Konstantego* (Recollections of a Cadet Officer from the Times of Grand Duke Constantine). Warsaw: 1900.
Koźmian, Andrzej E. *Wspomnienia* Recollections). 2 vols. Poznan: 1867.
Koźmian, Kajetan. *Pamiętniki* (Memoirs). 3 vols. Cracow: 1865.
Kraushar, Alexander (ed.). *Bajkow*. 2nd ed. Cracow: 1913.
Kukol'nik, P. (Anti-Tsiprinus). "Vospominanie o Novosil'tsov" (Recollections of Novosil'tsov). *Russkii Arkhiv* (1873):203-0200.
Lelewel, Prot. *Pamiętniki i diariusz domu naszego* (Memoirs and Diary of Our Household), ed. Irena Lelewel-Friemannowa. Wrocław: 1966.
Metternich, Prince Klemens. *Memoirs of Prince Metternich,* trans. A. Napier, ed., Richard Metternich. 5 vols. New York: 1881.
Morawski, Stanisław. *Kilka lat młodości mojej w Wilne (1818-1825) (Several Years of My Youth in Wilno, 1818-1825)*,eds. Adam Czartoryski and Henryk Mościcki. Warsaw: 1959.
Moroilles, Alexander. *Mémoires du Comte de Moriolles sur l'émigration, la Pologne et la cour du Grand-Duc Constantine (1789-1833).* 2nd ed. Paris: 1902.
Niemcewicz, Julian. *Pamiętniki* (Memoirs). 2 vols. Poznan: 1871.
Niemcewicz, Julian. *Pamiętniki czasów moich* (Memoirs of My Times). 2 vols. Warsaw: 1957.
Ogiński, Michael C. *Memoires de Michel Ogiński sur la Pologne et les Polonais depuis 1788 jusqu'à la fin de 1815.* 4 vols. Paris: 1827.
Orlov, M.F. "Primiechaniia M.F. Orlova, napisannyia v 1835" (M.F. Orlov's Comments, Written in 1835). *Russkaia Starina,* 20 (1877):657-662.
Potocka, Anna. *Pamiętniki* (Memoirs). Warsaw: 1898.
Przeclawski, C.A. (Tsirprinus). "Kaleidoskop vospominanii" (Kaleidoscope of Recollections). *Russkii Arkhiv* (1872):1705-1760.
Viazemskii, P.A. *Polnoe sobranie sochinenii Kniazia P.A. Viazemskago* (The Complete Collected Works of Prince P.A. Viazemskii), Vol. 1, *Avtobiograficheskoe vvedenie* (Autobiographical Preface), ed. S.D. Sherementev. St. Petersburg: 1878-1896.

IV. Contemporary Works

Constant, Benjamin. *Réflexions sur les constitutions.* Paris: 1816.
Gnorowski, S.B. *Insurrection of Poland in 1830-31; and the Russian Rule Preceding It Since 1815.* London: 1839.
Hoffman, Karol. *Rzut oka na stan polityczny Królestwa Polskiego pod panowaniem Rossyjskiem* (A Glance at the Political State of the Kingdom of Poland under Russian Rule). Warsaw: 1831.

Karamzin, N.M. *Karamzin's Memoir on Ancient and Modern Russia*, trans. and ed. Richard Pipes. New York: 1969.

Lelewel, Joachim. *Dzieła* (Works), ed. M.H. Serejski, et al., Vol. 8: "Nowosilcow w Wilnie w r. 1823/1824" (Novosil'tsov in Wilno in 1823/1824), pp. 545-606. Warsaw: 1961.

Niemojowski, Wincenty. *O monarchij konstytucynej i rękomach władz publicznych* (Con Constitutional Monarchy and the Guarantees of Public Authorities). Warsaw: 1831.

———. *O władzach publicznych w monarchij konstytucynej* (On Public Authorities in a Constitutional Monarchy). Warsaw: 1820.

Turgenev, Nicholas I. *La Russie et les russes*. 3 vols. Brussels: 1847.

Secondary Works

A. Books

Artz, Frederick B. *Reaction and Revolution, 1814-1832*. New York: 1934.

Askenazy, Szymon. *Dwa stulecia XVIII-XIX* (Two Centuries XVIII-XIX). 2 vols. 2nd ed. Warsaw: 1903.

———. *Łukasiński*. 2 vols. 2nd ed. Warsaw: 1929.

———. *Ministeryum Wielhorskiego 1815-1816* (Wielhorski's Ministry 1815-1816). Warsaw: 1898.

———. *Rosya-Polska 1815-1830* (Russia-Poland 1815-1830). Lwów: 1907.

———. *Szkice i portrety* (Sketches and Portraits). Warsaw: 1937.

Beauvois, Daniel. *Lumière et Société en Europe de l'Est: L'université de Vilna et les écoles polonaises de l'empire russe (1803-1832)*. 2 vols. Lille: 1977.

Beylin, Karolina. *Piętnaście lat Warszawy (1800-1815)* (Warsaw's Fifteen Years, 1800-1815). Warsaw: 1976.

Bieliński, Józef. *Królewski Uniwersytet Warszawski* (The Royal Warsaw University). 3 vols. Warsaw: 1907-1912.

———. *Uniwersytet Wileński* (Wilno University). 3 vols. Cracow: 1899-1900.

Black, J.L. *Nicholas Karamzin and Russian Society in the Nineteenth Century*. Toronto and Buffalo: 1975.

Blackwell, William L. "Alexander I and Poland: The Foundations of His Polish Policy." Ph. D. dissertation. Princeton University, 1959.

Bloch, Czesław. *General Ignacy Prądzyński, 1792-1850*. Warsaw: 1974.

Bogdanovich, Modest I. *Istoriia tsarstvovaniia Imperatora Aleksandra I* (History of the Reign of Emperor Alexander I). 6 vols. St. Petersburg: 1869-1871.

Bojasinski, Józef. *Rządy tymczasowe w Królestwie Polskiem, Maj-grudzień 1815* (Provisional Governments in the Polish Kingdom, May-December 1815). Warsaw: 1902.

Bortnowski, Władysław. *Kaliszanie: Kartki z dziejów Królestwa Polskiego* (The Kaliszites: Pages from the History of the Polish Kingdom). Warsaw: 1976.

―――――. *Wielki Książę Konstanty podczas powstania listopadowego* (Grand Duke Constantine during the November Insurrection). Warsaw: 1956.

Cieszkowski, S. *Aleksandr I a konstytucya* (Alexander I and the Constitution). Warsaw: 1909.

Dylągowa, Hanna. *Towarzystwo Patriotyczne i sąd sejmowy, 1821-1829* (The Patriotic Society and the Sejm Court, 1821-1829). Warsaw: 1970.

Feldman, Wilhelm. *Dzieje Polskiej myśli politycznej* (History of Polish Political Thought). Cracow: 1913.

Gąsiorowska, Natalia. *Wolność druku w Królestwie Kongresowem, 1815-30* (Freedom of the Press in the Congress Kingdom, 1815-1830). Warsaw: 1916.

Gołba, Zdzisław. *Rowój władz Królestwa Polskiego w okresie powstania listopadowego* (The Development of the Government of the Polish Kingdom in the Period of the November Uprising). Wroclaw: 1971.

Grimsted, Patricia Kennedy. *The Foreign Ministers of Alexander I*. Berkeley and Los Angeles: 1969.

Handelsman, Marceli. *Adam Czartoryski*. 3 vols. Warsaw: 1948-1950.

―――――. *Francja-Polska, 1795-1845* (France-Poland, 1795-1845). 2 vols. Warsaw: 1926.

―――――. *Kryzys r. 1821 w Królestwie Polskim* (The 1821 Crisis in the Kingdom of Poland). Lwów: 1939.

―――――. *Les idées françaises et la mentalité politique en Pologne au XIXe siècle*. Paris: 1927.

Ihnatowicz, Ireneusz. *Burżuazja Warszawska* (The Warsaw Bourgeoisie). Warsaw: 1972.

Kamiński, Alexander. *Polskie związki młodzieży 1804-1831* (Polish Youth Societies). Warsaw: 1963.

Karnovich, E.P. *Tsesarevich Konstantin Pavlovich*. St. Petersburg: 1899.

Kieniewicz, Stefan. *The Emancipation of the Polish Peasantry*. Chicago: 1969.

Kieniewicz, Stefan. *Historia Polski, 1795-1918* (History of Poland, 1795-1918). Warsaw: 1969.

———— and W. Kula (eds.). Vol. 2: *Historia Polski* (The History of Poland). Warsaw: 1960.

Kissinger, Henry A. *A World Restored.* New York: 1964.

Kizeweter, A.A. *Istoricheskie ocherki* (Historical Essays). Moscow: 1912.

Koberdowa, Irena. *Między Pierwszą a Drugą Rzecząpospolitą* (Between the First and Second Republic). Warsaw: 1976.

Koelichenówna, Stefanja. *Przejawy reakcji w działalności Towarzystwa do Dsiąg Elementarnych (1821-1830)* (Indications of Reaction in the Activity of the Society for Elementary Textbooks). Warsaw: 1929.

Kozłowski, W.M. *Autonomia Królestwa Polskiego (1815-1830)* (Autonomy of the Polish Kingdom (1815-1830)). Warsaw: 1907.

Kraushar, Alexander. *Miscellanea historyczne* (Historical Miscellanea). Vol. 15: *Panta Koina.* Warsaw: 1907.

————. *Miscellanea historyczne* (Historical Miscellanea). Vol. 54: *Senator Nowosilcow i cenzura za Królestwa Kongresowego (1819-1829)* (Senator Novosil'tsov and Censorship for the Congress Kingdom (1819-1829)). Cracow: 1911.

Kucharzewski, Jan. *The Origins of Modern Russia.* New York: 1948.

Kukiel, Marion. *Czartoryski and European Unity 1770-1861.* Princeton: 1955.

————. *Dzieje Polski porozbiorowe, 1795-1921* (History of Poland after the Partitions). 2nd ed. London: 1963.

Leslie, R.F. *Polish Politics and the Revolution of November 1830.* London: 1956.

Limanowski, Bolesław. *Historia demokracji Polskiej* (History of Polish Democracy). 3rd ed. Warsaw: 1946.

Łojek, Jerzy. *Studia nad prasą i opinią publiczną w Królestwie Polskim, 1815-1830* (Studies on the Press and Public Opinion in the Polish Kingdom, 1815-1830). Warsaw: 1966.

McConnell, Alan. *Tsar Alexander I.* New York: 1970.

Małachowski-Łempicki, S. *Raporty szpega Mackrotta o Wilnomularstwie Polskim 1819-1822* (Reports of the Spy Mackrott about Polish Freemasonry 1819-1822). Warsaw: 1931.

Manteuffel, Tadeusz. *Centralne władze oświatowe na terenie b. Królestwa Kongresowego (1807-1915)* (Central Educational Authorities on the Land of the Former Congress Kingdom (1807-1915)). Warsaw: 1929.

Manteufflowa, Marja. *J.K. Szaniawski: ideologia i działalność 1815-1830* (J.K. Szaniawski. Ideology and Activity 1815-1830). Warsaw: 1936.

Mazour, Anatole G. *The First Russian Revolution.* Stanford: 1937.
Mel'gunov, S.P. *Dela i liude Aleksandrovskogo vremeni* (Affairs and People of Alexander's Time). Berlin: 1923.
Mościcki, Henryk. *Pod znakiem orła i pogoni* (Under the Banner of the Eagle and the Hunt). Lwów: 1923.
Nechkina, M.V. *Russia in the Nineteenth Century,* trans. Bernard Pares and Oliver J. Frederiksen. Ann Arbor: 1953.
Nicolson, Harold. *The Congress of Vienna: A Study in Allied Unity: 1812-1822.* London: 1946.
Nikolai Mikhailovich, Grand Duke. *L'Empereur Alexandre Ier.* 2 vols. St. Petersburg: 1912.
———. *Graf Pavel Aleksandrovich Stroganov* (Count Paul Alexander Stroganov). 3 vols. St. Petersburg: 1903.
Offmański, Mieczysław. *Królestwo Polskie (1815-1830)* (The Kingdom of Poland (1815-1830)). Warsaw: 1907.
Olivier, Daria. *Alexandre Ier; Prince des Illusions.* Paris: 1973.
Ol'shaskii. P. *Dekabristy i Pol'skoe natsional'na-o*svobaditel'noe *dvizhenie* (The Decembrists and the Polish National Liberation Movement). Moscow: 1959.
Palmer, Alan. *Alexander I: Tsar of War and Peace.* London: 1974.
Pisarevskii, George. *Iz istorii Kongressovogo Tsarstva Pol'skogo* (From the History of the Polish Congress Kingdom). Smolensk: 1926.
Przelaskowski, Ryszard. *Sejm Warszawski r. 1825* (The 1825 Warsaw Sejm). Warsaw: 1929.
Pypin, A.N. *Obshchestvennoe dvizhenie v Rossii pri Aleksandr I* (Social Movement in Russia under Alexander I). 3rd ed. St. Petersburg: 1900.
Raeff, Marc. *Michael Speransky, Statesman of Imperial Russia, 1772-1839.* The Hague: 1957.
Rembowski, Alexander. *Pisma Aleksandra Rembowskiego* (The Writings of Alexander Rembowski). Vol. 1: *Nasze poglądy polityczne w 1818* (Our Political Views in 1818). Warsaw: 1901.
Rostocki, Władysław. *Korpus w gęsie pióra uzbrojony: Urzędnicy warszawscy, ich życie i praca w Księstwie Warszawskim i Królestwie Polskim do roku 1831* (A Corps Armed with a Quill Pen: Warsaw Officials, their Life and Work in the Duchy of Warsaw and the Polish Kingdom until 1831). Warsaw: 1972.
Shcherbatov, Prince M.M. *General-fel'dmarshal Kniaz Paskevich* (General Field-marshal Prince Paskevich). 7 vols. St. Petersburg: 1888.
Shilder, N.K. *Imperator Aleksandr I, ego zhizn i tsarstvovanie* (Emperor Alexander I, his Life and Reign). 4 vols. St. Petersburg: 1904.

Siegel, S. *Ceny w Warszawie w latach 1816-1914* (Prices in Warsaw, 1816-1914). Poznan: 1949.
Skowronek, Jerzy. *Antynapoleońskie koncepcje Czartoryskiego* (Czartoryski's Anti-Napoleonic Conceptions). Warsaw: 1969.
Smolka, S. *Polityka Lubeckiego przed powstaniem listopadowym* (Lubecki's Policy before the November Insurrection). 2 vols. Cracow: 1907.
Szacki, Jerzy. *Z historii rozwoju ideologii szlachecko-rewolucynej w Polsce drugiego i trzeciego dziesięciolecia XIX wieku* (From the History of the Evolution of Gentry-revolutionary Ideology in Poland during the Second and Third Decades of the Nineteenth Century). Warsaw: 1955.
Tokarz, Wacław. *Armia Królestwa Polskiego (1815-1830)* (The Army of the Polish Kingdom (1815-1830)). Piotrków: 1917.
Vernadsy, George. *La charte constitutionelle de l'empire Russe de l'an 1820*. Paris: 1933.
Wandycz, Piotr S. *The Lands of Partitioned Poland, 1795-1918*. Seattle and London: 1974.
Wawrykowa, Maria. *Ruch studencki w Niemczech, 1815-1825* (The Student Movement in Germany, 1815-1825). Warsaw: 1969.
Webster, Sir Charles. *The Congress of Vienna*. New York: 1966.
Więckowska, Helena. *Opozycja Liberalna w Królestwie Kongresowem 1815-1830* (The Liberal Opposition in the Congress Kingdom, 1815-1830). Warsaw: 1925.
Wołoszyński, Ryszard W. *Polsko-rosyjskie związki w naukach społecznych, 1801-1830* (Polish-Russian Contacts in the Social Sciences). Warsaw: 1974.
Zajewski, Władysław. *Józef Wybicki*. Warsaw: 1977.
Zdzitowiecki, Jan. *Xiążę-Minister Franciszek Xawery Drucki-Lubecki*(Princiszek Xawery Drucki-Lubecki). Warsaw: 1948.

B. Articles and Periodicals

Askenazy, Szymon. "Dwie rozmowy w Belwederze" (Two Conversations at Belvedere), in *Wczasy Historyczne* (Historical Holidays). Warsaw: 1910, pp. 228-247.
Beauvois, Daniel. "Adam Jerzy Czartoryski jako kurator wileńskiego okręgu naukowego" (Adam George Czartoryski as Curator of the Wilno Education District). *Przegląd Historyczny*, 1 (1974): 61-85.
Black, J.L. "Interpretations of Poland in Nineteenth Century Russian Nationalist-Conservative Historiography." *Polish Review*, 17 (1972), 4: 20-41.

Braunsteinówna, Helena Więckowska. "Charakterystyka braci Niemojawskich" (Characterization of the Niemojowski Brothers). *Przegląd Historyczny* (1922): 61-85.

Bujarski, George T. "Polish Liberalism, 1815-1823." *Polish Review*, 17 (1972), 2: 3-37.

Bychkov, I.A. "Aleksandr I i ego priblizhennye do epokhi Speranskago" (Alexander I and his Retinue to the Speranskii Era). *Russkaia Starina*, 113 (January-March 1903): 211-234.

Dubrovin, N. "Posle Otechestvennoi Voiny" (After the Fatherland War). *Russkaia Starina*, 117 (January-March 1904): 481-515.

Dylągowa, Hanna. "Towarzystwo Patriotyczne a Dekabryści" (The Patriotic Society and the Decembrists), in *Związki rewolucjonistów polskich i rosyjskich w XIX wieku* (Polish and Russian Revolutionary Contacts in the Nineteenth Century), pp. 33-50. ed. Wiktoria Sliwowska. Wroclaw: 1972.

Handelsman, Marceli. "The Polish Kingdom" in *The Cambridge History of Poland*, pp. 275-294, eds. W.F. Reddaway et al. Cambridge, 1941; reprint ed. New York, 1971.

Hass, Ludwik. "'Diaspora' polskiego wolnomularstwa, 1821-1908" (The "Diaspora" of Polish Freemasonry, 1821-1908). *Przegląd Historyczny*, 2 (1971): 197-224.

Kieniewicz, Stefan. "La culture politique polonaise au XIXe siècle" *Acta Poloniae Historica*, 33 (1976), pp. 141-164.

Kipa, E. "Stanisław K. Potocki jako Minister Wyznań Religijnych" (Stanisław K. Potocki as Minister of Religions). *Rocznik Historii Sztuki* (1956): 442-449.

Kraushar, Alexander. "Z tajnego archiwum Senatora Nowosilcowa: Uwagi nad konstytucya Królestwa z roku 1815" (From the Secret Archive of Senator Novosil'tsov: Observations on the Kingdom's Constitution from 1815). *Przegląd Historyczny*, 1 (1906): 108-115.

Leitsch, Walter. "Russians and Poles in the Nineteenth Century." *East European Quarterly*, 8 (1974), 3: 283-294.

Maikov, P.M. "Melkiia zamietki ob otnosheniiakh imperatora Aleksandra k Poliakam" (Small Notes about the Relations of Emperor Alexander to the Poles). *Russkaia Starina*, 116 (October-December 1903): 441-458.

――――. "Tsarstvo Pol'skoe posle vienskago kongressa" (The Kingdom of Poland after the Vienna Congress). *Russkaia Starina*, 113 (January-March 1903): 419-436; 115 (July-September 1903): 5-20; 120 (October-December 1904): 618-640; 121 (January-March 1905): 154-169.

Mencel, T. "Udział społeczeństwa w życiu politycznym Królestwa Polskiego w latach 1815-1830" (Participation of the Public in the Political Life of the Polish Kingdom in 1815-1830). *Przegląd Historyczny*, 4 (1968): 629-661.

Pogodin, A. "Pol'sha pered vosstaniem 1830 g." (Poland before the 1830 Insurrection). *Russkoe Bogatstvo*, 8 (1912): 36-52; 9 (1912): 43-65.

Popkov, B.S. "Vnimaet istinu iz ust tvoikh narod . . .' (Nauchno-pedagogicheskaia deiatel'nost I. Lelevelia v 1808-1830 gg. v otsenke pol'skikh sovremennikov)" ("Listen to the Truth from the Lips of Your People . . ." J. Lelewel's Scientific-Pedagogical Activity from 1808 to 1830 in the Estimation of Polish Contemporaries), in *Issledovaniia po istorii pol'skogo obshchestvennogo dvizheniia* (Investigations into the History of the Polish Social Movement), pp. 197-234. eds. V.A. D'iakov et al. Moscow: 1971.

Rose, J. Holland. "Napoleon and Poland" in *The Cambridge History of Poland*, pp. 208-219, eds. W.F. Reddaway et al. Cambridge, 1941; reprint ed. New York, 1971.

Russkii Biograficheskii Slovar. St. Petersburg: 1903. S.v. "Konstantin Pavlovich" by N. Chechulin.

Skowronek, Jerzy. "Skład społeczny i polityczny sejmów Księstwa Warszawskiego i Królestwa Kongresowego" (The Social and Political Composition of the Sejms of the Duchy of Warsaw and the Congress Kingdom). *Przegląd Historyczny*, 3 (1961): 466-494.

Sobociński, Władysław. "Quelques observations sur le bilan social de la Pologne en 1815: Questions juridiques et sociales." *Acta Poloniae Historica*, 14 (1966), pp. 105-116.

Walker, Franklin A. "Constantine Pavlovich: An Appraisal." *Slavic Review*, 26 (1967): 445-452.

Zawadzki, W. H. "Adam Czartoryski: An Advocate of Slavic Solidarity at the Congress of Vienna", in *Oxford Slavonic Papers* (new series) 10 (1977), pp. 73-97.

INDEX

Additional Article to the Polish Constitution, 119-122
Administrative Council, 17, 22-23, 25, 29-30, 38, 40, 62, 64, 94-95, 98, 133, 143-144
Alexander I, 3, 10-11, 21, 66, 71, 153n.; character and personality, 13, 24-25, 32-33, 37-39, 43-47, 53, 57-58, 78, 84, 90-92, 112, 120, 122, 137, 145, 147; additional article to the Polish constitution, 119-122; censorship, 60-61, 65, 76, 94-95, 133, 145; at Congress of Vienna, 11-14, 145-146; and Constantine, 21-25, 37-39, 81, 84-92, 169n.; constitutional project for the Russian Empire, 42, 44, 57-60, 80, 145; constitutionalism and liberalism of, 30-33, 46-47, 52-53, 57-58, 60, 65, 78, 87-88, 93, 119-122, 133, 145, 147-148, 152n.; and Czartoryski, 8-10, 83, 112, 129, 139, 154n.; death, 133, 139; formation of Congress Kingdom, 11-21; Liberal Opposition, 112-122, 136, 145-147; Lithuanian Question, 14, 42-47, 59-60, 88-92,113-114, 122, 138-139, 145-146; and Napoleon, 6, 10, 26; and Novosil'tsov, 26-30, 60, 79-82, 90-91, 106, 111-112, 123-125, 129-131, 168-169n.; opposed by Russian nationalists, 6-8, 11-13, 33-35, 47-50, 54, 58, 79, 137, 146; plans for Poland, 6-11, 13-14, 42-47, 54, 57-60, 76-84, 90, 93-94, 113-114, 123, 138, 145-148; Polish Sejm, 44-47, 52-53, 65, 73, 76-78, 80, 117-122; reform of education, 99, 101-102, 106, 128-129, 135, 146; secret societies, 123-126, 128-131, 145-147; Semenovskii mutiny, 93, 123; shaken by European events of 1820, 54, 57, 76, 79, 84, 123; Succession Crisis, 58, 76, 79, 81, 83-92.
Alexander II, 85

Arakcheev, A.A., 34, 122, 130
Askenazy, S., 59-60, 81

Baykow, L., 181n.
Benckendorf, A.K., 137
Bentham, J., 127
Berry, Duc de, 54
Burschenschaft, 66, 68, 123-124, 127. See also Student Secret Societies
Byron, G.G., 67

Capo d'Istria, I.A., 12-13, 45-46, 79, 95-96
Carbonari, 114, 123-125, 127. See also Student Secret Societies
Carlsbad Decrees, 95
Castlereagh, R.S., 11
Catherine the Great (Catherine II), 2, 8, 38, 55, 60, 150n.
Catherine Pavlovna, Grand Duchess, 55
Censorship, 77, 80, 93, 111, 144; after 1825, 132-133; and Alexander I, 60-61, 65, 94-95, 133, 145; attempts to co-ordinate with Russian Empire, 98-99, 132-133; attempts to regulate, 61-65, 94-99, 132-133; before 1815, 60-61; and Constantine, 94, 97-99, 132; examples of, 64-65, 94-98, 111; and Novosil'tsov, 94, 99, 132-133; and Polish constitution, 16, 61-65; and Szaniawski, 62, 98-99, 133; Zajaczek's decrees on, 64-65, 95, 98
Central Police Bureau, 110-111, 136
Chernyshev, A.I., II
Chevegrois-Schweizer, K. de. 128
Conspiracies. See Student Secret Societies
Constant, B., 70
Constantine Pavolovich, Grand Duke, 4 25, 59, 63, 66, 79, 108, 109-111; character and personality, 21, 36-39, 165n; and Alexander I, 24-25, 37-39, 81, 85-92, 138, 154n., 169n.;

INDEX

censorship, 94, 97-99, 132; commands Polish army, 10-11, 15, 21-24, 36-39, 80, 82, 89, 141; constitutionalism of, 51, 87, 118-119; and Czartoryski, 15, 21-23, 83, 141; evaluates Congress Kingdom, 33, 140-141; Liberal Opposition, 114-120; Lithuanian Question, 43, 59-60, 86, 88-92, 139-141; and Nicholas I, 109, 137-143; and Novosil'tsov, 89, 91, 112, 129-131; and Polish Decembrists, 141-144; position in Congress Kingdom, 21-25, 36-39, 81, 86-93, 112, 140-141, 147, 169n.; student secret societies, 127-129; Succession Crisis, 81, 83-92, 118-119, 140

Constitutional Project for the Russian Empire, 42, 44, 58-60, 80, 145
Constitutionnel, 97
Cracow University. *See* Jagiellonian University
Curator General, 104-109, 134
Czartoryski, A.J., 7, 21, 25, 70; character and personality, 7-8; and Alexander I, 8-10, 13, 83, 112, 129, 139, 145; at Congress of Vienna, 11-13; and Constantine, 15, 21-23, 83, 141; as Curator of Wilno Educational District, 8, 43, 128-130, 134; and Novosil'tsov, 27-29, 129-131; plans for Poland, 7-8, 14-15, 139-144; Polish Decembrists, 141-144, 169n.; at Polish Sejms, 51-52, 144; protests unconstitutional conduct, 15, 21-23, 26, 52, 82-83

Decembrists, 34-35, 48, 54, 132, 138
Dekada Polska, 127
Dmitriev, I.I., 48
Drucki-Lubecki, K., 82, 106, 133, 135
Dzieje Panowania Zygmunta III, 63

Education Reform, 62, 93, 111, 144; after 1825, 134-135; and Alexander I, 99, 101-102, 106, 145; changes in curricula, 106-107, 130, 134-135; Curator General, 104-109, 134; Educational Reform Committee, 102-106, 134-135; Elementary Book Society, 107-108, 135; and Stanislaw Grabowski, 96-98, 100, 105, 145; and Novosil'tsov, 90, 101-105, 107, 134-135; plans for Russification, 104, 130, 134-135, 139; Polish episcopate supports, 40-41, 99-100, 134-135; and Potocki, 40-41, 99-100; reactionary character of, 99-109, 111, 130, 136; reorganization of Religion and Education Ministry, 100-102; and Szaniawski, 100-101, 102, 104, 106-108, 135; Warsaw University, 41, 69, 102, 107-108, 135. *See also* Religion and Education, Ministry of
Educational Reform Committee, 102-106, 134-135
Elementary Book Society, 107-108, 135
Elizabeth Alekseevna, Empress, 139
Ermolov, A.P., 47

Fanshawe, J., 109
Filomats, 128-130, 180n.
Follen, K., 66
Freemasonry. *See* Polish Freemasonry

Gazeta Codzienna Narodowa i Obca, 63-64, 67
Gendre, A., 109
Glinka, F.N., 132
Golitsyn, A.N., 132
Gospoda Akademicka, 68
Grabowski, Stanislaw, 50, 96-98, 100-105, 107, 145
Grabowski, Stefan, 106
Gribovskii, A.M., 33
Grudzinska, J., 85

Hamburg Gazette, 63
Hauke, M., 24, 104
Heltman, W., 126-127

Imperial Commissioner. *See* N.N. Novosil'tsov
Interior, Ministry of, 18, 61, 64, 95, 97, 110-111

Jagiellonian University, 124
Jankowski, J., 129
Jezowski, J., 128
Journey to Darktown, 99
Justice, Ministry of, 18

Kalisz Provincial Council, 114, 116-117, 136
Karamzin, N.M., 33-48, 54-57, 137, 146
Kempen, I., 109
Kicinski, B., 63-64, 67
Kingdom of Poland. *See* Polish Congress Kingdom
Kiselev, P.D., 47-48
Kochubei, V.P., 27

INDEX

Korf, M.N., 29, 56
Kosciuszko, T., 21, 67
Kosciuszko's Revolt, 2, 8, 36, 160n.
Kotzebue, A. V., 54, 63, 123
Kozmian, A.E., 37
Kozmian, K., 29
Krakus, 97
Krasinski, W., 75
Kronika Drugiej Polowy Roku 1819, 64
Kucharzewski, J., 57
Kukiel, M., 24
Kurier Warszawski, 97

LaHarpe, F.C., 30, 38
Laibach, Congress of, 81, 82, 85, 93
Langeron, A., 27, 156n.
Lanskoi, V.S., 10, 11, 29, 150n.
Lebzeltern, L., 31
Lelewel, J., 181n.
Liberal Opposition, 4; after 1825, 136; membership, 70, 72-73, 136; origins, 65-66, 70; philosophy of, 65, 70-75, 136; at Polish Sejms, 50-52, 73-76, 120-122; under attack, 82, 112-122, 145-147. See also Niemojowski, B., Niemojowski, W.
Liberum Veto, 2, 150n.
Lithuanian Corps, 43, 138-140
Lithuanian Question, 14, 59-60; and Alexander I, 42-47, 75, 113-114, 122, 138, 145-146; and Constantine, 43, 59-60, 86, 88-92, 138-141; Lithuanian Corps, 43, 138-140; and Nicholas I, 138-141; Succession Crisis, 59-60, 86, 88-92
Lord Lieutenant, 16-19, 25-26. See also J. Zajaczek
Loyalty Oath, 125
Lubowidzki, M., 110-111, 125
Lunin, M.S., 35
Lukasinski, W., 109

Mackrott, H., 67-68, 109-110, 165n., 167n.
Mallet, J.C., 104
Maria Fedorovna, Dowager Empress, 54, 84
Mauersberger, L., 68-69
May Third Constitution, 8, 9, 68, 127, 128, 150n.
Memoir on Ancient and Modern Russia, 55
Metternich, K.v., 54, 63, 93, 95, 101

Mickiewicz, A., 128, 130
Mikhailovskii-Danilevskii, A.I., 47
Minerve Francaise, 71
Minister-Secretary of State for Poland, 16, 52, 112. See also Grabowski, Stefan, Sobolewski, I.
Mohrenheim, P., 124
Montesquieu, 67
Morawski, T., 63-64, 67
Mostowski, T., 62, 64, 111
Murav'ev, A.N., 35

Napoleon I, 3, 6, 8, 9, 10, 11, 15, 26, 96, 99, 103
Nesselrode, C.R., 7, 9, 12-13, 28-29, 99
Nicholas I, 7, 33, 59, 85, 89, 91, 109, 130, 132-144
Niemcewicz, J., 63, 100
Niemojowski, B., 121, 136. See also Liberal Opposition
Niemojowski, W., 51-52, 72-76, 114-116, 121, 136. See also Liberal Opposition
November Insurrection, 24, 26, 66, 110, 131, 136, 137, 144, 148
Novosil'tsov, N.N. 4, 14, 59, 63, 66; character and personality, 27-30, 129-131, 181n.; and Alexander I, 26-30, 60, 79-82, 90-91, 106, 110-112, 123-125, 129-131, 168-169n.; attacks secret societies, 69, 82, 90, 115, 122-131, 133-134; censorship, 94-98, 132-133; and Constantine, 89, 91, 112, 129-131; constitutionalism of, 80-81, 86-87, 90, 119-120, 168-169n.; creates Central Police Bureau, 110-111; criticizes Polish judicial system, 115-116, 124-126; and Czartoryski, 27-29, 129-131; education reform, 90, 101-105, 107, 134-135; evaluates Congress Kingdom, 80-82, 124; investigates Wilno Educational District, 127-131; Liberal Opposition, 82, 114-122; named Curator of the Wilno Educational District, 130-131, 134; prepares constitution for Russian Empire, 44, 58-60, 80; Polish Decembrists, 141-144; position in Congress Kingdom, 10, 26-27, 29-30, 60, 81, 91, 93, 105, 110-112, 129-131, 147; Succession Crisis, 86-91

Obszelwicz, D., 50
Oesterreichische Beobachter, 63
Oginski, M., 42-43

INDEX

Opinion of a Russian Citizen, 55-57
Orlov, M., 11, 34
Orzel Bialy, 94-95
Osterman-Tolstoi, P.A., 47

Panta Koina, 68-69
Paskevich, I.F., 47, 59
Patriotic Society, 141-142
Paul I, 8, 27, 83, 153n.
Peter the Great (Peter I), 2, 44, 83
Phillis, 63
Piatkiewicz, L., 126-127
Pielgrzym Nadwislanski, 97
Pietraszkiewicz, O., 128
Piotrkow *Sejmik*, 118
Pius VII, 125
Piwnicki, S., 121
Plater, L., 29, 62
Poland, partitions of, 2-3, 7, 9, 150n.
Police and spies, 77, 93, 122, 128; Central Police Bureau, 110-111, 136; Curator General, 104-109, 134; H. Mackrott, 67-68, 109-110, 165n., 167n; penetration of Polish life, 67-68, 108-111, 128, 136; M. Schley, 109-110
Polish Chamber of Deputies, 18-20, 77, 117-118, 121, 178n.
Polish Congress Kingdom, 4; Administrative Council, 17, 22-23, 25, 29-30, 38, 62, 64, 94-95, 98, 133, 143-144; army, 15, 21-24, 36-39, 80-82, 89, 145, 150n.; challenge to existence, 79-83, 90, 93, 111, 124; Constantine, position of, 21-25, 36-39, 81, 86-89, 91-92, 93, 112, 140-141, 147, 169n.; constitution of, 16-24, 30, 42, 52, 58, 61-65, 71, 75, 78, 79, 81-83, 86-88, 93, 115, 119-122, 133, 137, 145, 147, 178n.; formation of, 11-21; House of Deputies, 18-20, 71, 117-118, 121, 178n.; Interior, Ministry of, 18, 61, 64, 95, 97, 110-111; Lord Lieutenant, 16-19, 25-26; Minister-Secretary of State for, 16, 52, 112; Novosil'tsov, position of, 26-27, 29-30, 91-93, 105, 110-112, 129, 131, 133, 147; officials of, 16-27, 29-30, 36-39, 60-65, 116, 145; Provisional Government, 15, 29, 61; Religion and Education, Ministry of, 18, 40, 61-62, 64-65, 94-108, 135; Sejm, 18-20, 44-53, 73-80, 82, 113, 117-122, 144; Senate, 18-20, 74, 116-117, 121, 142-143, 178n.; State Council, 17-18, 62-65, 74-75, 77-78, 82; Treasury, Ministry of, 18
Polish Decembrists, 141-144, 169n.
Polish Episcopate, 40-41, 99-100, 134-135
Polish Freemasonry, 66, 69, 123, 125
Polish-Lithuanian Commonwealth, 1-2
Polish Revolution of 1830-1831. *See* November Insurrection
Polish Romanticism, 66, 140
Polish Senate, 18-20, 74, 77, 116-117, 121, 142-143, 178n.
Poniatowski, S.A., 100
Potocki, S.K., 70, 111; and censorship, 61-62, 64-65, 75, 94, 96-97; and education, 40-41, 99-100, 105, 108
Pozzo di Borgo, C.A., 12-13
Prazmowski, A., 101-102, 104, 135
Prefect System, 100, 136. *See also* Education, Reform of
Provincial Commissions, 113
Provincial Councils, 113-114, 117
Provisional Government of the Kingdom of Poland, 15, 29, 61
Pypin, A.N., 55

Radonski, O., 114-115
Raeff, M., 32
Reichenbach, Treaty of, 9
Religion and Education, Ministry of, 18, 40, 61-62, 64-65, 94-108, 135
Rimskii-Korsakov, A.M., 129
Roman Catholic Church in Poland. *See* Polish Episcopate
Rostopchin, F.V., 48
Rousseau, J.J., 67, 69
Rozniecki, A., 73, 94, 109-110, 125
Russian Constitution. *See* Constitutional Project for the Russian Empire
Russian Nationalism, 6-8; growth of, 3-4, 33-35, 47-50, 54-58, 137, 143, 146; Karamzin, articulated by, 33, 48, 54-57, 137, 146; opposed to Alexander I's plans for Poland, 11-13, 47-50, 146; Russian society, embraced by, 11, 33-35, 47-50, 54-58, 146
Russification, 13, 55, 104, 130-131, 134-135, 139
Russo-Turkish War, 138, 143

St. Petersburg Convention, 39, 43
Sand, K., 63, 123
Sanktpeterburgskii Vedomosti, 99

INDEX

Sass, Baron, 109
Schley, M., 109-110
Schmidt, J., 34, 110
Scott, W., 67
Sejm, 59, 94, 114, 115; description and composition, 18-20, 50-53, 152n.; *1818*, 44-53, 73; *1820*, 65, 73-80, 82, 113, 117, 165n., 167n.; *1822* (abortive), 117-119; *1825*, 118, 120-122; *1830*, 144
Semenovskii Mutiny, 93, 123
Shilder, N.K., 75
Shishkov, A.S., 130, 132
Sobolewski, I., 31, 113
Sobolewski, W., 62
Speranskii, M.M., 48-50
Staszic, S., 75
State Council, 17-18, 62-65, 77-78, 82
Stein, F.K.v., 12-13
Stolypin, A.A., 49
Stroganov, A.S., 27
Stroganov, P.A., 27
Student Secret Societies, 4, 108, 118, 122; after 1825, 131, 133-134; and Alexander I, 123-126, 128-131, 145-147; banned, 69-70, 125; and *Burschenschaft*, 66, 68, 123-125, 127; composition of, 65-66, 126-128; and Constantine, 127-129; *Filomats*, 128-130, 180n.; infiltrated by spies, 67-68, 128; and L. Mauersberger, 68-69; and Novosil'tsov, 69, 82, 90, 115, 122-131, 133-134; *Panta Koina*, 68-69; philosophy of, 65-67, 69-70, 126-128; radicalization of, 69-70, 126-128, 131; rituals of, 66-67, 126-128; *Union of Free Poles*, 126-127
Succession Crisis, 58, 76, 79, 81, 83-92, 118-119, 140
Suminski, T., 94-95, 97-98, 111, 118
Supreme Provisional Council, 9, 10, 14-15, 29
Syn Otechestvo, 6
Szaniawski, J.K., 145; and censorship, 62, 98-99, 133; and education, 100-108, 135

Tarnowski, J., 104
Treasury, Ministry of, 18
Troppau, Congress of, 78, 79, 81, 85, 93, 113
Trubetskoi, S.P., 34
Turgenev, N.I., 48
Tygodnik Polski i Zagraniczny, 63

Union of Free Poles, 126-127
University of Cracow. *See* Jagiellonian University
University of Warsaw. *See* Warsaw University
University of Wilno. *See* Wilno University
Uvarov, S.S., 130

Verona, Congress of, 93
Viazemskii, P.A., 48, 58-59
Viceroy. *See* Lord Lieutenant
Vienna, Congress of, 3, 11-14, 145-146
Voltaire, 67
La Vrai Liberal, 71

War, Ministry of, 18, 22-24
Warsaw, Duchy of, 6, 8, 9, 10, 11, 14, 20, 61
Warsaw University, 41, 62, 67-68, 69-70, 102, 107-108, 124, 135
Western *Gubernii*. *See* Lithuanian Question
Wielhorski, M., 22-24
Wilno Educational District, 8, 43, 128-130, 134, 139
Wilno Lyceum, 128, 130
Wilno University, 128-130, 134
Wloclawek *Sejmik*, 118

Yakushkin, I.D., 35

Zajaczek, J., 22-23, 29-30, 66, 93, 112, 113, 145; character and personality, 25-26; censorship, 63-65, 76, 95, 98; constitutionalism of, 16-19, 25-26; education reform, 100, 108; Liberal Opposition, 72, 116-119; loyalty oath, 125; Succession Crisis, 86-88. *See also* Lord Lieutenant
Zakrevskii, A.A., 47
Zan, T., 128

EAST EUROPEAN MONOGRAPHS

The *East European Monographs* comprise scholarly books on the history and civilization of Eastern Europe. They are published by the *East European Quarterly* in the belief that these studies contribute substantially to the knowledge of the area and serve to stimulate scholarship and research.

1. *Political Ideas and the Enlightenment in the Romanian Principalities, 1750-1831.* By Vlad Georgescu. 1971.
2. *America, Italy and the Birth of Yugoslavia, 1917-1919.* By Dragan R. Zivjinovic. 1972.
3. *Jewish Nobles and Geniuses in Modern Hungary.* By William O. McCagg, Jr. 1972.
4. *Mixail Soloxov in Yugoslavia: Reception and Literary Impact.* By Robert F. Price. 1973.
5. *The Historical and National Thought of Nicolae Iorga.* By William O. Oldson. 1973.
6. *Guide to Polish Libraries and Archives.* By Richard C. Lewanski. 1974.
7. *Vienna Broadcasts to Slovakia, 1938-1939: A Case Study in Subversion.* By Henry Delfiner. 1974.
8. *The 1917 Revolution in Latvia.* By Andrew Ezergailis. 1974.
9. *The Ukraine in the United Nations Organization: A Study in Soviet Foreign Policy. 1944-1950.* By Konstantin Sawczuk. 1975.
10. *The Bosnian Church: A New Interpretation.* By John V. A. Fine, Jr., 1975.
11. *Intellectual and Social Developments in the Habsburg Empire from Maria Theresa to World War I.* Edited by Stanley B. Winters and Joseph Held. 1975.
12. *Ljudevit Gaj and the Illyrian Movement.* By Elinor Murray Despalatovic. 1975.
13. *Tolerance and Movements of Religious Dissent in Eastern Europe.* Edited by Bela K. Kiraly. 1975.
14. *The Parish Republic: Hlinka's Slovak People's Party, 19391945.* By Yeshayahu Jelinek. 1976.
15. *The Russian Annexation of Bessarabia, 1774-1828.* By George F. Jewsbury. 1976.
16. *Modern Hungarian Historiography.* By Steven Bela Vardy. 1976.
17. *Values and Community in Multi-National Yugoslavia.* By Gary K. Bertsch. 1976.
18. *The Greek Socialist Movement and the First World War: the Road to unity.* By George B. Leon. 1976.
19. *The Radical Left in the Hungarian Revolution of 1848.* By Laszlo Deme. 1976.
20. *Hungary between Wilson and Lenin: The Hungarian Revolution of 1918-1919 and the Big Three.* By Peter Pastor. 1976.
21. *The Crises of France's East-Central European Diplomacy, 1933-1938.* By Anthony J. Komjathy. 1976.
22. *Polish Politics and National aReform, 1775-1788.* By Daniel Stone. 1976.
23. *The Habsburg Empire in World War I.* Robert A. Kann, Bela K. Kiraly, and Paula S. Fichtner, eds. 1977.
24. *The Slovenes and Yugoslavism, 1890-1914.* By Carole Rogel. 1977.
25. *German-Hungarian Relations and the Swabian Problem.* By Thomas Spira. 1977.

26. *The Metamorphosis of a Social Class in Hungary During the Reign of Young Franz Joseph.* By Peter I. Hidas. 1977.
27. *Tax Reform in Eighteenth Century Lombardy.* By Daniel M. Klang. 1977.
28. *Tradition versus Revolution: Russia and the Balkans in 1917.* By Robert H. Johnston. 1977.
29. *Winter into Spring: The Czechoslovak Press and the Reform Movement 1963-1968.* By Frank L. Kaplan. 1977.
30. *The Catholic Church and the Soviet Government, 1939-1949.* By Dennis J. Dunn. 1977.
31. *The Hungarian Labor Service System, 1939-1945.* By Randolph L Braham. 1977.
32. *Consciousness and History: Nationalist Critics of Greek Society 1897-1914.* By Gerasimos Augustinos. 1977.
33. *Emigration in Polish Social and Political Thought, 1870-1914.* By Benjamin P. Murdzek. 1977.
34. *Serbian Poetry and Milutin Bojic.* By Mihailo Dordevic. 1977.
35. *The Baranya Dispute: Diplomacy in the Vortex of Ideologies, 1918-1921.* By Leslie C. Tihany. 1978.
36. *The United States in Prague, 1945-1948.* By Walter Ullmann. 1978.
37. *Rush to the Alps: The Evolution of Vacationing in Switzerland.* By Paul P. Bernard. 1978.
38. *Transportation in Eastern Europe: Empirical Findings.* By Bogdan Mieczkowski. 1978.
39. *The Polish Underground State: A Guide to the Underground, 1939-1945.* By Stefan Korbonski. 1978.
40. *The Hungarian Revolution of 1956 in Retrospect.* Edited by Bela K. Kiraly and Paul Jonas. 1978.
41. *Boleslaw Limanowski (1835-1935): A Study in Socialism and Nationalism.* By Kazimiera Janina Cottam. 1978.
42. *The Lingering Shadow of Nazism: The Austrian Independent Party Movement Since 1945.* By Max E. Riedlsperger. 1978.
43. *The Catholic Church, Dissent and Nationality in Soviet Lithuania.* By V. Stanley Vardys. 1978.
44. *The Development of Parliamentary Government in Serbia.* By Alex N. Dragnich. 1978.
45. *Divide and Conquer: German Efforts to Conclude a Separate Peace, 1914-1918.* By L. L. Farrar, Jr. 1978.
46. *The Prague Slav Congress of 1848.* By Lawrence D. Orton. 1978.
47. *The Nobility and the Making of the Hussite Revolution.* By John M. Klassen. 1978.
48. *The Cultural Limits of Revolutionary politics: Change and Continuity in Socialist Czechoslovakia.* By David W. Paul. 1979.
49. *On the Border of War and Peace: Polish Intelligence and Diplomacy in 1937-1939 and the Origins of the Ultra Secret.* By Richard A. Woytak. 1979.
50. *Bear and Foxes: The International Relations of the East European States 1965-1969.* By Ronald Haly Linden. 1979.
51. *Cxechoslovakia: The Heritage of Ages Past.* Edited by Ivan Volgyes and Hans Brisch. 1979.

52. *Prima Minister Gyula Andrassy's Influence on Habsburg Foreign Policy.* By Janos Decsy. 1979.
53. *Citizens for the Fatherland: Education, Educators, and Pedagogical ideals in Eighteenth Century Russia.* By J. L. Black. 1979.
54. *A History of the "Proletariat": The Emergence of Marxism in the Kingdom of Poland, 1870-1887.* By Norman M. Naimark. 1979.
55. *The Slovak Autonomy Movement, 1935-1939: A Study in Unrelenting Nationalism.* By Dorothea H. El Mallakh. 1979.
56. *Diplomat in Exile: Francis Pulszky's Political Activities in England, 1849-1860.* By Thomas Kabdebo. 1979.
57. *The German Struggle Against the Yugoslav Guerrillas in World War II: German Counter-Insurgency in Yugoslavia, 1941-1943.* By Paul N. Hehn. 1979.
58. *The Emergence of the Romanian National State.* By Gerald J. Bobango. 1979.
59. *Stewards of the Land: The American Farm School and Modern Greece.* By Brenda L. Marder. 1979.
60. *Roman Dmowski: Party, Tactics, ideology, 1895-1907.* By Alvin M. Fountain, II. 1980.
61. *International and Domestic Politics in Greece During the Crimean War.* By Jon V. Kofas. 1980.
62. *Fires on the Mountain: The Macedonian Revolutionary Movement and the Kidnapping of Ellen Stone.* By Laura Beth Sherman. 1980.
63. *The Modernization of Agriculture: Rural Transformation in Hungary, 1848-1975.* Edited by Joseph held. 1980.
64. *Britain and the War for Yugoslavia, 1940-1943.* By Mark C. Wheeler. 1980.
65. *The Turn to the Right: The Odeological Origins and Development of Ukrainian Nationalism, 1919-1929.* By Alexander J. Motyl. 1980.
66. *The Maple Leaf and the White Eagle: Canadian-Polish Relations, 1918-1978.* By Aloysius Balawyder. 1980.